PERSPECTIVES
— ON —
MARKETING MANAGEMENT

ADVISORY BOARD

PERSPECTIVES ON MARKETING MANAGEMENT

VOLUME 1 1991

Edited by
Michael Baker
Department of Marketing, University of Strathclyde

JOHN WILEY & SONS
Chichester · New York · Brisbane · Toronto · Singapore

Perspectives on Marketing Management
ISSN 1051–1806

Published annually by John Wiley & Sons

Volume 1 — 1991 £50/$90 (Institutions)

Personal subscription at reduced rate available for prepayment direct to the publisher. For details telephone 0243 770 397 or write to The Journals Subscriptions Department, John Wiley and Sons Ltd, Baffins Lane, Chichester, West Sussex PO19 1UD, England.

Future volumes will be invoiced to subscribers prior to publication, and subscriptions may be cancelled at any time.

British Library Cataloguing in Publication Data
Perspectives on marketing management.
Vol. 1, 1991
658.8

ISBN 0-471-92858-5

Typeset by Inforum Typesetting, Portsmouth
Printed and bound in Great Britain by Biddles Ltd, Guildford, Surrey

CONTENTS

LIST OF CONTRIBUTORS

Douglas T. Brownlie
Glasgow Business School, Department of Management Studies, University of Glasgow, 53–59 Southpark Avenue, Glasgow, G12 8LF

Adamantios Diamantopoulos
European Business Management School, University of Wales — Swansea, Singleton Park, Swansea, SA2 8PP

Paul Fifield
The Winchester Consulting Group, St Thomas House, St Thomas Street, Winchester, SO23 9HE

Susan Hart
Department of Marketing, University of Strathclyde, Stenhouse Building, 173 Cathedral Street, Glasgow, G4 0RQ

Amr Kheir-El-Din
Department of Marketing, University of Strathclyde, Stenhouse Building, 173 Cathedral Street, Glasgow, G4 0RQ

Patricia Snelson
Grant Thornton, Chartered Accountants, 112 West George Street, Glasgow, G1

Introduction to Volume 1

This book is the first volume in a new series to be published on an annual basis. Its objective is to present an authoritative survey of the latest thinking on issues of interest and concern to students of marketing, who, for our purposes, are defined broadly as persons wishing to increase their understanding of and professional competence in the field of marketing. In other words students, academics, and practitioners with inquiring minds.

In an increasingly crowded marketplace it is becoming more difficult to find an opportunity for scholars to share their thinking, insights, and research findings with others. This series is seen as improving this opportunity by providing a forum for contributions of greater length than the typical journal article but of lesser magnitude than a book (which said, two of the contributions to this volume are certainly of monograph proportions!). A great deal of material of this type is to be found in academic research (doctoral and master's dissertations) and is also believed to exist in support of unpublished practitioner research. Often it will be of the kind which is consigned to appendices because it is concerned with summarizing the current state of knowledge or with techniques and/or methodology. Hopefully, the introduction of this series will encourage the authors of such work to consider publishing it for the benefit of a wider audience.

Given the primary objective of publishing original and timely contributions, it follows that the Editorial Board's selection must be guided by the nature and quality of the material submitted to it. For future years it is hoped to attract a proportion of the contributions to a pre-identified theme ('Marketing strategy and planning', for 1991 and 'Europe — the implications of a single market' for 1992), with the balance of the volume made up of the best of the material addressing other themes. However, for this first, inaugural volume the theme 'Managing the marketing mix' has been chosen to reflect the scope of the selected material rather than being a prior attempt to attract submissions on this theme.

The volume comprises five contributions, two of which (Chapters 3 and 5) are subdivided into several parts:

1. The contribution of marketing to competitive success
2. Putting the management into marketing management
3. Pricing: Theory and evidence
4. Product policy: Perspectives on success
5. Managing the mix in Europe

Chapter 1 — 'The contribution of marketing to competitive success' — is by Amr Kheir-El-Din, a lecturer from Ain-Shams University in Egypt and currently a post-doctoral fellow at the University of Strathclyde, where he is conducting research into Japanese marketing strategies in Europe. This inquiry is but one element of an ongoing research programme at Strathclyde and a number of other UK universities and polytechnics into the nature of competitiveness in international trade and, specifically, the role which marketing appears to play. As Kheir-El-Din observes, the quest for improved competitiveness has led many analysts and commentators to assign considerable importance to marketing and a marketing orientation, but often without spelling out just what the role of marketing is and what evidence there is to support this supposition in the first place. Kheir-El-Din seeks to answer some of these questions.

The first section of his chapter is concerned with exploring the most significant environmental changes that have made marketing a priority and with which marketers must learn to deal. This analysis is reinforced in the next section, which seeks to explain the key role which marketing can play in business success as reflected in both academic and practitioners' writings. The third section seeks to answer the question whether successful companies are really marketing oriented and, if they are, how marketing has contributed to their success. The concluding section of the chapter outlines the contribution of different marketing factors in achieving competitive success and shows the role of the marketing function in competitive strategy formulation.

Douglas Brownlie of Glasgow University picks up this theme in his chapter 'Putting the management into marketing management', which is seen as a first cut at an attempt to reflect on the literature on the subject of marketing management which has accumulated over the past 30 years or so and has the appearance of a body of knowledge with pretensions to the status of theory.

While the problems of theory development may seem arcane and even irrelevant to the marketing practitioner, they are the source of considerable soul-searching for the marketing academic — especially when challenged by the practitioner to operationalize his findings and speculations. The issues are not new and have been experienced by all the applied disciplines, particularly medicine and engineering, in which the first step to professional acceptability (and thereby respectability) has been the codification of a body of knowledge which can be communicated much more cost effectively to would-be practitioners than would be possible through extended experiential learning. In turn, the value of the knowledge base is largely judged on the basis of its relevancy, and a key criterion in assessing this is the extent and degree to which it can help guide future decisions through the statement of logical relationships and dependencies (theories!).

In seeking to chart the currently perceived gap between the present state of the theory of marketing management and its effective organizational implementation, Brownlie argues that the way ahead must lie in a better understanding of the managerial dimensions of the marketing job. Thus the purpose of his chapter is to extend understanding of the roles of marketing management and the nature of its work by bringing to the discussion informative insights and explanations from the management and organizational theory literature.

On the basis of his analysis, Brownlie calls for fundamental revisions to be made to current models of and approaches to the subject of marketing management, including consideration of a competency-based view of the function as opposed to the conventional emphasis on analysis and planning.

The third contribution to this volume — 'Pricing', by Adamantios Diamantopoulos (Senior Lecturer at Swansea University) — is much the most extensive and, indeed, might have justified publication as a small book in its own right. Fortunately, the Editor was also the author's supervisor for his doctoral dissertation and made a pre-emptive strike before another publisher could offer such a suggestion. In the opinion of the Editor and Professors Peter Doyle and Michael Thomas who examined the thesis, Diamantopoulos' literature review comprises the most extensive, thorough and up-to-date evaluation of the current state of thinking on the subject of pricing written from the perspective of a marketer.

While distribution has been termed the Cinderella of the marketing mix, pricing is undoubtedly seen as the 'blunt instrument of competition'. Despite the emphasis given it in economic theory as the mechanism for achieving a balance between supply and demand, this equilibrium assumes the provision of homogeneous goods, which is largely antithetical to the marketer's concern to provide differentiated goods tailored to the needs of different kinds of consumers. In part, of course, this desire to be seen as a differentiated supplier is driven by the supplier's wish to exercise some control over market forces and be a 'price-maker' rather than a 'price-taker'. But if one is to be proactive rather than reactive in one's pricing strategy, it is essential that one has a sound grasp of both the underlying theories and the empirical evidence — Diamantopoulos provides both.

In the Introduction the meaning, functions and importance of price are discussed together with an overview of the pricing literature to provide a lead-in to the examination of price theories. These (price theories) are considered in five groupings:

Conventional price theory
Extensions of conventional price theory
Industrial organization theory
Managerial theories
Behavioural theories

Given his review of the various pricing theories, the author concludes with an examination of pricing in practice which incorporates both a methodological assessment of empirical pricing studies and the evidence provided by them.

The fourth contribution on 'Product policy' by Pat Snelson and Susan Hart of Strathclyde University stems from their current interests in product policy and represents an analysis based upon decision outcomes rather than having the conventional focus, which emphasizes the description of decision variables in normative decision processes.

In the authors' view, the marketing literature dealing with product policy suffers from two crucial shortcomings. First, most marketing textbooks concentrate solely upon new product development and so neglect management of the product portfolio and particularly the *elimination* of unsatisfactory products. Secondly, the accepted normative model of new product development represents a task-stage model which differs significantly from the evidence of recent empirical research showing the process to be dynamic and flexible with inputs from all key functions throughout. To address these important issues the chapter is divided into two sections.

First, the issues of new product development (NPD) are dealt with by summarizing and analysing the 'success literature' and feeding back salient success factors into the authors' conception of the NPD process. Secondly, marketing literature and thought in the field of product deletion are summarized in such a way as to focus on how procedures of product deletion might generate successful outcomes.

To break the mould thus far, the final contribution is from a management consultant — Dr Paul Fifield of the Winchester Consulting Group. It is, however, based upon the doctoral dissertation he completed at the Cranfield School of Mannagement.

In 'Managing the mix in Europe' the author is concerned with the question of international market segmentation, particularly in its application to the Western European market. The chapter begins by considering current company practice and the alternatives open to the international organization. From a critical appraisal of the latest applicable theory, the work concludes that personal values are determined by cultural background and that culture offers a practical segmentation base in an international context. The considerable benefits of moving from national to cultural segments in Western Europe are identified.

The author then makes a case for using spoken language as a descriptor of existing cultural groupings in Western Europe and proceeds to test statistically the relationship between personal values and language.

The significance of the relationships exposed allows the author to conclude that personal values are affected by culture. The chapter finishes by outlining in some detail the form of the research now required if the effect of culture is to be measured accurately and exploited as an international segmentation base.

Taken together, the contributions contained in this first *Perspectives on Marketing Management* represent the distillation of many years of hard work and focused research. They also represent an overriding concern that scholarly endeavour in the field of marketing should be directed towards, and be seen as relevant and useful to, marketing practitioners. In terms of both quality and relevance I believe this first volume has set a challenging standard for future contributors to follow. Hopefully, this challenge will be taken up; the Editorial Board looks forward to a continuing flow of similar material in the future.

Michael J. Baker
Strathclyde University
November 1990

CHAPTER 1

The Contribution of Marketing to Competitive Success

Amr Kheir-El-Din

Department of Marketing, University of Strathclyde

INTRODUCTION

Major economic and social changes during the 1980s have made marketing a priority for many firms. Marketing, it is argued, can help companies to win against severe national and international competition. It can also provide companies with strategic weapons to achieve success. In fact, the importance of marketing in achieving business success has been the subject of several studies recently. However, any attempt to stress the role of marketing in achieving success should try to answer some fundamental questions, such as what are the significant changes that have made marketing a priority; what are the theoretical dimensions within which marketing can contribute to competitive success; are successful companies really marketing oriented; what is the role of different marketing factors in achieving success; and finally, what is the role of the marketing function in competitive strategy formulation?

This review will address itself to answering these questions. It will be divided into the following sections.

The first section is concerned with exploring the most significant environmental changes that have made marketing a priority, and with which marketers must learn to deal.

The second section explains the key role of marketing in contributing to business success as reflected in both academic and practitioners' writings.

The third section seeks to answer the question whether successful companies are really marketing oriented and, if they are, how marketing has contributed to their success.

Perspectives on Marketing Management, Volume 1.
Edited by M.J. Baker

The fourth section outlines the contribution of different marketing factors in achieving competitive success and shows the role of the marketing function in competitive strategy formulation.

MARKETING AMIDST RAPID CHANGE

Vast economic and social changes have made marketing an imperative. Realization of this fact has led companies of every type to look for a president with marketing experience who understands such concepts as target markets, market segmentation, product life cycles, and developing product strategies. Companies are seeking a renewal of the risk-taking, entrepreneurial spirit that they need if they are to be successful (*Business Week*, 1983).

These changes include a rapidly altering business environment, a critical need by business to understand markets and competition and a challenge to managers to adjust marketing strategies to changing conditions (Cravens and Woodruff, 1986).

Gumpert (1985) summarizes four of the most challenging areas of change that have made marketing an imperative, and that have combined to make the marketing manager's job increasingly challenging and complex, as being: (1) a rapidly changing national and international order; (2) an increasingly competitive marketing environment; (3) changing attitudes to what comprises effective management; and (4) the technology–information revolution.

On the other hand, a *Business Week* article entitled 'Marketing: The new priority' summarizes the vast social and economic changes that have altered the shape of competition as:

1. The emergence of a fragmented consumer population
2. Intense international competition
3. Rapid technological change
4. The maturing or stagnation of certain markets

Changing conditions, it is argued, have given marketing one of the key roles — if not the key one — in corporate strategy (*Business Week*, 1983).

In fact, more rapid changes in the practice of marketing are expected to take place in the future. These have led Michaels to suggest that marketing will be tomorrow's competitive cutting edge (Michaels, 1982).

Cravens and Woodruff (1986) predict that the nature and scope of social and economic changes in the future are likely to develop at a much faster rate than in the past. Intense global competition, increasing complexity of people's needs and wants, emergence of new firms, and application of modern marketing practices by less developed countries are all seen as factors contributing to this quickened pace.

To quote Cravens and Woodruff (1986):

> Looking ahead to the next twenty years, the fiercely competitive business environment that is expected to prevail simply will not allow firms in many industries to succeed unless they develop and maintain strong marketing capabilities.

In fact, some years ago, Baker (1979) pointed this out and said:

> . . . change is inevitable; in order to survive, organizations must anticipate and adapt to change, and the responsibility for anticipating and responding to changes belongs with management.

Similarly, Kotler and Singh (1981) predict that marketing competition will heat up in the years ahead.

The reasons for change in the business environment are diverse. Incomes fluctuate; technology progresses; people's living patterns change; the age distribution of the population changes; and so on (Itami, 1987).

Perhaps the accelerating technological change in recent years has had one of the most profound effects on businesses. The pace of technology has been rapid, and its impact in most cases has been dramatic. The eighties produced astonishing leaps in technological growth. Technological advances have had a substantial effect on the variety of goods and services available to consumers. For example, digital watches now account for a substantial share of all timepieces sold. Digital records offer a new high level of fidelity and clarity. Digital television is on the horizon (Bennett, 1988). Companies must monitor those technologies most likely to affect their goals and efforts. They must be ready to modify their plans in response to the ever-changing needs of consumers. One foundation of good marketing is the effective management of change. Better managed companies manage change instead of being 'shocked' by it (Tofler, 1970). Managers should wake up every morning uncertain about the marketplace, because it is invariably changing (McKenna, 1988).

It is logical to hypothesize then that companies emerging from this complicated situation will be those that understand better the new marketing and consumer environment.

Finally then, if there is a conclusion to be drawn from this opening section, it is clear that businesses are facing dramatic changes in the external environment. These changes should have an impact on their strategies and tactics. Businesses need to pay closer attention than ever before to changing political, economic, social, and technological trends. It is clear that the fast pace of environmental change creates both marketing opportunities and threats. Good marketing, it is argued, can help companies to win against the rapid change in the external environment, providing them with strategic weapons to achieve success.

In summary, Buzzell (1983) really encapsulates the whole argument when he says:

> If you have to change how to compete, then all of a sudden marketing is a very important function.

THE KEY ROLE OF MARKETING IN ACHIEVING SUCCESS

Having shown that our current environment is changing continuously, and that marketing has become a priority for many businesses, it is the objective of this section to explain the theoretical dimension within which marketing can contribute to success.

Levitt (1983) in *The Marketing Imagination* says:

> The world of competitive enterprises openly facing each other in open markets is clearly a world of constant change. The marketing concept alerts us to this fact with the prescriptive injunction that to keep up requires studying and responding to what people want and value, and quickly adjusting to choices provided by competitors.

Levitt argues that successful enterprises know that the requisites of competitive success are as follows:

1. The purpose of a business is to create and keep a customer
2. To do that the business has to find a niche and produce and deliver goods or services at competitive prices
3. To continue to do that the enterprise must have a sound financial base and a thorough knowledge of its markets
4. To achieve this, the enterprise has to clarify its purposes, strategies, and plans, clearly communicate and frequently review them
5. Finally, there should be a system of control to ensure that what is intended gets done properly and, when it is not, that it gets quickly rectified.

In fact, the role of marketing in helping to achieve success was appreciated many years ago. Eppert (1965) stressed the key role of marketing in sustaining America's progress. He indicated that 'more than ever before, the economic future of the US is vested in the marketing process and future American progress will be determined largely by marketing management's success in the new frontier: the world market'.

Twenty years later other writers still share the same view, as Stanton and Futrell (1987) indicated: 'Now as we approach the end of the 1980s, it is increasingly clear that marketing is the name of the game in both business and non-business organisations'.

In the same vein, Cravens and Woodruff (1986) suggest that 'as the world moves toward 1990 the analysis, planning, and implementation of effective marketing strategies will be essential to the successful performance of business and other organizations'.

Schwartz (1981) makes a very simple and straightforward statement when he says:

> Because marketing managers are responsible for both implementing the 4Ps and adapting to the uncontrollable elements in the environment, the key to a firm's success rests with its marketing managers.

Further evidence of the key role of marketing is expressed by Cunningham *et al.* (1987) as they say: 'In many ways, effective marketing is the key to success in business'. They add: 'In the free enterprise market place, the consumer decides who wins and who loses'.

However, it is important to note here that in our discussion we do not relate business success to marketing factors alone; in fact doing this is considered to be unsatisfactory, as Baker and Hart (1987) indicate. They argue that the reasons for the performance of a company are manifold and overlapping.

Barry (1986) expresses the same view when he suggests that the managerial talent across all functional areas is the prime determinant of a firm's long-run success or failure. In fact, he goes on to say that there are some production-oriented as well as finance- or sales-oriented firms and some of them are successful. However, he admits that they could be more successful with a marketing-oriented philosophy. In his own words:

> We propose, however, that they could be more so (successful) with a more customer-oriented philosophy.

In a *Harvard Business Review* article, Shapiro (1988) argues that the term 'market-oriented' represents a set of processes touching on all aspects of the company. It is far more than 'getting closer to the customer'. A company can be termed market driven only if information on all important buying influences permeates every corporate function; strategic and tactical decisions are made interfunctionally and interdivisionally; and finally, divisions and functions make well-coordinated decisions and execute them with a sense of commitment.

The key role of marketing in achieving success is not only found in academics' writings; increasingly, practitioners tend to share the same view.

A survey (Webster, 1981) conducted with 21 of the largest American corporations concluded that 'chief executives believe that marketing is the most important management function in their businesses, and they see it becoming more important in the future'. Several respondents expressed the opinion that the financial management orientation that once tended to dominate corporate strategy may have created a weakened position *versus* what corporations can do with effective marketing.

Accepting the proposition that companies can perform better with effective marketing raises the question of whether successful companies are really marketing oriented and, if they are, how marketing has contributed to their success.

ARE SUCCESSFUL COMPANIES REALLY MARKETING ORIENTED?

Before answering such a question, it is necessary to define what we mean by success.

In fact, success has many dimensions. At a simple level it may be viewed as the consistent achievement of company objectives, which varies from a definition of the role that the company seeks to play in its industry to targets related to innovation and technology. However, it is a common view that the most usual type of company objectives are finance-related, like sales volume, market share, return on investment. Looking at the major studies designed to test what it is that distinguishes successful companies, we find that they all use financial criteria as means of measuring successful performance (Baker *et al.*, 1986).

In addition, some other studies have considered softer measures such as 'quality of management', 'quality of products or services', 'ability to attract, develop, and keep talented people', 'community and environmental responsibility', and 'innovativeness' (Schultz, 1988).

Whatever the merits and demerits of each type of measurement, Baker *et al.* (1986) summarize the major conditions that measurement criteria should meet as follows:

1. It is helpful if the measures can be verified from sources such as company reports, to minimize the effects of respondents' errors and to simplify the research questionnaire.
2. The measures should not vary from one industry to another where industries are to be compared.

3. The measures should vary as little as possible from company to company.
4. It is helpful to have measures which can be calculated and compared longitudinally.

Finally, it is important to note here that whatever the company objectives are, the presumption is that companies can do better with a marketing-oriented philosophy.

Peters and Waterman (1982) in *In Search of Excellence* identified about 50 businesses that had a history of successful performance. Two traits that every one of these companies had were (1) a drive to provide a superior service and quality to customers and (2) a drive to innovate — to develop new products and services. Peters and Waterman found that excellent companies exhibit, among other factors, closeness to customers. While closeness to customers seems a cliché of modern business, it is apparent that only a few companies adhere to it. These are the excellent ones. Peters and Waterman uncovered that 'excellent companies are really close to their customers. Other companies talk about it; the excellent ones do it'.

They also indicated that the excellent companies are obsessed with service, quality and reliability and these characteristics comprise an essential part of their value system. In fact, Peters and Waterman found that the secret of many excellent companies lies in their service, especially after-sales service. In their own words, they concluded that:

> In fact, one of our most significant conclusions about the excellent companies is that, whether their basic business is metal bending, high technology, or hamburgers, they all defined themselves as service businesses.

Procter & Gamble provides an interesting example on how to get really close to the customer. In one of their factories, workers are given letters from customers who have problems with the products. In another factory, customers are called up to talk directly to line workers (Doyle, 1989).

Further evidence comes from Clifford and Cavanagh (1985) in *The Winning Performance*. They concluded that the majority of winning performers exhibit among their strategic traits:

- Emphasis on innovation
- Creating and serving niches defined by customers' needs
- Ability to identify and build on distinctive strengths
- Recognition that the value of product or service, not just price, spells success

They found that continuous market-driven innovation underpins the success of the winning performers. They also found that successful companies compete by producing and delivering a product that supplies superior value to customers rather than one that just costs less. They indicated as well that in successful companies profit was not viewed as the prime objective; instead, there was a view of profit and wealth creation as inevitable by-products of doing other things well.

A similar view was indicated by Peters and Waterman (1982) when they pointed out that the prime objective of excellent companies was service excellence and that profitability naturally follows.

Buchan and Marsh (1989) examining the successful performance of Merck, the world's biggest pharmaceuticals group, found that a key to Merck's winning mix in drug research is a close involvement by marketing staff in new research projects. There are continual meetings between scientists working on a new product and the people who will eventually sell it. According to J.L. Huck, Merck's ex-chairman, '. . . this ensures that when the drug comes to the market it will meet a real need'.

It is not only in the USA that business success has been associated with a marketing orientation. McBurnie and Clutterbuck (1987) in *The Marketing Edge* found that all companies which have achieved success in the marketplace have made marketing the foundation-stone of their business. Whether these companies were service companies, consumer goods companies or manufactured durables companies, successful ones were found to be clearly market driven.

Marketing as the foundation-stone of successful companies was reflected in their corporate strategies, where you often find such statements as:

- Providing the highest level of service to all customers
- Responding quickly and sensitively to the changing needs of present and potential customers

In fact, one big consumer goods company attributed its success to four particular factors:

- Creative marketing
- Every one in the company is going in the same direction
- Concentrating on areas where the company has expertise
- Commitment of the total management team

Saunders and Wong (1985) indicated that excellent companies in the UK placed emphasis on providing customer satisfaction through product quality and service. The main feature of the better performers was offering superior quality products and services at competitive prices.

Hooley and Lynch (1985) in their study of 1504 British companies found that more successful ones, called the 'high-flyers', shared three common characteristics to a degree which the less successful companies, called the 'also-rans', could not match. These characteristics were:

1. A genuine market orientation
2. A strategic sensitivity and responsiveness
3. Particular emphasis on product quality and design to a larger extent than on price

The genuine market orientation of the 'high-flyers' appeared significantly in their greater use of market research in its many forms from the less to the more sophisticated.

Michaels (1982), examining the characteristic features of leading consumer packaged goods companies, identifies five features. These are:

1. The most effective organizations are consumer oriented
2. They take an integral view on planning
3. They look further ahead — at least three to five years
4. They have highly developed marketing systems
5. Marketing dominates the corporate culture

Ogilvy (1983) looking for the reasons for Procter & Gamble's overwhelming success indicated that they are really marketing oriented. They apply marketing principles and techniques like marketing research and marketing segmentation in every basic meaningful way. Their test marketing is particularly thorough and patient. They tested one product for regional expansion, from the west to the east coast of the USA, for six years.

In fact, evidence supporting the key role of marketing in achieving success is not only limited to the industrial sector. Further evidence comes from Davis' (1987) study *Excellence in Banking*. He found that:

> The excellent banks have been driven by their customers to reevaluate their client priorities, organisational structure, information base and delivering systems. They are much closer to their customers in the sense of physical contact, formal and informal market research and the use of relationship managers who are assuming an increasingly important role in customer interface.

Moreover, the role of marketing is not limited to the size of the company. Both large and small firms can benefit from the strategic weapons marketing provides.

Chaganti and Chaganti (1983), comparing the key features of the product and market strategies of profitable and not-so-profitable small businesses, found that the most profitable firms achieve this status by identifying a niche in the marketplace.

Seller (1987) investigated the reasons why one American beer company was performing so well and increasing market share steadily unlike any major competitor. She found the secret in the application of marketing techniques more vigorously and imaginatively than its competitors. The company's most important techniques were its target marketing and its obsession with quality.

Finally, Baker and Hart (1989) found that successful companies have a number of differences from the less successful ones. At the strategic level:

1. These companies have greater commitment to strategic planning
2. They quantify objectives to a greater extent
3. The period covered by strategic plans is generally longer
4. They add value to their products to a significantly greater extent

At the tactical level:

The more successful companies are more actively involved in market research and information gathering, market segmentation and promotion

Certainly lessons can be learned by examining the factors that have contributed to the failure of some businesses.

One study (Clark, 1979) followed the activities of unsuccessful organizations. Reasons for failure included:

1. An inability to adjust to changing times and consumer needs
2. Improper execution of marketing, finance, and production techniques
3. Inability to develop a distinctive, positive image in the marketplace
4. Implementing radical changes too late
5. An ineffective drifting in the marketplace; a lack of understanding of company strengths and weaknesses

At first glance, it is not difficult to conclude that basically most of these factors reflect poor marketing performance. It is apparent that these companies were unable to understand and implement marketing principles and techniques. In short, they were not marketing oriented.

A more recent study (Bruno *et al.*, 1987) entitled 'Why firms fail' supports the above findings. Among the reasons cited for failure of some high-technology firms were:

- Wrong product timing and design
- Ineffective distribution relations
- Unclear business definition
- Too great a reliance on one customer

Another study (Doyle, 1985) examined how four large Dutch enterprises had, after a long period of decline, been turned around into profitable businesses. Among the factors identified for the revitalization of the businesses were:

- Development of clear marketing strategy defining target markets, and differentiated advantage
- Determining clear product market priorities for action

It is apparent from the above studies that poor marketing is regarded as a main cause of failure in business. In fact, it is seen that the lack of effective marketing is a main reason behind the decline of British producers in world markets.

One study (NEDO, 1981) assessing the marketing efforts pursued by the British industrial sectors in both home and overseas markets has identified the lack of commitment to marketing as the single most important constraint on improvement in the UK's market share.

Another study (Stacey, 1962) concludes that the neglect of marketing functions, including market research, advertising and public relations abroad, was one of the main reasons causing Britain to lose her share in world markets.

Further evidence comes from a study by Johnson (1982), where he concludes that Britain's lack of competitiveness is reflected not only in the production function but also in marketing performance. He argues that British producers make products which are comparable to their competitors, but that their marketing is not as aggressive as that of foreign producers.

In the same vein, another study (Turnbull *et al.*, 1981) about marketing and purchasing practices in five European countries came to the conclusion that British firms are slow in offering new products, less likely to initiate joint product development with their customers, cannot be relied upon to supply products of consistently high quality or to provide customers with technical information, and finally are regarded as slow and very unreliable in delivery.

In an article entitled 'Marketing and the competitive performance of British industry: Areas for research', Doyle (1985) suggests that poor marketing has been an important contributor to the decline of Britain's competitive market position. He argues that instead of investigating macroeconomic factors as a cause of the UK's poor performance, attention should be paid to the examination of factors within individual firms, for example lack of commitment to marketing.

Finally, McBurnie and Clutterbuck (1987) state that:

> The plain fact is that if even half the major (let alone the minor) companies in Britain understood and reacted to customers' needs as well as they should, the entire economy would be far stronger than it is now — and the Japanese would be trooping here to find out how it was done.

Before closing our discussion, insights can be gained by examining the factors that have contributed to the success of some specific companies. IBM and Amstrad will be examined from the consumer electronics business, with Reebok and Hi-Tec from the leisure and sport business.

IBM

The information technology business is one of the most complex and competitive markets, demanding high R&D capabilities, technological innovation, manufacturing excellence, financial soundness, and aggressive marketing.

IBM is an excellent example of a company which has remained highly competitive through all the changes that have affected the industry.

Its founder, Thomas J. Watson (1963), articulated IBM's philosophy in three simple beliefs:

1. Respect for the individual
2. Superior service to the customer
3. Pursuit of excellence as a way of life

The key element in IBM's success is their superior service to the customer. Throughout the company the message is made clear: 'Remember, the customer pays your salary'. The company is clearly market driven. Markets are extensively researched, analysed, and segmented in a meaningful way.

McBurnie and Clutterbuck (1987) observe:

> It is, quite simply, a strongly market-driven, well-managed organization which knows exactly where it intends to go and how it will get there — a formidable combination with a high likelihood of success.

AMSTRAD

Amstrad, founded only in 1968, has grown rapidly and is now considered one of the most successful consumer electronics companies in the UK (*Financial Times*, 1988a).

Its founder, Alan Sugar (*Financial Times*, 1988a), describes his company as a 'marketing company'. He believes that it is mainly marketing that has contributed to his company's success.

What Amstrad does is very simple and can be termed 'creative imitation'. Amstrad waits until a product shows signs of taking off. By looking hard at the existing offerings, it comes up with simpler designs, often adding some innovative features of its own.

The product, usually priced cheaply enough to undercut all opposition, is pushed by a large advertising budget often directed at people who are price-sensitive.

REEBOK

Reebok International, the sports shoes manufacturer, has grown dramatically in the 1980s to acquire one-third of the athletic footwear market in the USA and is now growing rapidly overseas (*Financial Times*, 1988b). The secret of Reebok's success, it is argued, lies in its analysis of what consumers want from their sports shoes. Reebok, studying carefully market trends in the USA, discovered it is the leisure area which determines success or failure in the industry.

Reebok left rivals behind, sweeping the market in the States with its fashionably oriented shoes of soft leather, appealing strongly to women. In the words of Rene Jaeggi (*Financial Times*, 1988c), chairman of Adidas, one of Reebok's competitors, 'Reebok discovered females'. He added: 'A new product was created. It was actually a very simple idea, but excellently and consistently marketed'.

HI-TEC

Hi-Tec is another company in the leisure and sport business which provides an excellent example of a company founded only in 1974 and now placed very close to the market leader (McBurnie and Clutterbuck, 1987).

It is argued that the company has achieved this position through its marketing orientation. Technology in sports shoe manufacture is widely known so the competitive edge, it is argued, has to come from styling and quality of construction to ensure performance to the standard required.

In a relatively short period of time, the company has established itself in the core sport segments and it is now extending its brand into fashionable footwear. It positioned itself to exploit a market gap between an inactive Dunlop and an expensive Adidas. Hi-Tec's chief executive summarizes the main features of the company's successful strategy as follows:

- Being better informed and wider awake than the competition
- Having the best product for money in the market
- Consistently providing the right colours and cosmetic appeal
- Being more creative and imaginative than others in the marketplace

Accepting the fact that companies can do better with a marketing orientation, and demonstrating that successful companies can only do this by meeting the needs of the marketplace, it is now proposed to discuss the role of different marketing factors in achieving competitive success.

THE ROLE OF DIFFERENT MARKETING FACTORS IN ACHIEVING SUCCESS

Having discussed the key role of marketing in determining the positions of competing firms, it is appropriate now to outline the role of different marketing factors in achieving success.

Some of the major factors will be discussed to see how each factor may affect the position of competing firms in the marketplace.

THE ROLE OF MARKETING RESEARCH

In essence, marketing research is undertaken to help marketing managers make better decisions. In today's highly competitive environment, the effective use of information is a critical managerial weapon. Moreover, marketing research is taken to be more important in foreign markets, where the risks are certainly greater.

Tookey (1964), Shankleman (1975) and McFarlane (1978) found that the inefficiency of the marketing research function is one of the major causes of some companies' lack of competitiveness.

On the other hand, Baker and Abou-Zeid (1982) found that 86% of the companies with a high record of export performance carried out export market research.

Support for the above findings is found in a NEDO report (1979) which showed that gathering detailed and reliable information is a major factor behind success in these markets. By contrast, an ITT report (1975) considered lack of market research activities as a major constraint on export growth.

Finally, Hooley and Lynch (1985) indicated that successful companies made much greater use of all types of market research than did less successful ones. Market research techniques used included customer surveys, qualitative research, field experiments and laboratory experiments.

THE ROLE OF THE PRODUCT

Baker *et al.* (1986) state that ultimately company success is dependent upon its product policy. In the same vein, Kent (1984) indicates that price is the price of the product, distribution is the distribution of the product, and advertising is the advertising of the product.

In considering the role of the product in achieving business success, we will deal with the following issues:

- Product differentiation
- Product quality
- Product innovation

Product Differentiation

Levitt (1980), in his article 'Marketing success through differentiation of anything', states that 'there is no such thing as a commodity, all goods and services are differentiable'. Levitt attributes the success of companies like IBM, Xerox, Texas Instruments and ITT to the amount of careful analysis, control and fieldwork that characterizes their management of marketing. Their success, he argues, is related to their ability to differentiate the most commodity-like products.

Hall (1980) studying the financial performance of leading firms in eight old-established industries, found that over a significant period of time the top firms in these industries outperformed well-known growth industry leaders. The explanation for their superior performance was that they pursued meaningful differentiation in their offerings.

Levitt (1980) suggests that 'meaningful differentiation is competitively more effective and enduring than low cost production alone'.

Support of Levitt's suggestion comes from all the major empirical studies conducted to explain the success of top performers (Peters and Waterman, 1982; McBurnie and Clutterbuck, 1987; Clifford and Cavanagh, 1985).

In the study by Clifford and Cavanagh (1985), one CEO of the top performers stated:

> The lesson to be learned is that no matter how commonplace a product may appear, it does not have to become a commodity. Every product, every service can be differentiated.

In fact, one of the three strategies for a company to pursue identified by Porter (1980) in his *Competitive Strategy* is differentiation. In this strategy, the company concentrates on creating a highly differentiated product line and marketing programme so that it comes across as the class leader in the industry. Most customers will prefer to buy this brand if its price is not too high.

Saunders and Wong (1985) found in their survey that excellent companies were better at product differentiation than less successful ones.

A business and its products can be differentiated in various ways. Among the favourable routes are providing superior product quality and offering innovative features. These will be discussed next.

Product Quality

El-Morsy (1986) indicates that the role of product quality represents the most important aspect of product-related factors, and is considered the main method of achieving competitiveness.

According to John A. Young (speaking in 1984), CEO of Hewlett-Packard, 'In today's competitive environment ignoring the quality issue is tantamount to corporate suicide'.

In fact, product quality, it is argued, is a powerful ingredient in a successful competitive strategy. Quality can increase productivity and profitability by lowering costs and increasing sales (Shetty, 1987).

Shetty (1987) in his study of the relationship between product quality and profitability found that a strategic focus on quality is one of the best ways to gain a sustainable competitive advantage.

Another study by Ross and Shetty (1985) supports the above findings. It was found that quality has a direct impact on both market share and profit margins.

Further evidence is found in Schoeffler, Buzzell and Heany's study (1974). They provided quantitative data concerning the link between quality and profitability. They found that both rate of return on investment and net profit as a percentage of sales rose as quality increased.

They further discovered that businesses that improved quality increased their market share five or six times faster than those whose products declined in quality.

Along similar lines, a study by Buzzell and Wiersema (1981) investigating the relationship between advertising, price, product quality, and market share found that quality improvement is the most powerful in building market share.

The study showed that:

- Changes in product quality had the strongest relationship to changes in market share
- Advertising had only a modest relationship to share changes
- Price changes had no relationship to share changes

Shetty and Buehler (1983) using case studies involving several companies showed that quality can increase profits by lowering costs, increasing sales, and improving the firm's competitive position.

It is worth noting here, however, that superior quality is not synonymous with high or sophisticated technology. Successful companies always sacrifice an unproven technology for something that works (Peters and Waterman, 1982).

In fact, Takeuchi and Quelch (1983) argue that quality is more than making a good product. They say that it is also a matter of keeping close tabs on changing consumer values and after-sales service.

Garvin (1981) in one of his several studies attributes the decline of American competitiveness relative to Japan to high-quality imports and relative lack of emphasis on quality by American firms.

With respect to British experience, similar evidence of the importance of quality is documented in many studies.

A NEDO (1983) study stresses the importance of quality to British producers. It states that 'price, though important, is not everything in today's international markets. What is just as important in world markets is quality'. The report adds: 'The most effective way of increasing our share of world markets is to give the customer the quality he demands at a price he is prepared to pay'.

It is important to emphasize that quality improvement is a continuous process, for there is no such thing as top quality. Every day, each product or service is getting relatively better or worse compared to competition (Peters, 1988).

Finally, companies using product quality as a competitive strategy should define quality from the customer's perspective. Quality, Garvin (1987) contends, means pleasing customers, not just protecting them from annoyances. He says that customers' complaints play an important role because they provide a valuable source of product information. He adds that some customers' preferences should be treated as absolute performance standards. In other words, customers define quality and management should accept the perception of customers. To identify customers' requirements, however, successful companies use customer surveys, customer comments, focus groups, and constant interaction with the customer (Shetty, 1987).

Product Innovation

One basic role of the marketing function is helping and assisting new products to achieve success in the marketplace.

Baker (1988), in an article entitled 'Innovation — key to success', claims that the key strategy to achieve competitiveness is innovation, and that it should receive the most attention from top management.

In fact, with shorter product life cycles, intense international competition, and complexity and variety of consumer needs and wants, innovation turns out to be a necessity, not just an afterthought.

Wilson (1984) indicates that if the processes of innovation are to be successful, they must run in parallel with a deeper and consistent study of the innovative concept or product, that is, the customer.

Pearson (1988) contends that what distinguish successful competitors from less successful ones are two basic principles. First, successful competitors know that consistent innovation is the key to a company's survival. Secondly, they understand that the most successful innovations they can make are those that create value for the current and potential customers.

Support for this view has been provided by Von-Hippel (1982), who argues that customers rather than manufacturers are often the actual developers of successful new products.

Among the most extensive innovation studies has been the SAPPHO project (Project SAPPHO, 1972). It came to the conclusion that successful firms pay more attention to the market than do failures. Successful innovators innovate in response to market needs, involve potential users in the development process, and understand user needs better.

Support of the above findings is found in the McKinsey study of America's high-growth midsized companies. Successful companies, it was found, see their role as taking note of customer needs and meeting those needs in a distinctive way by innovating on their behalf (Clifford and Cavanagh, 1985).

Cooper (1979) identifies three factors that contribute to new product success. These are poor marketing and managerial synergy, strength of marketing communications and launch effort, and market needs, growth, and size. It is clear that these factors describe a strong marketing orientation.

On the other hand, poor marketing is regarded as a chief factor in the failure of new product innovation.

Cooper (1975) in another study refers to marketing as a major cause of failure of new industrial products.

Millmans (1982) indicates that the lack of market orientation and breakdown in communication are the reasons for British industry failing to complete the product innovation cycle and achieve full commercial exploitation.

In the same vein, Wilson (1984) argues that Britain's economic failure has not been caused by shortage of creative ability, but by inability to exploit inventions.

In his article entitled 'Marketing and competitive performance of British industry: Areas for research', Doyle (1985) states that:

> The marketing success stories are not the Concordes, Hovercrafts, Prestels or EMI scanners, but the Sony Walkman, Honda Accord, McDonalds and Komatsus — conventional technologies, superior marketing.

THE ROLE OF PRICE

Udell (1964), in an article entitled 'How important is pricing in competitive strategy', tried to ascertain the key elements of business success in the marketplace. In his survey of 200 producers of industrial and consumer goods, one half of the respondents did not select pricing as one of the five most important strategy areas in the firm's marketing success.

According to Udell, three factors probably account for the relatively low ranking of pricing. These are (1) little or no freedom for a company to deviate from the market price; (2) today's consumers are interested in more than just price; (3) it is through successful product differentiation that a manufacturer may obtain some pricing freedom.

A similar view is shared by Posner and Steel (1979), who indicated that non-price factors are more important in advanced manufacturing countries.

On the other hand, some other studies stressed the critical role of price. One study (Central Policy Review Staff, 1975) indicated that British car manufacturers must equalize their cost base to that of the competition if they are to achieve success.

In the same spirit, Mikesell and Farah (1980) reported that the decline in the US share of markets in less developed countries was mainly due to price factors.

However, being the low-cost producer alone is not enough; price competitiveness makes sense when it is combined with competitiveness in all other factors (Levitt, 1983). Along similar lines, Baker *et al.* (1986) concluded '. . . price is important if and when the quality of the rest of the package is comparable to the competition. Otherwise the cost benefit trade-off must be considered'.

THE ROLE OF DISTRIBUTION

It is widely accepted that the selection of effective channels of distribution is often a critical factor in a firm's differential advantage in world markets.

Blackwell (1982) indicated the importance of distribution when he stated that:

> In an environment of technological parity, effective market coverage becomes even more important in determining competitiveness, and choosing the best channels to serve specific market segments becomes a critical and complex decision.

Stern and Sturdivant (1987) stated that:

> Of all marketing decisions, the ones regarding distribution are the most far reaching. A company can easily change its prices or its advertising. It can hire and fire a market research agency, revamp its sales promotion, even modify is product line. But once a company sets up its distribution channels, it will generally find changing them to be difficult.

They further argued that distribution, too often, is the neglected side of marketing. Many companies lose large shares of their markets because they resist making changes in their existing distribution network or because they reach their markets in outmoded or outdated ways.

Similarly, Nadel (1987) wrote:

> One of the most vital and powerful parts of the product mix is distribution, and companies that control distribution control almost everything.

Slijper (1978) supported the above finding. He concluded that better distribution may often be the means of facing intensive competition in world markets.

Walsh (1979) indicated that distribution was the most effective way for British producers to enter the German market.

On the other hand, the Central Policy Review Staff study (1975) concluded that a poor distribution network is one of the chief factors contributing to British car manufacturers' lack of competitiveness.

In short, it is clear that the ability of the firm to choose and manage the appropriate channel of distribution will ultimately influence its success or failure.

THE ROLE OF PROMOTION AND ADVERTISING

Relatively few studies have emphasized promotion as a factor for achieving competitive success.

Nevertheless, Slatter (1977) in his study of the pharmaceutical industry claims that promotion is a major factor leading to increase in market share.

Suzuki (1980) in his study of Japanese advertising in the USA reveals that there is some correlation between the sales volume of four sectors and the increase of advertising expenditure, which means that advertising had some effect on export performance in the US market.

Johnson (1982) indicates that failure to create the right image and effectively communicate the benefits of the product is one of the major reasons behind the British car industry's lack of competitiveness.

On the other hand, Michell (1979) reported that only 3% of the firms he surveyed claim that advertising is a vital factor for success in foreign markets.

Increasingly, however, it seems that companies are now considering successful advertising to be a prerequisite for profitable international operations. A successful advertising campaign is seen to be the critical factor in achieving sales goals (Roth, 1982).

Killough (1978), in an article entitled 'Improved payoffs from transnational advertising', argues that if advertising succeeds in establishing and maintaining the desired market image, it can pave the way for expansion.

In brief, promotion and advertising activities if used effectively can create a perceptive effect and can have a key role in achieving business success.

Before closing our discussion of the role of different marketing factors in achieving success, we will deal briefly with the role of the marketing function in competitive strategy formulation.

Levitt (1983) points out that 'there can be no corporate strategy that is not in some fundamental fashion a marketing strategy'. Ohmae (1988) argues that the first principle of strategy is not to beat the competition but to serve customers' real needs. He states that it is important to take the competition into account only after management recognizes that the heart of strategy is creating and delivering value for customers. Ohmae (1989) argues that getting back to strategy and focusing on providing value for customers lies at the heart of the competitive challenge facing managers today.

Accepting the idea that the purpose of the business is to create and keep a customer, it follows that an effective corporate strategy should predict and respond to what customers are willing to pay at a certain price.

Schendal and Hofer (1979) identify four distinct levels of strategy formulation:

1. Enterprise strategy. This level of strategy formulation is concerned with the overall social, political, and legal environment of the firm. It deals with such issues as government relations, the social responsibility of business, policy towards stockholders, ethical conduct, and the like.
2. Corporate strategy. Strategy formulation at this level is concerned with selecting the portfolio of business for the firm. It provides a way for management to answer more effectively the questions: what business is the firm in, and what business should it be in? In general, corporate strategy serves to integrate the activities of such critical management areas as marketing, finance and production.
3. Business strategy. This level of strategy formulation is concerned with the selection of overall competitive goals and tactics by the business unit within a specific industry. At the business level, the major purposes of strategy are to identify the major opportunities and threats a business will face, and the key resources and skills around which it can develop a strategy that will exploit these opportunities and meet these threats in a way which will satisfy its goals within its existing structure.

4. Functional strategy. Corporate strategy, by definition, constrains all administrative and operational decisions throughout the organization. Because of the size and complexity of these functional areas, such as marketing, finance and production, it is not surprising that each in turn seeks to develop its own strategy which constrains the action within its group. Each of these functional strategies is an element of corporate strategy and when aggregated they provide a substance and meaning to the firm's overall strategy.

Perhaps the work by Porter (1980) on *Competitive Strategy* is the most comprehensive in the area.

Porter proposed three generic strategies that a company can pursue within a market.

Overall cost leadership. Here the company works hard to achieve the lowest cost of production and distribution so that it can price its products lower than its competitors and win a large market share.

Differentiation. Here the company concentrates on creating a highly differentiated product line and marketing programme so that it comes across as the class leader in the industry. Most customers will prefer to buy this brand if its price is not too high. Companies pursuing this strategy have major strength in R&D, design, quality control and marketing.

Focus or market segmentation. Here the company focuses its effort on serving a few market segments well rather than going after the whole market. The company gets to know the needs of the segments and pursues either cost leadership or product differentiation, or both, within each chosen segment.

Although Porter did not address marketing directly in his discussion, it can, however, be safely concluded that at least two of these strategies are marketing oriented (El-Morsy, 1986).

For example, focus strategy is by definition a marketing strategy. In fact, the concepts of market segmentation and its counterpart, positioning, are seen as marketing's most important contribution to strategic thinking in general and competitive strategy in particular (Briggadike, 1983).

With reference to the second strategy, which is a differentiation strategy, a business is differentiated when some value-added activities are performed in a way that leads to perceived superiority along dimensions that are valued by customers (Day and Wensley, 1988).

Among the most favoured routes to differentiate a business or its products are: providing superior service, using a strong brand name, offering innovative features, and providing superior product quality.

It is obvious that such a strategy, to achieve success, needs in the first place a strong marketing orientation.

In fact, Levitt (1980) points out marketing's ability to differentiate anything.

From this brief discussion, it is not difficult to conclude, then, that marketing provides a key input to the competitive strategy formulation process.

SUMMARY AND CONCLUSION

The purpose of this chapter was to shed light on the contribution of marketing to competitive success. It has been already concluded that companies need to pay closer attention than ever before to changing political, social, economic and technological trends. Marketing, it is argued, can help companies win against severe international competition. Yet, for all the lip service companies give to being marketing oriented, it is remarkable how few of them appear to adhere to this. Successful companies, on the other hand, have made marketing a distinctive element in their business strategies. They view it as a major factor to gain market power and competitive strength. Lastly, it was made clear that marketing is a key element in competitive strategy formulation.

REFERENCES

Baker, M.J. (1979) Export myopia. *The Quarterly Review of Marketing*, Spring, pp. 1–10.

Baker, M.J. (1988) Innovation — key to success. In Thomas, M.J. and White, N.E. (eds) *The Marketing Digest*. Heinemann, London, pp. 129–145.

Baker, M.J., and Abou-Zeid, E.D. (1982) *Successful Exporting*. Westburn, Helensburgh.

Baker, M.J., Hart, S.J., Black, C.D., and Abdel-Mohsen, T.M. (1986) The contribution of marketing to competitive success. University of Strathclyde Working Papers.

Barry, T.E. (1986) *Marketing: An Integrated Approach*. Dryden Press, London.

Bennet, P.D. (1988) *Marketing*. McGraw-Hill, New York.

Blackwell, N. (1982) How to market technology. *Management Today*, December, pp. 70–75.

Briggadike, E.R. (1983) *The Contribution of Marketing to Strategic Management*, 2nd edn., Allyn Bacon, Boston.

Bruno, A.V. *et al.* (1987) Why firms fail. *Business Horizons*, March–April, pp. 50–58.

Buchan, J., and Marsh, P. (1989) The winning mix in drug research. *Financial Times*, January 27, p. 16.

Business Week (1983) Marketing: The new priority. November 21, pp. 66–73.

Buzzell, R. (1983) Quoted in Marketing: The new priority. *Business Week*, November 21.

Buzzell, R., and Wiersema, F.D. (1981) Successful share-building strategies. *Harvard Business Review*, January–February, pp. 135–144.

Central Policy Review Staff (1975) *The Future of the British Car Industry*. HMSO, London.

Chaganti, R., and Chaganti, R. (1983) A profile of profitable and not so profitable small businesses. *Journal of Small Business Management*, July.

Clark, J. (1979) *Business Today: Success and Failures*. Random House, New York.

Clifford, D.K. Jr, and Cavanagh, R.E. (1985) *The Winning Performance: How America's High Growth Midsized Companies Succeed*. Sidgwick and Jackson, London.

Cooper, R.G. (1975) Why new industrial products fail. *Industrial Marketing Management*, **4**, December, pp. 315–326.

Cooper, R.G. (1979) The dimensions of industrial new product success and failure. *Journal of Marketing*, **43**, Summer, pp. 93–103.

Cravens, D.W. and Woodruff, R.B. (1986) *Marketing*. Addison-Wesley, Reading, MA.

Cunningham, W.H. *et al.* (1987) *Marketing: A Managerial Approach*. South Western Publishing Company.

Davis, S. (1987) Quoted in T. McBurnie and D. Clutterbuck, *The Marketing Edge: Key to Profit and Growth*. Weidenfeld & Nicolson, London.

Day, G.S., and Wensley, R. (1988) Assessing advantage: A framework for diagnosing competitive superiority. *Journal of Marketing*, **52** (2), April, 1–20.

Doyle, P. (1985) Marketing and competitive performance of British industry: Areas for research. *Journal of Marketing Management*, **1** (1), 87–98.

Doyle, P. (1989) Markets and innovation. *European Management Journal*, **7** (4), 413–421.

Dumaine, B. (1989) P & G rewrites the marketing rules. *Fortune*, November 6, pp. 34–43.

El-Morsy, G.M. (1986) Competitive marketing strategy: A study of the competitive performance in the British Common Market. Unpublished PhD dissertation, Department of Marketing, University of Strathclyde.

Eppert, R.R. (1965) Passport for marketing overseas. *Journal of Marketing*, April, pp. 5–6.

Financial Times (1988a) Just add sugar. Monday, July 4.

Financial Times (1988b) Reebok sprints into foreign markets. Tuesday, May 24.

Financial Times (1988c) The going gets tough, so Adidas gets going. Friday, February 19.

Garvin, D.A. (1981) Product quality: An important strategic weapon. *Business Horizons*, **27** (3), May–June.

Garvin, D. (1987) Competing on the eight dimensions of quality. *Harvard Business Review*, November–December, pp. 101–109.

Gumpert, D.E. (1985) Introduction. In *The Marketing Renaissance*. Harvard Business Review Executive Book Series. Wiley, New York.

Hall, W.K. (1980) Survival strategies in a hostile environment. *Harvard Business Review*, September–October, pp. 75–85.

Hooley, G.J., and Lynch, J.E. (1985) Marketing lessons from the UK's high flying companies. *Journal of Marketing Management*, **1** (1), Summer, pp. 67–74.

Johnson, H. (1982) Beware the challenge of importers: An example of the importers advertising activity in motor car industry. *Journal of Advertising*, **1** (3), 273–276.

Itami, H. (1987) *Mobilizing Invisible Assets*. Harvard University Press, Cambridge, Mass.

ITT Research Ltd (1975) *Concentration on Key Markets*. Betro Trust, London.

Kent, R. (1984) Marketing faith and marketing practice: A study of product range in the Scottish food processing industry. Unpublished MSc thesis, Department of Marketing, University of Strathclyde.

Killough, J. (1978) Improved payoffs from transnational advertising. *Harvard Business Review*, July–August.

Kotler, P., and Singh, R. (1981) Marketing warfare in the 1980s. *Journal of Business Strategy*, Winter.

Levitt, T. (1980) Marketing success through differentiation of anything. *Harvard Business Review*, January–February, pp. 83–91.

Levitt, T. (1983) *The Marketing Imagination*. Free Press, New York.

McBurnie, T., and Clutterbuck, D. (1987) *The Marketing Edge: Key to Profit and Growth*. Weidenfeld & Nicolson, London.

McFarlane, G. (1978) Scots Queen's Award winners don't excel. *Marketing*, April.

McKenna, R. (1988) Marketing in the age of diversity. *Harvard Business Review*, September–October, pp. 88–95.

Michaels, E.G. (1982) Marketing muscle. *Business Horizons*, May–June, pp. 63–74.

Michell, P. (1979) Infrastructure and international marketing effectiveness. *Columbia Journal of World Business*, **14** (4), 91–104.

Mikesell, R.F., and Farah, M.G. (1980) *US Export Competitiveness in Manufacturers in The Third World Markets*. The Centre for Strategic and International Studies, Washington DC, Georgetown University.

Millmans, A.F. (1982) Understanding barriers to product innovation at the R&D/marketing interface. *European Journal of Marketing*, **16** (5), 22–34.

Nadel, J. (1987) *Cracking the Global Market: How To Do Business Around the Corner and the World*. AMACOM, New York.

NEDO (1979) *Growth Through Exports*. National Economic Development Council, HMSO, London.

NEDO (1981) *Industrial Performance: Trade Performance and Marketing*. National Economic Development Council, London.

NEDO (1983) *Standard, Quality and Competitiveness*. National Economic Development Council, London.

Ogilvy, D. (1983) *Ogilvy on Advertising*. Orbis, London.

Ohmae, K. (1988) Getting back to strategy. *Harvard Business Review*, November–December, pp. 125–132.

Ohmae, K. (1989) Companyism and do more better. *Harvard Business Review*, January–February, 125–132.

Pearson, A.E. (1988) Tough minded ways to get innovative. *Harvard Business Review*, May–June, pp. 99–106.

Peters, T.J. (1988) *Thriving on Chaos*. Macmillan, London.

Peters, T.J., and Waterman, R.H., Jr (1982) *In Search of Excellence*. Harper & Row, New York.

Porter, M.E. (1980) *Competitive Strategy: Techniques for Analysing Industries and Competitors*. Free Press, New York.

Posner, M., and Steel, A. (1979) Price competitiveness and performance of manufacturing industry. In Blackaby, F. (ed.) *De-Industrialisation*. Heinemann Educational Books, London.

Project SAPPHO (1972) *Success and Failure in Industrial Innovation*. Science Policy Research Unit, University of Sussex; Centre for the Study of Industrial Innovation, London.

Ross, J.E., and Shetty, Y.K. (1985) Making quality a fundamental part of strategy. *Long Range Planning*, **18** (1), 53–58.

Roth, R.F. (1982) *International Marketing Communications*. Crain, Chicago.

Saporito, B. (1984) Hewlett-Packard discovers marketing. *Fortune*, October 1, pp. 50–52.

Saunders, J., and Wong, V. (1985) In search of excellence in the UK. *Journal of Marketing Management*, **1** (2), Winter, 119–137.

Schendal, D.E., and Hofer, C.W. (eds) (1979) *Strategic Management: A New View of Business Policy*. Little Brown, Boston.

Schoeffler, S., Buzzell, R., and Heany, D. (1974) Impact of strategic planning on profit performance. *Harvard Business Review*, March–April, pp. 137–145.

Schultz, E. (1988) America's most admired corporations. *Fortune*, January 18, pp. 26–33.

Schwartz, D.J. (1981) *Marketing Today*, 8th edn. Harcourt Brace Jovanovich, New York.

Seller, P. (1987) How Busch wins in a doggy market. *Fortune*, June 22, pp. 67–74.

Shankleman, E. (1975) *Britain's Post War Export Performance*. NEDO, London.

Shapiro, B.P. (1988) What the hell is 'market oriented'? *Harvard Business Review*, November–December, pp. 119–125.

Shetty, Y.K. (1987) Product quality and competitive strategy. *Business Horizons*, May–June, pp. 46–52.

Shetty, Y.K., and Buehler, V.M. (ed.) (1983) *Quality and Productivity Improvements: US and Foreign Company Experience*. Manufacturing Productivity Centre, Chicago, pp. 46–52.

Slatter, S. (1977) *Competition in the Pharmaceutical Industry*. Croom-Helm, London.

Slijper, M. (1978) Why we must wake up to distribution. *Marketing*, May, pp. 45–52.

Stacey, N. (1962) Problems of export marketing. *Planning*, No. 459, February.

Stanton, W.J., and Futrell, C. (1987) *Fundamentals of Marketing*, 8th edn. McGraw-Hill, New York.

Stern, L.W., and Sturdivant, F.D. (1987) Customer driven distribution systems. *Harvard Business Review*, July–August, pp. 34–41.

Suzuki, N. (1980) The changing pattern of advertising strategy by Japanese business firms in the US market: Content analysis. *Journal of Internation Business Studies*, **11** (3), Winter, 63–72.

Takeuchi, H., and Quelch, J.A. (1983) Quality is more than making a good product. *Harvard Business Review*, July–August, pp. 139–145.

Tofler, A. (1970) *Future Shock*, Bantam Books, New York.

Tookey, D. (1964) Factors associated with success in exporting. *The Journal of Management Studies*, **1**, March, pp. 48–66.

Turnbull, P.W. *et al.* (1981) *International Marketing and Purchasing*. Macmillan, London.

Udell, J.G. (1964) How Important is pricing in competitive strategy. *Journal of Marketing*, **28**, January, pp. 44–48.

Von-Hippel, E. (1982) Get new products from customers. *Harvard Business Review*, March–April, pp. 117–122.

Walsh, L. (1979) How Compair went into Germany. *Marketing*, February, pp. 18–22.

Watson, T.J. (1963) *A Business and its Beliefs: The Ideas that Helped Build IBM.* McGraw-Hill, New York.

Webster, F.E. (1981) Top management's concerns about marketing: Issues for the 1980's. *Journal of Marketing*, **45**, Summer, pp. 9–16.

Wilson, A. (1984) Innovation in the marketplace. *Management Today*, June, pp. 78–82.

CHAPTER 2

Putting the Management into Marketing Management

Douglas T. Brownlie

Glasgow Business School, University of Glasgow

INTRODUCTION

The origin of this chapter can be traced back to the author's time as an undergraduate student of marketing, when he would ponder what it would be like to be a marketing manager and what he would be required to do. Those questions lingered with him through four years of marketing management classes. And they seemed to loom larger as it became clear that very little was being said about the job of management in marketing. The marketing manager's job had been reduced to a simple model of analysis, planning and control. At the centre of it was the marketing mix and a sophisticated analytical technology that made marketing management seem as if it was a matter of turning the knobs of a pre-programmed machine in the indicated direction to get a desired effect.

Gradually the idea has taken root that if the prevailing model of marketing management was incomplete or even invalid in some way, then how could we possibly design and run courses whose purpose is to train tomorrow's marketing managers? Many aspects of industrial and commercial activity have changed since the times when the early and perennial models of marketing management were developed. And perhaps the skills and competencies that marketing managers require have also changed.

It was often remarked that marketing was too important to be left to the marketing department; the corollary being that in a truly market-driven organization everyone makes decisions based on their impact on the customer. Customer considerations should then be factored into every management decision. So marketing is first and foremost a general management responsibility and individual executives should put the interests of the customer at the top of their priorities. And so the litany would proceed.

Perspectives on Marketing Management, Volume 1
Edited by M.J. Baker

The author has often suspected that implicit to this remark were insights about the organizational role and power of the marketing function and the skills of its managers that have never been adequately explicated by marketing scholars. Indeed, most studies of marketing management focus on the technical, or decision-making content of the job, neglecting the broader managerial elements. Others, notably Bonoma (1984), Hutt, Reingen and Ronchetto (1988), Walker and Ruekert (1987), Deshpande and Webster (1989) and Piercy (1986a, 1989) have recently come by different routes to a similar conclusion.

Perhaps, as this view seems to be gaining some popularity among marketing academics, now is the time to begin to explore its implications and ramifications. But in some respects there are broader forces at work which heighten the urgency of the task.

A VIEW OF MARKETING MANAGEMENT

The rhetoric of market forces argues that competition in domestic and international markets will continue to intensify and that further opportunities for profitable growth and innovation will demand more sophisticated and skilled marketing. Marketing and innovation are pinpointed as the vital skills management must master if it is to secure competitive advantage in the 1990s.

The popularity of this rhetoric suggests that the importance of skilled marketing to every nation's industrial and commercial prosperity is becoming more widely appreciated. Indeed, several surveys have found marketing to be an area of management that at least British and American executives feel they should know more about (Lynch, Hooley and Shepherd, 1989; Cowell, 1987; Doyle, 1987; Webster, 1981; Hooley and Lynch, 1985).

Yet surprisingly little is known about the extent and nature of marketing practice in British industry and commerce. Surveys count heads and do point to a lack of marketing skills and professionalism. But for these surveys, which do tend to verify the predispositions of the researchers, there has been little systematic in-depth study of the work of marketing managers. Consequently, benchmarks of best management practice do not yet exist which could guide individual firms and their executives towards more effective marketing practice.

Indeed, it is surprising how little is known about the skills and competencies that marketing managers bring to organizations. We know they should be innovative, forward thinking, flexible and able to communicate. But how do they develop and apply skills in these areas to good effect? And how do they put the ideas of marketing into practice so that they make an effective contribution to the organization's development? There is a wealth of material telling us *what* to do, but rarely *how* to do it.

One wonders how marketing can be put to good use in organizations in the absence of such knowledge. It could be argued that the route to effective marketing, and thus competitiveness, must lie in a robust understanding of how to implement marketing ideas in an organizational context. So the qualities of effective marketing management are those that calibrate the organization's ability to implement its marketing strategies.

Clearly there are organizations that have successfully worked out an approach to managing marketing that suits their needs — usually through trial and error rather than planning. In many sectors it is common practice to subcontract much of the organization's marketing to marketing services consultants, including advertising agencies, design houses, public relations groups, market research agencies, sales promotions consultants, new product development specialists, domestic and overseas wholesale or retail distributors, or even a management consultant.

You might then be forgiven for wondering what the marketing manager does. It may seem to involve negotiating a brief, managing a budget, coordinating the various marketing efforts of subcontractors and evaluating their performance. And the successful execution of those tasks would employ the managerial skills of any marketing executive. But the conventional wisdom has it that the marketing manager identifies unfulfilled needs and wants; defines and measures their magnitude; determines which target markets the organization can best serve; decides on appropriate products, services and programmes to serve these markets; and calls upon everyone in the organization to think and serve the customer.

Marketing management is then thought of as a process which takes the manager through a logical sequence of activities. The execution of this process defines the marketing manager's areas of responsibility and therefore circumscribes the nature of his work. In Kotler's (1988) terms, marketing management is the process of analysing marketing opportunities, researching and selecting target markets, designing marketing strategies, planning marketing programmes, and organizing, implementing and controlling marketing efforts. He adds that the marketing manager plans and executes the conception, pricing, promotion, and distribution of ideas, goods and services to create exchanges that satisfy individual and organizational objectives. So the job involves managing particular marketing resources with well-defined tasks and responsibilities in the areas of advertising, sales promotion, market research, distribution, product development and pricing.

But for the task of realizing the marketing concept, the marketing manager would seem to spend much of his time in analysis and planning duties in support of his decision-making.

The notion of the marketing manager as a decision-maker is initially simple and easily derived from the classical school of management thought. But this simple notion only holds if we choose to forget about the organizational and managerial aspects of the job. While most writers on management are not now prepared to accept this condition, most writers on marketing management are, even if only by default. Consequently, abstracted from the context of management, models of marketing management would have us presume that marketing managers act rationally in their decision-making: i.e. they collect adequate and appropriate information and then process it to its logical conclusion, thereby coming to a choice of the option that promises to lead to the best result.

This review of marketing management is firmly embedded in the writings of Kotler (1988) and those whose work builds on his ideas. He sees marketing management as the most significant functional contributor to the strategic planning process. He ascribes to it leadership roles in defining the business mission; analysing the market environment, including competition; developing objectives, goals and strategies; and defining product, market, distribution and quality plans to implement the business' strategies. But without a concept of organization it is difficult to see how those roles can be enacted and the manager empowered.

Kotler promotes a view of the marketing management process as one that is driven by marketing planning. Indeed, he states that the marketing plan is the central instrument for directing and coordinating the marketing effort. So organizations that want to improve their marketing effectiveness must learn how to create and implement sound marketing plans.

The basis of Kotler's view of best marketing management practice is derived from a normative model of marketing management which has not been tested. It lays considerable emphasis on formal analysis and planning and the application of sophisticated marketing technology to the collection and processing of information. Indeed, this is reflected in the contents of his famous marketing management text. Approximately 95% of the book is devoted to the discussion of marketing analysis, planning and the application of marketing technology to decision-making. The remaining 5% deals with the subject of implementation: i.e. making it all happen both within and outwith organizations.

Kotler has developed a metrology for testing marketing management which has been very influential and is still popular. It is enshrined in his famous article (Kotler, 1977) on the marketing audit which prescribes universal benchmarks against which to judge marketing practices. And while the process of conducting a marketing audit may itself be a very useful managerial exercise, it enters dangerous and difficult intellectual and political waters when it comes to passing judgement on management activities and assumptions.

The inability to specify, *a priori*, good managerial practice in marketing puts in jeopardy the concept of the SWOT analysis, which supports the marketing planning process, and the marketing audit, which informs it. Without a metrology with which to measure good practice, the audit becomes a self-fulfilling prophecy. Or, where off-the-shelf benchmarks are used, such as Kotler's (1988) marketing audit prescriptions, automatic judgements are arrived at on the basis of vague generalizations, making it difficult to come to any specific conclusions. Implicit to the metrology of the marketing audit and the judgements of the internal appraisal must be a model of best management practice in marketing.

The step that seems to be missing in the audit methodology is that which asks specific questions about the nature of the management job in marketing in the organization and about the kind of person likely to be effective in it. Answers would provide a template which could be used for decisions such as the selection of marketing staff, the appraisal of their performance, their promotion and the design and assignment to marketing management development activities. Without this sort of knowledge it is difficult to see how anyone can attribute organizational success to anything in particular.

The pervasiveness of Kotler's views has led many with him to the belief that better marketing decision-making demands better analytical tools. And even when making a small concession to the view that marketing thinking and action involves processes not easily amenable to analysis and planning, he adds the rider that to strengthen marketing practice and thought we must develop improved strategic theory and sharper tools of analysis (Kotler, 1988). Bonoma (1984) strongly rejects this view and widely criticizes the obsession of marketing scholars with strategy formulation. He argues that relevancy in the 1990s will demand that increased attention be paid to marketing practice and to the signposts of good marketing management. In his view, the formulation and the implementation of strategy are inextricably entwined.

Bonoma (1984) believes that the key to managerial effectiveness is the ability to put strategies into action. And you could argue that in the 1990s what top management will need of marketing is not new analytical techniques to answer questions about strategy formulation, but increased attention to marketing practice and to the signposts of effective marketing management.

In a review of 17 marketing management texts which includes Kotler's, Bonoma (1985) is surprised to find that very little emphasis is placed on marketing practice and implementation. Indeed, what he finds by way of a description of the activities of marketing managers are clearly extensions of the analysis, planning and control paradigm. So the conventional wisdom is that marketing managers spend their time using sophisticated marketing technology to help them take their decisions and lay their plans. And the attractiveness of this view is perhaps enhanced by the seemingly rational work habits and viewpoints which computers induce.

The embedded rationality of Kotler's view of marketing management has its origins in the scientific management school. Simon (1957) widely criticizes the tenets of this school of thought, partly on the basis of the individual's inability to be completely rational even when he intends to be. Simon tells us that the rationality of the individual is strictly bounded. He offers further criticism on the basis of the individual's limited ability to collect, then process the information he needs to its purely rational conclusions.

Child (1972) criticizes classical management theory on the basis of its dismissal of what he considers to be the primary management task, i.e. the resolution of the plurality of interests represented within the organization. He uses the term 'strategic choice' to denote the task, which he describes as a complex and inherently political activity. Spender (1989a) continues the line of criticism by questioning the classical management theory's imputation of a unique rationality. He argues that the rationality of this theory is simply one of a whole universe of possible rationalities.

Spender (1989b) draws our attention to the important role of individual rationality, or judgement, in any model of management. Kotler's definition of the roles and responsibilities of the marketing manager in terms of analysis, planning and decision-making overlooks the part played by judgement in marketing decision-making.

King (1985) writes that judgement will always be more important than technique in marketing. In his view, marketing is different from finance and production, where operations research and econometrics have been applied so forcefully and effectively. The data on which marketing decisions are based are always unreliable: consumers are irrational; competitors confound cause–effect models; rules are broken. To focus on marketing techniques is in King's (1985) view to sacrifice relevancy.

At first sight, the management task in marketing seems to have been reduced to one of analysis and planning. And while this may be broadly true in junior brand management jobs in fast moving consumer goods (FMCG) organizations, one wonders if it can be representative across levels of managerial responsibility, across sectors and sizes of organizations. Moreover, analysis and planning only provide umbrella headings under which many more specific managerial activities could be organized. The chapter argues that this categorization of managerial work in marketing is not powerful enough to serve as a guide to the design of marketing jobs and, therefore, to the evaluation of marketing performance and effectiveness.

On the basis of studying the responsibilities of managers in particular jobs, several writers on management have developed more specific lists of the activities of managers and have used them to arrive at profiles of the qualities of successful managers. The management development work of Burgoyne and Stuart (1976) has led them to the following list of qualities, or attributes, which forms the basis of their recipe for successful management:

1. Command of the basic facts
2. Relevant professional knowledge
3. Continuing sensitivity to events
4. Analytical, problem-solving, decision/judgement-making skills
5. Social skills and abilities
6. Emotional resilience
7. Proactivity
8. Creativity
9. Mental agility
10. Balanced learning habits and skills
11. Self-knowledge

As Pedler, Burgoyne and Boydell (1978) note, these qualities fall into three groups which constitute three different levels. Numbers 1 and 2 form the foundation level and represent two kinds of basic knowledge and information that a manager may need in his job. Numbers 3–7 are specific skills and attributes that directly affect management behaviour and performance. Numbers 8–11 are those qualities which allow the manager to develop and deploy his skills and resources in particular circumstances.

Some marketing writers, including Piercy (1986b), Thomas (1984), Cowell (1987), Doyle (1987) and Middleton and Long (1988) have studied the responsibilities of marketing managers. Table 2.1 lists the responsibilities of chief marketing executives which Piercy (1986b) found in his study. Thomas (1984) and Cowell (1987) have also produced lists of the skills and qualities that marketing managers seem to need to possess in order to successfully discharge their duties and responsibilities. Table 2.2 reproduces Thomas' (1984) list. From a content

Table 2.1 Chief marketing executive responsibilities

Marketing mix
Market research
Advertising
Marketing staffing
Marketing training
Marketing planning
Sales promotion
New product development
Sales forecasting
Product planning
Pricing
Packaging
Field sales force
Price discounts
Product design
Distributor negotiations
Warehousing
Transport
Corporate strategy
Corporate/strategic planning
R&D strategy
Diversification studies
Investment appraisal

Source: Piercy (1986b). Reproduced by permission.

Table 2.2 Skills and abilities needed by marketing managers

Planning skills
Environmental awareness
Organizational ability
Segmentation – product development skills
Behaviour analysis skills
Market research commissioning skills
Information analysis skills
Innovation management skills
Strategic thinking skills
Sales & advertising management and productivity
Management skills
Marketing mix optimization skills
Interdepartmental cooperation and conflict resolution skills
Financial management skills
Systems-thinking skills
The ability to comprehend the long-term interests of the company
The ability to 'market' marketing enthusiastically

Source: Thomas (1984). Reproduced by permission.

analysis of 100 job advertisements for marketing managers, the author has derived lists of the attributes, skills and job activities as expressed in the copy of the advertisement. These lists are reproduced in Tables 2.3, 2.4 and 2.5 respectively. Kotler (1988) has also recently taken to providing lists of the skills that marketing managers need in the area of implementation: these he lists as allocating skills, monitoring skills, organizing skills and interacting skills.

Clearly it would be a simple task to organize the contents of those

Table 2.3 Attributes

Ambitious	Cool head
Professionalism	Resourceful
Innovative	Flair
Creative	Maturity
Flexible	Tact
Experienced	Effectiveness
Intellect	Work under pressure
Keen for extra responsibility	Practical
High calibre	Imaginative
Impressive	Work without supervision
Entrepreneurial	Breadth of vision
Young	Rapid success
Energetic	Fast paced
Self-motivated	Successful

Table 2.4 Skills

General	Specific
Numeracy	Advertising planning
Analytical	Print campaigns
Organizational	Below-the-line promotions
Strategist	Evaluating response
Implementational	Distribution
Strategic planning	Selling
Man management	Trade negotiations
Information handling	New product development
Interpersonal	Incentive activities
Business development	Conferences/exhibitions
Coordination	Brand support
Liaising	Developing/implementing promotional strategy
Languages	Direct marketing/mail
Communications	Campaign planning
Team building	Brochure production
	Public relations
	Press briefings
	Marchandise planning

Table 2.5 Job activities

Plan trade promotions and promotional strategy
Achieving bottom-line profit
Develop and implement marketing and sales strategies
Plan and execute direct marketing and direct mail activities
Product selection
Brochure production
Campaign planning and execution (press/poster)
Link creative, commercial and sales functions
Organize/coordinate promotional activities
Liaise with national marketing department
Provide company with new impetus and direction
Take full control of all aspects of the marketing mix
Guide all commercial activity
Bring new products/services to market
Work closely with corporate management team
Develop medium–long term strategy
Help sales managers address regional market needs
Manage full range of marketing activities
Support operational activities
Report to director (MD/sales/marketing)
Total involvement in the development of new products/services from design concept to launch
Manage sizeable department
Stimulate new phase of growth
Develop UK and international information system
Manage commercial contacts with a large number of companies
Bring an innovative approach to business development
Seek out new business opportunities
Control UK corporate promotional activities
Client liaison
Organizing and evaluating promotions
Coordinate direct mail
Strengthen the marketing department
Developing marketing systems
Collaborating between marketing, sales, research and production
Input into NPD and promotional activity conception/organization of in-house incentive activity
Arranging conferences and exhibitions
Developing/implementing short/long term marketing objectives

various lists according to the 4Ps rubric, so specifying the content of the marketing management job; and the analysis, planning, control and implementation rubric, which specifies the marketing management process. In so doing you would discover the real value of those models: i.e. as broad headings under which to arrange basic teaching material of a descriptive, but not prescriptive nature.

The author has two reservations about this approach. First, it accumulates a comprehensive list of qualities, skills and activities which in a circular way provides a basis on which to describe a very general model of marketing management. But, as Piercy (1986b, c) found, only in a very few UK firms will you find a marketing department with responsibility for all of those activities and, therefore, where all of those skills and qualities are employed. Across sectors and sizes of firms there may also be significant variations of emphasis on the activities of marketing managers, and thus the skills and qualities they employ.

Secondly, the research method which is utilized tends to ask the marketing manager what he does, whether by means of a postal survey questionnaire or by interview. To do so puts the manager in the position of the researcher. He is expected to translate complex reality, as he perceives it, into meaningful abstraction. And as Mintzberg (1973) notes, there is no evidence to suggest that managers can do this effectively. Indeed, he cites numerous empirical studies of the work of managers which in his view provide ample evidence that managers are poor estimators of their own activities. So, despite their convenience, the interview and the questionnaire are only useful instruments for gathering data on managers' perceptions of their own job. Other research approaches must be employed if we are to discover what marketing managers really do. We might also need to ask new questions.

It is not surprising that the results of empirical research diverge from the conventional model of marketing management. Much of the material on marketing management that has been published during the last 20 years is normative and derivative of the analysis, planning and control paradigm. The description it offers of both the content and the processes of marketing management is distant from what marketing managers say they do. Yet there is no shortage of abstract descriptions of marketing management that, while lacking the hard data of empirical research, are also encrusted with convictions that merit further scrutiny.

In several incisive articles writers have recorded the disappointment of organizations with the results achieved by their efforts at marketing. Many feel that its promise is largely unfulfilled (Webster, 1981, 1988; Hayes and Abernathy, 1980; Bennett and Cooper, 1981), while others believe that it has never really been tried (Baker, 1989; Samli *et al.*, 1987). But if we do not understand what constitutes the marketing manager's job, how can we measure his effectiveness and how can we be clear about what we should attribute success or failure to? Yet as long as the lessons of these organizations remain unavailable to the wider management audience, it seems that the wheel of the conventional model of marketing management will continue to be reinvented time after time.

CHANGING CONTEXTS, CHANGING COMPETENCIES

Effective management is attributable to the skills and competencies of executives, whose behaviour is itself greatly influenced by the organizational setting they find themselves in. Managerial decision-making is therefore inextricably linked to the individual manager's responsibility and place in the organization (Spender, 1989). And as organizations adapt to new circumstances and change their structures, systems, practices and cultures, so the job of the manager changes as do the skills and competencies he must bring to his work.

This has changed in recent years and looks likely to continue to do so as new corporate cultures, strategies and organizational structures emerge in the 1990s. Yet existing models of marketing management are based on studies of the structures, systems and practices of organizations reflecting the circumstances of the 1960s.

During the early 1980s, in response to recessionary pressures and intense competition, many UK organizations greatly reduced their staffing levels (Deloitte, Haskins and Sells, 1989). The ranks of middle management dwindled. Management structures have become leaner, and the need for broader based management skills has become clear. Since then corporate structures and ways of working have continued to change, particularly in response to the increasing speed of change in the markets that organizations serve and the products they deliver.

In an attempt to get closer to their customers and to be more responsive to their needs, organizations are creating more fluid structures through decentralization and devolved decision-making. As a result of flatter structures and more flexible ways of organizing work, many organizations are becoming more adaptable and responsive (Ashridge Management Research Group 1988). But decentralization and fragmentation put pressure on managers to provide the integrating force through overall corporate strategy, culture and information technology.

A recent study (Ashridge Management Research Group, 1988) concluded that the context of managerial activity would change substantially in the 1990s. It found that managers will increasingly be concerned with cross-functional issues of quality, service and new technology. And consequently, managers will need to become more skilled in horizontal management, i.e. managing lateral relationships, networking, team building, working on projects in groups, using influence and negotiation rather than power, being tolerant of ambiguity and change; and all those rather than the management of hierarchical relationships based on power and organizational status.

Indeed, Nulty (1987) foresees the rise of what he calls the value-added manager. It is his view that as the number of middle managers dwindles, those that remain will become less bound up in the bureaucratic tasks of writing reports and filling out forms. They will act more as coaches to the troops below and as coordinators who exchange information horizontally with other middle managers, rather than relaying it between upper and lower ranks.

The premise of this chapter is that there is genuine doubt about what marketing managers really do for their organizations. The conventional wisdom says that they analyse and plan and take decisions. But, as Spender (1989) reminds us, this simple idea implies not only a chosen theory of the organization, but also of the external context and of society at any point in time. And each theory of the organization implies a specific place and function for its management. If the context changes, so does the organization, so does the management job within it and so do the skills and competencies of the effective manager.

In an era of change, it does not seem unreasonable to expect the nature of organizations to change and the nature of management work also to change. None have argued more vehemently than Kanter (1983) that the assumptions that we hold about organizations, which have survived for decades and in which our existing view of management is embedded, are now invalid. The cumbersome hierarchies, segmentalism and differentiation of the 1960s and 1970s must now be replaced by integrative assumptions about organizations. Like others (Greenwood and Hinings, 1987), she argues that the ability to manage change is the challenge of the 1990s. She goes on to offer new assumptions about organizations that reflect the needs of an era of transformation.

So the legitimacy of existing models of marketing management is open to question for many of the same reasons that are driving changes in management in general. The author believes them to be oversimplified and mechanistic, reflecting large company structures and roles of the 1960s. And they may not be appropriate in the 1990s, where organizational structures will be flatter and more fluid and where management tasks look likely to be project based, involving a mixture of operational and strategic duties.

So perhaps we do need to ask new questions, such as what is the content of the marketing manager's job? How does he spend his time? What role does he play? What relationships does he have with others in the organization? What operational and strategic responsibilities does he have? What skills, behaviours and qualities does the effective marketing manager bring to his organization? And how does the organizational setting influence the application of his skills?

The author believes that current answers to those questions are inadequate. If you agree, then you will share the author's interest in advancing our understanding of the skills and competencies required for effective marketing management. It will also generate insights into the roles and character of marketing executives in British firms, so providing more robust benchmarks of best management practice on which to base the development of marketing management and managers in organizations. But we also need new ways of finding answers to the questions.

CULTURE, CHANGE AND THE MARKETING CONCEPT

Drucker's (1954) original articulation of the marketing concept emphasizes that marketing is not a separate management function but the whole business as seen from the customer's point of view. In other words, the marketing concept defines a distinct organizational culture, a fundamental set of shared beliefs and values that put the customer in the centre of the firm's thinking about strategy and operations.

Deshpande and Webster (1989) argue that despite this centrality of organizational culture to marketing management issues, there has been relatively little scholarly study of its impact in a marketing context — the recent work of Dunn, Norburn and Birley (1985), Morgan and Piercy (1989) and Birley, Norburn and Dunn (1987) perhaps being in the vanguard. But the lack of scrutiny perhaps reflects Ruekert, Walker and Roerring's (1985) wry observation that greater attention is given to customer than to organizational issues in marketing in general.

Of course, other writers have made similar observations about the limitations of marketing's customer focus, including Oxenfeld and Moore (1975), Henderson (1981), Wind and Robertson (1983) and Day and Wensley (1983, 1988). All agree on the need to take a wider perspective, especially to encompass the measurement and analysis of competitive advantage. But issues of internal organization, culture, management and implementation are rarely considered.

In spite of such esoteric academic concerns, many have recently been converted to the broad view of marketing as a management philosophy. Indeed, marketing may even have been rediscovered by others in the 1980s (Webster, 1988; Baker, 1989). In some organizations the marketing concept has become a symbol of organizational change and development as well as an instrument of general management policy. Clearly the pressures of intense competition are driving organizations towards marketing. But they might also be rediscovering the view that marketing is itself ill equipped to effect the important organizational changes that in many cases are necessary preconditions to the development of a customer-focused, market-driven culture. In other words, they may find themselves eagerly embracing the trappings of marketing at the expense of its substance (Ames, 1970).

In theory, the realization of the marketing concept is the property and task of marketing. Yet, unless the necessary cultural changes occur throughout the organization, it is likely that marketing will be thwarted in its efforts. Tampering with the structure of the organization will not guarantee success. Marketing should be empowered to carry the task through, especially if it is to be held accountable for profit or growth. But, as Piercy (1986b) argues, the implementation of the marketing concept does not necessarily imply any particular set of organizational arrangements. Prescriptive material often advocates that the realization of the concept requires the existence of a marketing manager and a marketing department. Piercy (1986b) disputes this on the following grounds:

1. The realization of the marketing concept requires a change in management attitudes rather than simply organizational arrangements
2. Firms can be found that are marketing oriented but have no formal marketing organization
3. The context predefines the arrangements that will best suit the needs of each individual firm

Piercy (1986b) found that in many organizations, despite board representation, the corporate position of marketing was weak. The abdication of top management responsibility for marketing can only emasculate its strategic role and with it its contribution to organizational development. If the chief marketing executive lacks the organizational power and status to make substantive changes to the organizational culture, structure and systems, then only symbolic changes will be made. In such cases the marketing organization controls little more than the budget for advertising and promotion, and is unlikely to have a decisive influence when it comes to approving it.

On the basis of existing evidence, there is no clear way to integrate marketing into the organization's systems, processes and culture. Indeed, Piercy (1986b) found the tendency for marketing departments to disintegrate as firms grew in size and their marketing budgets increased. This is in direct contrast to the textbook view of the organization of the marketing function.

And while it may be true that active top management support is a precondition of cultural change in an organization, the nurturing of customer-oriented values and beliefs also demands the willing involvement and participation of other managers (Davis, 1984; Sathe, 1983). The top-down view of the process of cultural change is important as it defines the leadership role of top management in the short term. But in the longer term the troops have to be involved and in so doing will also mould the culture that eventually emerges.

The crude use of organizational power may be irresistible given the immovable object of the organizational inertia. And where those unfortunate circumstances are combined with the need to turn an organization around very quickly, it is common to replace the chief executive and his top management team, thus accelerating the implementation of the changes needed (Grinyer, Mayes and McKiernan, 1988). But it is a blunt instrument of change, often with unavoidable and brutal side-effects for many in the organization (Schwartz and Davis, 1981).

The ability to manage organizational change and transformation has been said to be the management challenge of the 1990s (Child and Smith, 1987). Yet the marketing concept has always called for constant change as market conditions evolve. It is not surprising then that many organizations have found the implementation of the concept a difficult and problematic managerial task. It has always struggled for acceptance in organizations where the culture, structure and systems were not ready for change. So for such reasons the realization of the marketing concept may indeed be an issue that is bigger than the marketing department.

The marketing discipline has yet to come to terms with the language and concepts of the management of change. It has had little to say about the management processes by which the marketing concept can be introduced and promoted in an organization. Despite the pioneering work of Walker and Ruekert (1987) and Piercy (1986a), the nature of marketing's role as an agent of change in the organization is not well understood. Yet without this understanding, how can the marketing management process ever be effective?

The marketing concept is a central tenet of the popular and successful management development and training programmes on customer care and total quality management. Some firms, including British Gas, British Telecom, British Rail, SSEB and many retail banks, have used these programmes in recent years as instruments of organizational change and development. And it would seem that, for those firms at least, the realization of the marketing concept has become more of an issue for personnel or organizational development than marketing.

The marketing managers of the 1990s will need to know how to realize the marketing concept. The imperatives of rapid changes in an increasingly hostile competitive climate have set the right context in which the role of marketing should grow. Organizations are learning that marketing is not sales, nor is it corporate strategy or planning (Webster, 1988). Top managers are espousing the view that serving customers and markets is the first priority for all functions. But perhaps the marketing concept itself also needs to grow.

The quest for greater competitiveness is not only enacted in the marketplace of customers. Many organizations are now building internal market structures so that internal marketing is becoming an important competitive weapon. And the acceptance of a broader view of marketing demands a similarly broader view of customers. Customers are not only those who purchase the goods and services provided by the organization. All stakeholders can also be seen as customers. And within the organization itself one employee can be thought of as the customer for the products and services of other employees.

Fellow marketers will appreciate that the language of customer care, internal markets, market orientation, quality and managing change has always been well within the domain of marketing management. Yet the realization of the concepts that this language describes has recently been advanced by work which takes a human resource perspective, not a marketing-derived one (Whipp, Rosenfeld and Pettigrew, 1988a, b; Rosenfeld, 1988). Conceptual and practical developments have been made in areas as diverse as management development (Brownlie *et al.*, 1988), operations management (MacBeth and Southern, 1989) and human resources management (Hendry, 1987).

The author believes that the convergence of cognate disciplines on marketing-related issues provides opportunities for the migration (Brownlie, 1989) of new ideas, concepts and methods into the field of marketing. In this way, marketing might evolve promising new perspectives and conceptual frameworks that could help to close the gap between theory and marketing practice.

MARKETING IS MANAGEMENT TOO

This chapter is written at a time when management development is percolating onto the strategic agenda of British industry. The Handy (1987) and Constable (Constable and McCormick, 1987) reports have drawn our attention to the question of how best to facilitate the development of British managers so as to improve their professionalism. They have also helped propagate the belief that existing models of managerial professionalism may need to be updated if they are to accurately embody the skills and competencies being demanded of managers now and forward into the 1990s.

It takes the view that marketing is management too, and that many of the issues raised by Handy and Constable are relevant to the continued development of marketing professionalism. The argument at the heart of the chapter is that new contexts demand organizational change and new management competencies. And if strategic management is about the management of change, then strategic marketing must be about the role of marketing management in effecting such change. This places management, and thus implementation, at the core of strategic marketing, not at the periphery.

In 1982, the Institute of Marketing commissioned a survey (Hooley, West and Lynch, 1984) of the practice and performance of marketing in Britain. In the context of a biting economic recession, the quality of British industry's marketing practices had become a matter for parliamentary consideration. It was becoming more widely appreciated that international competitive advantage was not only a question of productivity and cash management, but also of innovative marketing.

The Institute's survey covered 1800 senior executives, and the main findings concerned the qualities which distinguish marketing excellence from mediocrity and incompetence. These qualities were found to include:

- Genuine marketing orientation
- Heightened environmental sensitivity
- Organizational flexibility and adaptability
- Increased marketing professionalism

The authors of the report described these findings as 'effectively a summary of the conventional wisdom on marketing excellence'. This was in effect a rediscovery of what was already known about what firms should be doing to make their operations more competitive.

But this study left some significant gaps in our understanding of contemporary marketing practice. The questions which were not addressed in the report included:

1. What is the nature of the marketing manager's job, in practice, in the 1980s?
2. To what extent does contemporary marketing management differ from textbook models, which are largely based on the experience of American firms in the 1960s?
3. How can we expect the nature of the marketing manager's job to change in the 1990s?
4. What is known about the skills, competencies, roles and qualities of effective marketing managers?
5. What competencies are required by marketing managers to deal effectively with change in their organizations?

That the nature of managerial work in marketing is perhaps misrepresented in existing material must, to a great extent, reflect the preconceptions of researchers, who have perhaps approached the subject with readily operationalized views of what marketing management should be about.

The popular research model in the field of marketing is the direct questioning approach, where managers are asked to say what they think they do in their job. This they do through the medium of mail questionnaires and structured interviews, rather than through observation, audio diaries, critical incident analysis, or even scripts.

But large, cross-sectional, questionnaire-based surveys of management activities do provide external validity, perhaps at the expense of internal validity. They place excessive reliance on what the respondents, i.e. managers, think and say about their jobs. It was previously observed that by doing so the researcher leaves it up to the respondents to conceptualize their behaviour when they might not have the knowledge or skills to do so.

Nevertheless, this approach has many attractions for researchers eager to quantify their work and pursue the correlations that they believe to be the currency of imputed causality. Such studies often take a fragmented view of marketing management as a decision-making process, focusing on one major marketing decision at a time, such as the selection of new products or the elimination of others, neglecting the overlaps and synergies. The use of attitude surveys in such studies tends to verify the researcher's predispositions, so that the researcher is more likely to get caught up in the mythology of the organization than see the real process of management in action.

The five questions listed above deal with the context and process of marketing management and not the content of marketing decisions and plans. Answering them will require a grounded approach. They are unlikely to be found with a research approach that has prior assumptions about what the nature of good marketing practice should be. Perhaps it is therefore appropriate at this time to consider marketing management as it is understood and practised by marketing managers, and not as the conventional theory would have it be. Our understanding will surely be confined to the domain of self-fulfilling prophecies if we continue to approach these questions with preconceived notions about the reality of marketing management.

The author believes that answers to those kinds of questions will be found by structured observation of the work of marketing managers. Of course, there have been many studies of what managers do, including the seminal works of Stewart (1967), Mintzberg (1973), Kotter (1982), Mumford (1988), Hirsh and Bevan (1988) and Boyatzis (1982). These writers have shown how some managers spend their time, what roles they play, and what skills and qualities they possess. And despite this effort, as Cox and Cooper (1988) remind us, very little is still known about what many managers actually do.

There has been no attempt to study the work of marketing managers in this fashion. And perhaps this is not surprising, given the tendency of writers such as Drucker (1954) to describe some of the duties of marketing managers as inherently non-managerial. As previously discussed, the survey-based work of marketing researchers has largely been inconclusive. But it is suggested here that it would be a fruitful and long overdue exercise to observe the management of marketing in the fashion of Mintzberg (1973).

A VIEW OF MANAGEMENT WORK

There can be no doubting the value of managerial skills. And whatever can be done to alleviate their scarcity has become an issue of strategic importance. In his most recent book, Mintzberg (1989) argues that management is the key human resource. Yet in our haste to solve the technical problems of marketing we may have overlooked the problems associated with the managerial and organizational aspects of marketing. Marketing management is therefore biased towards strategy-making, analysis and planning. It assumes that whatever answer the analysis throws up will be magically converted into action that will lead to satisfactory outcomes. And by dehumanizing the market management process it might suggest that marketing is a management-free zone.

But if the content of the marketing management job does differ from what the conventional wisdom says it should be, what might it involve? What specific activities, tasks, roles and relationships might the marketing manager be responsible for?

If for the sake of argument we assume that marketing is not a management-free zone, then it might be reasonable to assume that the management of marketing will have some things broadly in common with the management of other areas. But what, then, do other managers do? In the words of Henry Fayol (1949), managers *plan, organize, coordinate, command and control.* In various forms, often by adding to the number of present particles to include staffing, directing and budgeting, this kind of definition of management dominates writing on the subject. The influence of engineering as an applied discipline is not hard to detect, as the models are always linear and logical. And most models of management that have found their way into the marketing imagination still focus on combinations of these broad aspects of the manager's job: planning, organizing, motivating, directing and controlling. So the manager then contributes foresight, order, purpose, integration of effort, and effectiveness to the work of others (Mintzberg, 1973).

These classical definitions of management, like those of marketing management which are derivative of them, describe what managers ought to aim to achieve, not what they do. They are the product of the search for universal prescriptions with which to direct managers to the one best way of managing. This quest characterizes Taylor's (1947) pioneering efforts to combat inefficiency and managerial incompetence. He believed that effective managerial processes were essentially the same for all managers in all kinds of organizations. Fayol (1949) shared Taylor's quest, although he believed that by recording and codifying the experiences of succeeding generations of managers we would be able to prescribe best management practice.

Yet if a marketing manager is holding a weekly management meeting with his team and discusses a particular problem with a key customer, he may be involved in all the processes described by Fayol. But managerial actions need to be seen in more specific terms, including the questions the marketing manager asks, the information and advice he imparts, the way he involves other staff in the meeting and empowers them with tasks and accountabilities. It is such specific behaviour which describes what the marketing manager needs to do effectively. So we must be able to answer specific questions such as those in Table 2.6 before we can expect to be able to describe the nature of management work in any detail.

The studies of Carlson (1951), Stewart (1967), Mintzberg (1973) and Kotter (1982) provide fundamental insights into the nature of managerial life which have helped to answer some of those questions in specific situations. The focus of their enquiries did shift from the search for universal principles to a detailed examination of the manager's job. Of course, their work does assume that useful generalized statements about the nature of management work can be made.

In the author's view, the findings and method of their studies are both relevant to the problem of defining what it actually is that we want marketing managers to be able to do. It is also worth repeating that those studies made use of various research instruments in combination, including interviews, diaries, critical incident analysis, structured and unstructured observation. This they did rather than relying on a detailed questionnaire, or hypothetical constructs about how managers might behave if they were not answering a questionnaire.

One of the earliest studies of what managers actually did was conducted by Carlson (1951). He observed the working lives of nine

Table 2.6

1. What kinds of activities does the marketing manager perform?
2. What kinds of information does he process?
3. With whom must he work? Where and how often?
4. What are the distinguishing characteristics of managerial work in marketing? What is of interest about the communications media the marketing manager uses, the activities he/she prefers to engage in, the flow of these activities during the workday, his/her use of time, the pressures of the job?
5. What basic roles can be inferred from a study of the marketing manager's activities? What roles does the marketing manager perform in moving information, in processing it, in making decisions, in dealing with people?
6. What variations exist among marketing management jobs? To what extent can basic differences be attributed to the situation, the incumbent, the job, the organization and the environment?
7. To what extent does marketing management conform to the basic systems model attributed to it? To what extent is the marketing manager's work repetitive, systematic and predictable, i.e. programmed and programmable? To what extent can marketing science reprogramme marketing management work?

Swedish managing directors. And in his account of their behaviour he used the phrase 'diary complex' to describe the way in which the top managers used their appointments diaries in an attempt to control the apparent randomness and unpredictability of their working day.

Stewart (1967) has been studying the work of many British senior and middle managers over almost 30 years. The main features of the findings of her work can be summarized as follows: few management jobs have a daily cycle; most managers do not have the time to think; they do not work to the neat, well-organized themes of the classical management school; managers spend most of their time interacting with other people in informal discussion; their activities are characterized by brevity, variety and fragmentation; they work at a brisk and continuing pace with little free time; and they are continually bombarded with requests for one thing after another.

In his seminal study, Mintzberg (1973) spent five days shadowing five CEOs as they went about their work. This also included about a month of preparatory data collection for each participant. The study yielded six characteristics of management work and a 10-part cluster of managerial roles. Like Stewart, Mintzberg found a number of different activities likely to be common to all management jobs. But he also discovered important differences which existed within what he saw as a similar structure of roles. Mintzberg found that the differences in job performance were influenced by factors such as the organization itself, the industry and its environment; factors specific to the particular job; and the impact of the job holder in terms of personal qualities and management style.

Again, like Stewart, Mintzberg found that managers' work was characterized by brevity, fragmentation and variety. He also found that they preferred activities that were current, specific, well defined and possibly non-routine, rather than the provision of time to think. A great proportion of their time was spent in oral communications and this was much preferred to written forms. Face-to-face contact was thought to be the best process of communication and they spent much time engaged in it. Managers had a wide variety of contacts with superiors, subordinates, peers and outsiders. Table 2.7 summarizes the conclusions he drew from the findings of his study.

Mintzberg's (1973) view of the essential similarities of managers' jobs was expressed through 10 roles which he identified as follows:

Interpersonal roles
Figurehead
Leader
Liaison

Information roles
Monitor
Disseminator
Spokesman

Decisional roles
Entrepreneur
Disturbance handler
Resource allocator
Negotiator

While proposing that all managers do in fact exercise those roles, Mintzberg recognizes that different managers will give different priorities to them. More recently, Kotter (1982) spent one month observing the work of each of 15 general managers. He found that the participants were not strategic, proactive or well organized. He explained this with reference to the following responsibilities which they needed to discharge as part of their jobs:

- Setting goals in conditions of uncertainty
- Allocating resources among competing claims

Table 2.7

1. Managers' jobs are remarkably alike and can be described in terms of 10 basic roles and six sets of working characteristics — irrespective of level, function and organizational context.
2. The differences that do exist in managers' work can be described largely in terms of these common roles and characteristics.
3. Much of the manager's work is challenging and non-programmed. But every manager has his share of regular, ordinary duties to perform, particularly in moving information and maintaining a status system. Almost all activities managers engage in relate back to their role as manager.
4. The manager is both a generalist and a specialist. In his own organization he is a generalist — the focal point in the general flow of information and in the handling of general disturbances. But as a manager he is a specialist.
5. Much of the manager's power derives from his information. With access to many sources of information, some of them open to no one else in his organization unit, the manager develops a database that enables him to make more effective decisions than his employees. Unfortunately, the manager receives much of his information verbally, and lacking effective means to disseminate it to others, he has difficulty delegating responsibility for decision-making. Hence, he must take full charge of his organization's strategy-making system.
6. The prime occupational hazard of the manager is superficiality. Because of the open-ended nature of his job and because of his responsibility for information processing and strategy-making, the manager is induced to take on a heavy load of work and to do much of it superficially. Hence, his work pace is unrelenting and his work activities are characterized by brevity, variety and fragmentation. The job of managing does not develop reflective planners; rather it breeds adaptive information manipulators who prefer a stimulus–response milieu.
7. Managers work with verbal information and intuitive processes. The management scientist has had almost no influence on how the manager works.
8. The manager is in a vicious circle. The pressures of the job force him to adopt work characteristics (e.g. fragmentation of activity, verbal communication) that make it difficult for him to receive help from the management scientist and that lead to superficiality in his work. This leads to more pronounced work characteristics and increased work pressures. As the problems facing large organizations become more complex, senior managers will face even greater work pressures.
9. The management scientist can help break this loop. He can provide significant help for the manager in information processing and strategy-making, provided he can better understand the manager's work and can gain access to the manager's verbal database.
10. Managerial work is enormously complex, far more so than a reading of the traditional literature would suggest. There is a need to study it systematically and to avoid the temptation to seek simple prescriptions for its difficulties. We shall improve it significantly only when we understand it precisely.

- Fire fighting, problem solving, identifying solutions
- Organizing informal cooperation
- Implementing decisions rather than making them
- Motivating and controlling large groups of subordinates

Like Mintzberg, Kotter saw that the demands of the management job applied to all participants in his study. However, their application did vary in intensity and effectiveness in different situations. And while the participants were never as well organized or systematic in their approach to their work as the classic models suggest, Kotter did find the characteristics of effective general management to include the following:

- Building networks
- Developing agendas
- Execution
- Establishing values and norms
- Maintaining relationships
- Working through meetings and dialogues
- Establishing multiple objectives
- Spending time with others
- Using rewards to secure support and desired behaviour

In Mumford's (1988) view, Kotter's phrase 'the efficiency of seemingly inefficient management behaviour' accurately describes the work of managers. It refers to the fact that the managers in his study rarely planned their day's work in advance in much detail. Rather, they reacted to each day's needs through short and often disjointed conversations on a variety of issues. This may be inefficient compared to the classical models of management. But Kotter found that this apparently accidental and opportunistic way in which managers operated was efficient in practice. This approach was found to provide managers with information, understanding and contact, which was an essential part of their job. So, while being responsive to the needs of others, the manager can in fact direct his attention to issues on his personal agenda, highlighted by apparently accidental experiences.

In a study of senior managers Isenberg (1984) came to similar conclusions. He found that the managers he studied had to deal with a context of ambiguity, inconsistency and surprise, and that they did so by managing a network of interrelated problems rather than working on neatly identifiable and separate problems.

At the same time as the results of Kotter's study were published, Boyatzis (1982) published the results of his very extensive and thorough study of management competencies. It involved discussion and analysis with about 2000 American managers at different levels of seniority and in different kinds of organizations. It identified 20 characteristics, or skills, which all successful managers had in common. These are reproduced below:

- Efficiency orientation
- Proactivity
- Diagnostic use of concepts
- Concern with impact
- Self-confidence
- Use of oral presentations
- Logical thought
- Conceptualization
- Use of socialized power
- Positive regard
- Managing group process
- Accurate self-assessment
- Developing others
- Use of unilateral power
- Spontaneity
- Self-control
- Perceptual objectivity
- Stamina and adaptability
- Concern with close relationships
- Specialized knowledge

The findings of this study have been used to generate management development programmes. Boyatzis recommends that rather than working from someone else's idea of what managers should know, organizations should work from an explicit model of management which has been tested in the particular organization. The competencies he identified can be used to define both the level of performance required in any particular job and the level of performance in that competency which individual managers have attained. He does produce another generalized list of required skills and abilities which all successful managers require. But his views are qualified to the extent of saying that there will necessarily be variations of requirements in different organizations.

The fundamental features of these studies lead to the conclusion that any view of management which emphasizes discrete activities, organized thinking processes, neatness and freedom of choice is likely to be out of phase with the reality of management as managers find it. So the traditional lists of what managers ought to do, do not sufficiently embrace the confused and chaotic reality of management. The work of Mintzberg (1973) and Kotter (1982) is important to the study of marketing management because it reveals the complicated ways in which managers actually do make things happen. And they seem to have very little to do with sophisticated analyses, articulated decision-making processes and formal planning systems of the kind so popular in marketing management texts.

It has been widely accepted (Mumford, 1988; Cox and Cooper, 1988; Hughes, 1988) that the observational approaches of Kotter (1982), Stewart (1967) and Mintzberg (1973) have much to commend them. They have produced data that are relevant, real and grounded in the observed behaviour of practising managers. Reservations (Hughes, 1988) have been expressed on the small samples of those studies. There is also the question that the studies are from another time and culture and that the management behaviour which is their subject lies at the top of the organization. Only Stewart's (1967) work emanates from a UK culture and is sufficiently wide ranging to encompass the differences, as well as the similarities, between managerial jobs, both across as well as up and down the organization.

Since there are so many differences in the nature of management work, not only functional and hierarchical but also in terms of content and emphasis, considerable room remains for replication. In the author's view, this cursory examination of the work of a selected group of management scholars is sufficient to initiate a new methodological and substantive agenda for research in the area of marketing management.

PACKAGING OR PARADIGM SHIFT

The previous sections have argued for the adoption of new research methods in the area of marketing management and the formation of new questions to research. To some this combination of assertions might suggest a discipline in crisis. But there is a movement gathering pace which clearly points to other tangible evidence of such crisis.

Anyone who has the habit, or the duty, of following the academic marketing journals will find it difficult to refute the view that much of what passes for knowledge on the subject of marketing management has been written by researchers for other researchers. King (1985) eloquently records his despairing incomprehension of much of the esoterica that are the subject of the academic marketing literature. And as a practitioner he bemoans his failure to derive any benefit whatsoever from this writing. Little of it is contributed by practising marketing managers and rarely do their problems seem to provide the subject or the object for discussion. And while prescriptions for better marketing management practice are often eschewed, it is seldom that any clear commitment to managerial action is provided.

Of course, academic research has yielded knowledge that does provide marketing managers with useful insights. But often this knowledge can only be true in the limited sense that it is at one point in time a valid representation of reality as seen from the perspective of the researcher. And one wonders if it has any prescriptive value or if it merely provides a way of illuminating and interpreting particular managerial experiences retrospectively. To be relevant to the perceived needs of practising managers, the knowledge is expected to be reliable in application. Yet the sizeable and persistent gap between the theory as propounded by the scholarly researcher and practice as experienced by the working marketing manager would seem to be evidence of unreliability in specific applications.

So conventional models of marketing management are predicated on what *ought* to be, rather than what *is*. The premise of this chapter is then that conventional models of marketing management are distant from the reality of what practising managers do, in terms both of the content of the job and the managerial processes they ascribe to it. Of course, there may be several reasons for this. The author explores what he believes to be the key reason: i.e. an incomplete representation of the work of marketing managers based on conceptual frameworks which draw on outmoded concepts of organization and management.

Those readers who accept the premise might worry about its logical implications for marketing education and the development and training of marketing managers. This is a concern that King (1985) shares and gives expression to in his observation of people emerging from various institutions with qualifications in marketing but not remotely suited to any of the marketing jobs he knows about. For if the reality of how marketing managers carry out their jobs and the central content of what they do needs to be defined differently, then both the content and the processes of formal marketing management development might need to be similarly redefined.

It is generally held that the substance of classroom education is based on prior research. To the extent that this is the case in marketing management education, there are several legitimate concerns about the future relevancy of current marketing management education. Much existing knowledge on marketing management is derived from research which is based on the traditional positivistic science model for generating knowledge so successful in the physical sciences. But the appropriateness of this approach is increasingly being called into question in marketing (Brownlie, 1989) in particular and the management and organizational sciences in general (Arndt, 1985). Indeed, the issue has been clearly presented by Evered (1981):

> The epistemology underlying much of our managerial and organisational research is not adequate for the job required. There is an epistemological crisis in our field because it has adopted the positivistic model of science as the ultimate model of what is best for our field. It is now clear to many in the field that this crisis of epistemology is generating a crisis of relevancy in our research findings. The researcher's task is therefore to examine the epistemological assumptions underlying our research and to revise our core paradigm of inquiry . . . we must move beyond the objective, analytic, reductionist, number-oriented, optimising and fail-safe approaches to future problems, and learn to think with equal fluency in more subjective, synthesising, holistic, quantitative, option increasing and fail-safe ways.

Marketing is an eclectic discipline. It finds application in a diverse array of contexts and is concerned with a wide variety of issues within those contexts. At the same time, marketing represents a setting in which theories are developed and tested, particularly through application. And yet despite this rich source of diversity, or perhaps because of it, the discipline has been accused of taking a defensive and insecure view of its thinking.

Dholakia and Arndt (1985) characterize the dominant thinking methodology in marketing by its positivistic approach to enquiry and a heavy reliance on traditional exchange theory. These rules of intellectual engagement are thought to provide a point of reference and stability which enables the discipline to organize its thoughts about a diverse array of contexts, issues and theories. And some observers have attributed the dominance of logical empiricism to the abiding insecurity of marketing thought.

While being tolerant of diversity, the marketing discipline is accused of being less tolerant of alternative thinking methodologies. The dominant approach facilitates empirical enquiry and much of it is guided by positivist precepts. But the discipline faces a diverse array of contexts, issues and ideas that are changing rapidly. Further insights into marketing phenomena may need the pluralism of mixed scanning (Etzioni, 1967) and its wide set of viewing lenses that has been embraced by strategic management (Thomas and McGee, 1986).

Arndt (1985) believes that a growing number of scholars in the marketing discipline are expressing their concern that the knowledge system of marketing is in turmoil. The technical sophistication of research efforts is evidently increasing, as a cursory glance at any of the academic marketing journals will testify. Yet despite this, the range of problems examined by marketing scholars and the research philosophies they use remain constricted. And while marketing may appear to outsiders to be very controversial and dynamic, some argue that it remains precariously placid and intellectually barren on the inside.

Arndt argues that marketing thinking is profoundly dominated by the empiricist world view, which emphasizes rationality, measurement and problem solving, and that as a result the insights it generates are limited. He suggests that a cure for its anaemia is for the prevailing wisdom to embrace alternative paradigms which offer the foundations for richer conceptual frameworks.

Of course, this clarion call is neither new nor original. It is now almost 20 years since Dawson (1971) first suggested the need for a comprehensive review of marketing paradigms on finding the following symptoms of a discipline approaching a crisis:

- The inability of practitioners to define the field
- The neglect of the most pressing economic and social issues
- The discrepancies between reality and marketing's view of the world

Yet despite those observations, the debate in marketing regarding acceptable paradigms has lacked the critical intensity of that in some areas of the social sciences (Arndt, 1985). Notwithstanding this, there has been a conceptual broadening and subsequent redefinition of the subject which was initiated by Kotler and Levy (1969) and chronicled by Hunt (1976 and 1983). The migration of ideas between marketing and cognate disciplines has gathered pace (Brownlie, 1989) and is bringing new concepts and methodologies to bear on topic areas such as marketing management. This chapter is evidence of that.

CONCLUSION

Given the changing context of management, it is an appropriate time to revisit marketing management, to consider it as it is, and not as we would have it. Our understanding will be confined to the domain of self-fulfilling prophecies if we continue to approach the study of marketing management with preconceived notions about the reality as it was found to be in a different era and context. We need an improved understanding of the work that marketing managers actually do in dealing with the complexity and transformation of organizations in the late 1980s and early 1990s.

We know what marketing should be. But we know very little about how to make it work, and about how to implement the results of grand strategic analyses. We also know what the strategic role of marketing management should be: to generate profitable growth opportunities for the business; and so to initiate change, sometimes strategic; and to ensure that the conditions for organizational flexibility persist. But what do we know about how marketing management sees its initiatives for strategic change through?

Although much has been written about the development of market strategy and decision-making about the marketing mix elements themselves, little has been written about the implementation of marketing strategy and the nature of marketing management itself.

When Mintzberg (1973) published his book *The Nature of Managerial Work*, the management literature was in much the same position. Mintzberg wrote:

> Although an enormous amount of material has been published on the manager's job, we continue to know very little about it. Much of the literature is of little use, being merely endless repetition of the same vague statements.

Mintzberg's observation of the abundance of abstract generalities about management and the shortage of the hard data of empirical research can still be found to be true these days in the area of marketing management. This chapter attempts to ask some searching questions about why this should continue to be the case for much longer. It also offers methodological and substantive ideas for changing the situation.

REFERENCES

Ames, C. (1970) Trappings versus substance in industrial marketing. *Harvard Business Review*, **48** (4), 93–102.

Arndt, J. (1985) The tyranny of paradigms: The case for paradigmatic pluralism in marketing. In Dholakia, N., and Arndt, J. (eds) *Changing the Course of Marketing*. JAI Press, Greenwich, CT, pp. 2–25.

Ashridge Management Research Group — Foundation for Management Education (1988). *Management for the Future*. Ashridge Management Research Group, Ashridge.

Baker, M.J. (1989) Marketing — a new philosophy of management? *Quarterly Review of Marketing*, March, 1–4.

Bennett, R., and Cooper, R. (1981) The misuse of marketing. *Business Horizons*, November/December, 51–60.

Birley, S., Norburn, D., and Dunn, M. (1987) *Marketing Effectiveness and its Reliability to Customer Closeness and Market Orientation: The British Experience*. Proceedings MEG Conference, University of Warwick, 1987.

Bonoma, T.V. (1984) *Managing Marketing*. Free Press, New York.

Bonoma, T.V. (1985) *The Marketing Edge: Making Strategies Work*. Free Press, New York.

Boyatzis, R. (1982) *The Competent Manager*. Wiley, Chichester.

Brownlie, D., McCalman, J., Paton, R., and Southern, G. (1988) Annotated bibliography of management development. Glasgow Business School Working Paper.

Brownlie, D. (1989) The migration of ideas between strategic management and marketing. *European Journal of Marketing*, **23**, 12.

Burgoyne, J., and Stuart, R. (1976) The nature, use and acquisition of managerial skills and other attributes. *Personnel Review*, **5** (4), 19–29.

Carlson, S. (1951) *Executive Behaviour*. C.A. Stromberg, Stockholm.

Child, J. (1972) Organisation structure, environment and performance. *Sociology*, **6**, 1–21.

Child, J., and Smith, C. (1987) The context and process of organisational transformation — Cadbury Limited in its sector. *Journal of Management Studies*, **24**, Part 6, 555–593.

Constable, J., and McCormick, R. (1987) *The Making of British Managers*. BIM/CBI, London.

Cowell, D. (1987) Some insights into the background and training and marketing executives in the UK. *Journal of Marketing Management*, **3** (1), 51–60.

Cox, C., and Cooper, C. (1988) *High Fliers*. Blackwell, Oxford.

Davis, S.N. (1984) *Managing Corporate Culture*. Ballinger, New York.

Dawson, L. (1971) Marketing science in the Age of Aquarius. *Journal of Marketing*, **35**, 66–72.

Day, G. and Wensley, R. (1983) Marketing theory with a strategic orientation. *Journal of Marketing*, **47**, 79–89.

Day, G., and Wensley, R. (1988) Assessing advantage: A framework for diagnosing competitive superiority. *Journal of Marketing*, **52**, 1–20.

Deloitte, Haskins, and Sells (1989) *Management Challenge for the 1990s: The Current Education, Training and Development Debate*. Training Agency, HMSO, Sheffield.

Deshpande, R., and Webster, F. (1989) Organisational culture and marketing: Defining the research agenda. *Journal of Marketing*, **53**, 3–15.

Dholakia, N., and Arndt, J. (eds) (1985) *Changing the Course of Marketing: Alternative Paradigms for Widening Marketing Theory*. JAI Press, Greenwich, CT.

Doyle, P. (1987) Marketing and the British Chief Executive. *Journal of Marketing Management*, **3** (2), 121–132.

Drucker, P.F. (1954) *The Practice of Management*. Harper & Row, New York.

Dunn, M., Norburn, D., and Birley, S. (1985) Corporate culture: A positive correlate with marketing effectiveness. *International Journal of Advertising*, **4**, 65–73.

Etzioni, A. (1967) Mixed scanning: A third approach to decision-making. *Public Administration Review*, December, 385–391.

Evered, R. (1981) Management education for the year 2000. In Cooper, C. (ed.) *Developing Managers for the 1980s*. MacMillan, London.

Fayol, H. (1949) *General and Industrial Management*. Pitman, London.

Greenwood, R., and Hinings, C. (1987) Organisational transformations, special issue. *Journal of Management Studies*, November, 591–594.

Grinyer, P., Mayes, D., and McKiernan, P. (1988) *Sharpbenders*. Blackwell, Oxford.

Handy, C. (1987) *The Making of Managers*. MSC/NEDO/BIM, London.

Hayes, R., and Abernathy, W. (1980) Managing our way to economic decline. *Harvard Business Review*, July/August, 67–77.

Henderson, B.D. (1981) The anatomy of competition. *Journal of Marketing*, **47**, 7–11.

Hendry, C. (1987) Strategic change and human resource management in retail banking and financial services: An overview. Centre for Corporate Strategy and Change, University of Warwick Working Paper.

Hirsh, W., and Bevan, S. (1988) *What Makes a Manager?* Institute of Manpower Studies, Report No. 144.

Hooley, G., and Lynch, J. (1985) Marketing lessons from the UK's high-flying companies. *Journal of Marketing Management*, **1** (1), 65–74.

Hooley, G., West, C., and Lynch, J. (1984) *Marketing in the UK: A Survey of Current Practice and Performance*. Institute of Marketing, London.

Hughes, J. (1988) The body of knowledge in management education. *Management Education and Development*, **19** (4), 301–310.

Hunt, S. (1976) *Marketing Theory: Conceptual Foundations of Research in Marketing*. Columbus, Ohio.

Hunt, S. (1983) *Marketing Theory: The Philosophy of Marketing Science*. Irwin, Homewood.

Hutt, M., Reingen, P., and Ronchetto, J. (1988) Tracing emergent processes in marketing strategy formation. *Journal of Marketing*, **52**, 4–19.

Isenberg, D. (1984) How senior managers think. *Harvard Business Review*, Nov–Dec, 81–90.

Kanter, R. (1983) *The Change Masters*. Unwin, London.

King, S. (1985) Has marketing failed or was it never really tried? *Journal of Marketing Management*, **1** (1), 1–20.

Kotler, P. (1977) The marketing audit comes of age. *Sloan Management Review*, Winter, 25–44.

Kotler, P. (1988) *Marketing Management: Analysis Planning, Implementation and Control*, 6th edn. Prentice Hall, New York.

Kotler, P., and Levy, S. (1969) Broadening the concept of marketing. *Journal of Marketing*, **33**, 10–15.

Kotter, J. (1982) *The General Managers*, Free Press, New York.

Lynch, J., Hooley, G., and Shepherd, J. (1989) *The Effectiveness of British Marketing: Resume of Preliminary Findings*. Proceedings MEG Conference, Glasgow, 1989, ed. L. Moutinho *et al.*, pp. 106–126.

MacBeth, D., and Southern, G. (1989) Advanced manufacture and services: Common issues — common approaches. *International Journal of Operations & Production Management*, **9**, 5

Middleton, B., and Long, G. (1988) *Towards an Understanding of Marketing Skills*. MEG Conference Proceedings, pp. 578–603.

Mintzberg, H. (1973) *The Nature of Managerial Work*. Harper & Row, New York.

Mintzberg, H. (1989) *Mintzberg on Management*. Free Press, New York.

Morgan, N., and Piercy, N. (1989) *Corporate Culture, The Formalisation of Marketing and Marketing Effectiveness*. Proceedings MEG Conference, July 1989, pp. 225–255.

Mumford, A. (1988) *Developing Top Managers*. Gower, London.

Nulty, P. (1987) How managers will manage. *Fortune*, February 2, 39–41.

Oxenfeld, A.R., and Moore, W.L. (1975) Customer or competitor: Which guideline for marketing? *Management Review*, August, 43–48.

Pedler, M., Burgoyne, J., and Boydell, T. (1978) *A Manager's Guide to Self Development*. McGraw-Hill, New York.

Piercy, N. (1986a) *Marketing Budgeting*. Croom Helm, London.

Piercy, N. (1986b) The role and function of the Chief Marketing Executive and the marketing department. *Journal of Marketing Management*, **1** (3), 265–289.

Piercy, N. (1986c) The model of organisation. *Marketing*, May 15, 34–36.

Piercy, N. (1989) *Managing Strategic Change in Marketing*. Proceedings EMAC Conference, Athens, April 1989, ed. G.J. Avlonitis, pp. 91–106.

Rosenfeld, R. (1988) *Strategies and Past Actions: Management Awareness of Competitive Precedents*. Business Archives Council Annual Conference, London, June 1988.

Ruekert, R., Walker, O., and Roerring, K. (1985) The organisation of marketing activities. *Journal of Marketing*, **49**, 13–25.

Samli, A., Palda, K., and Barker, A. (1987) Towards a mature marketing concept. *Sloan Management Review*, **28** (2), Winter, 45–51.

Sathe, V. (1983) Implications of corporate culture: A manager's guide to action. *Organisational Dynamics*, Autumn, 5–23.

Schwartz, H., and Davis, S. (1981) Matching corporate culture and business strategy. *Organisational Dynamics*, Summer, 30–48.

Simon, H. (1957) *Administrative Behaviour*. Macmillan, New York.

Spender, J.-C. (1989a) What do managers really do for their organisations? *European Management Journal*, **7** (1), 10–22.

Spender, J.-C. (1989b) *Industry Recipes: An Enquiry into the Nature and Sources of Managerial Judgement*. Blackwell, Oxford.

Stewart, R. (1967) *Managers and their Jobs*. Macmillan, London.

Taylor, F. (1947) *Scientific Management*. Harper & Row, London.

Thomas, H., and McGee, J. (eds) (1986) Introduction: Mapping strategic management research. In *Strategic Management Research*. Wiley, Chichester.

Thomas, M. (1984) The education and training of marketing managers. *The Quarterly Review of Marketing*, Spring, 27–30.

Walker, O., and Ruekert, R. (1987) Marketing's role in the implementation of business strategies. *Journal of Marketing*, **51**, 15–33.

Webster, F. (1981) Top management concerns about marketing: Issues for the 1990s. *Journal of Marketing*, Summer, 9–16.

Webster, F. (1988) The rediscovery of the marketing concept. *Business Horizons*, May-June, 29–39.

Whipp, R., Rosenfeld, R., and Pettigrew, A. (1988a) Understanding strategic change processes: Some preliminary British findings. In *The Management of Strategic Change Processes*. Blackwell, Oxford.

Whipp, R., Rosenfeld, R., and Pettigrew, A. (1988b) *The Management of Strategic and Operational Change: Lessons for the 1990s*. Strategic Management Society Conference, Amsterdam, October 1988.

Wind, Y., and Robertson, T. (1983) Marketing strategy: New directions for theory and research. *Journal of Marketing*, **47**, 12–25.

CHAPTER 3

Pricing: Theory and Evidence — A Literature Review

Adamantios Diamantopoulos

European Business Management School, University of Wales — Swansea

PART 1. INTRODUCTION — THE NATURE OF PRICE

THE MEANING OF PRICE

Given the high visibility of prices in everyday life (e.g. display of price information in shops, product catalogues and the media), the fact that everybody in modern society learns to understand the significance of price at a very early age (e.g. spending pocket money) and the persistent interest of all sectors of society — consumers, firms, trade unions, academics, government — in the function and implications of prices (e.g. inflation, distribution of income, profitability), it is hardly surprising that 'price is so frequently treated as a simple and unequivocal fact' (Committee on Price Determination, 1943, p. 33). Thus, 'if one were to ask a group of randomly selected individuals to define "price", many would reply that price is an amount of money paid by the buyer to the seller of a product or service' (Harper, 1966, p. 1). However, as will be argued below, price is not an unambiguous concept (Silberston, 1970) and simple definitions such as the one just considered, while intuitively appealing, are constrained in their ability to provide a comprehensive understanding of price in the context of any particular transaction. The reason for this is that 'when one attempts to specify those terms of a transaction that are part of the price of a commodity, serious questions, both accounting and theoretical arise. Furthermore, any concern with the meaning of price soon reveals how closely attached are the difficulties of providing . . . a definition that is at the

This chapter is based on the author's doctoral dissertation in the Department of Marketing, University of Strathclyde, under the supervision of Professor Michael J. Baker.

Perspectives on Marketing Management, Volume 1
Edited by M.J. Baker

same time theoretically valid and empirically useful' (Committee on Price Determination, 1943, p. 33).

At a conceptual level, 'price is a ratio of quantities: the amount of some other good Y that must be given up to obtain a unit of desired good X' (Hirschleifer, 1980, p. 27). Since in modern economies price is usually expressed in money terms, price can be formally denoted by the following ratio:

$$\text{Price} = \frac{\text{Quantity of money (and/or goods/services) given up by the buyer}}{\text{Quantity of goods/services provided by the seller}} \quad (1)$$

Inspection of the above ratio reveals that any transaction involves some 'sacrifice' from both parties. In this context, price can be conceived as representing the buyer's sacrifice, in that it shows 'how much must be given up for the acquisition of a product' (Simon, 1982, p. 5). The seller's sacrifice, on the other hand, is represented by the loss in ownership/possession of the product/service under consideration. In other words, 'to the consumer the structure of prices indicates the terms on which he can acquire the goods for which he spends his money income. To the producer the structure of prices indicates the terms on which he may dispose of his goods or services or acquire the goods and services of others' (Mason, 1940, p. 45). Consequently, whether a transaction will in fact take place depends on the extent to which the sacrifice to be incurred by the buyer and that to be incurred by the seller overlap sufficiently to produce what is known as the 'range of mutual benefit' (Boulding, 1966). In the example shown in Figure 3.1, exchange is only possible within the price range £15–28; at prices outside this range, one of the parties will not benefit from the transaction and thus the latter will not take place.

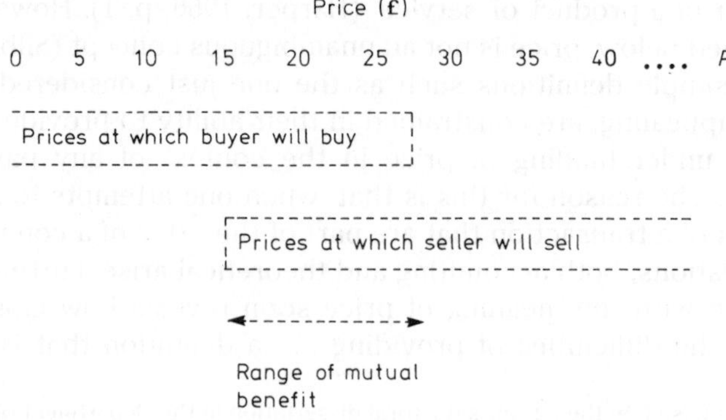

Figure 3.1 The range of mutual benefit (adopted with modifications from Boulding, 1966, p. 34)

Unfortunately, the conceptualization of price along the above lines does little beyond indicating that one man's price is another man's cost (Brown, 1967), as 'the *amount by which* the parties to the exchange feel that they gain, depends . . . upon *where* the price falls within this range' (Boulding, 1966, p. 34, emphasis in the original). The main problem with the definition of price in ratio (1) is that the latter can assume a variety of values depending upon the impact of *other* factors which are *not* represented in the ratio. Table 3.1 provides a list of factors which must be taken into account before the 'true' price of a product or service can be determined; whenever any of the associated elements changes, so does price (Harper, 1966). This augmented concept of price is aptly summarized by Cox (1946) in his classic article on price measurement: 'Price, then, must be considered as an agreement between buyer and seller whose full meaning depends not only upon the numbers given but also upon a complicated group of understandings lying outside of the formal ratio. . . . A price under this concept is changed not only when the number of monetary units or the number of commodity units changes, but also when any of the underlying understandings change' (pp. 375, 377).

Bearing the above in mind, a comprehensive definition of price must somehow make provision for the diversity of influences that are excluded from the formal ratio of quantities and money. A definition that appears to accomplish this has been offered by Cox (1946); despite its age, it is substantially superior to definitions that have appeared in the more recent pricing literature (e.g. Alpert, 1971; Marshall, 1979; Simon, 1982). Thus:

> Price can be defined . . . as an agreement between seller and buyer concerning what each is to receive, embodied in a formal ratio between quantities of money and quantities of goods or services modified by formal and explicit or informal and implicit understandings as to:
>
> 1. The quality of the goods or services to be provided, or, alternatively, the premiums and discounts to be applied to deliveries whose quality varies from a specified standard.
> 2. The times and places at which the privileges and responsibilities of (a) possession and (b) ownership are to pass from seller to buyer.
> 3. The particular form of money to be rendered in payment.
> 4. The times and places at which payments are to be made and accepted.
> 5. The services furnished by the seller without extra charge, such as advertising, servicing the product, and return privileges. (Cox, 1946, pp. 376–377)

From an empirical/practical perspective, further complications arise in any attempt to define and measure price as a result of the following.

Table 3.1 Elements influencing the 'true' price in a transaction

Element	Examples	Author
Size/quantity	No. of items Weight	Till (1937); Oxenfeldt (1951); Monroe (1979); Simon (1982)
Quality	Durability Reliability	Till (1937); Cox (1946); Oxenfeldt (1951); Harper (1966); Monroe (1979)
Transfer of ownership	Immediate delivery Free delivery	Committee on Price Determination (1943); Cox (1946); Monroe (1979)
Time of payment	Payment in advance Interest-free period	Cox (1946); Harper (1966); Monroe (1979)
Form of payment	Cash only Credit facilities	Till (1937); Committee on Price Determination (1943); Cox (1946); Harper (1966); Monroe (1979); Simon (1982)
Discounts	Trade discounts Quantity discounts	Till (1937); Committee on Price Determination (1943); Cox (1946); Oxenfeldt (1951); Harper (1966); Silberston (1970); Monroe (1979); Simon (1982)
Allowances	Trade-in allowances Promotional allowances	Till (1937); Committee on Price Determination (1943); Cox (1946); Silberston (1970)
Premiums	Trading stamps Gifts	Till (1937); Monroe (1979)
Guarantees	Quality guarantees Price guarantees	Oxenfeldt (1951); Harper (1966); Simon (1982)
Other services	Technical advice Returnable policies	Till (1937); Cox (1946); Simon (1982)

First, 'the "published", "quoted", "announced", or "list" price of a product or service may, in reality, not be the price actually paid' (Harper, 1966, p. 2). Especially in industrial/organizational markets, it is a well-documented fact that, in many cases, list prices bear hardly any relationship to actual or 'transaction' prices (McAllister, 1961; Flueck, 1961; Stigler, 1962; Stigler and Kindahl, 1970; Sultan, 1974). A major reason for this discrepancy is that prices are, more often than not, subject to negotiation between an individual buyer and his suppliers. For example, 85% of the 500 industrial buyers surveyed by Farmer and Farrington (1979) indicated that negotiation is a key phase in purchase price management, while a number of studies have shown that the price charged is influenced by the degree of delegation of pricing authority to the sales force and the negotiation strategies adopted by the latter (Woodside and Davenport, 1976; Stephenson, Cron and Frazier, 1979; Patton and Puto, 1979; Zarth, 1981; Plinke, 1985). A related point concerns the practice of making concealed price concessions to some or all buyers (*Business Week*, 1963). Nelson and Keim (1941) list no fewer than 36 different arrangements by means of which concessions may be concealed; such practices are likely to go largely undetected because 'companies neither record nor generally talk about all the "under the table" prices and other valuable concessions they make' (Burck, 1972, p. 8). The divergence between list and transaction prices has both managerial and methodological implications. On the one hand, the uncertainty facing an individual firm in the market is increased, as a comparison between one's prices *vis-à-vis* the competition becomes extremely difficult (Simon, 1982). On the other hand, it becomes questionable whether valid inferences about industrial pricing behaviour can be drawn from studies based on official (i.e. published) sources (Cocks and Virts, 1974).

A second problem relates to the distinction between relative (or real) and absolute (or money) prices. In comparing prices between different products or suppliers, it is relative prices that should be considered, a relative price of a good being defined as 'the ratio of its absolute price to the average price of all other goods (except money)' (Miller, 1978, p. 7). In periods of rapid inflation, however, fixed-price contracts tend to be modified by escalator clauses or replaced altogether by 'price-at-delivery' and 'renegotiated' price arrangements (Allen, Tatham and Lambert, 1976; Tatham and Allen, 1976; Long and Varble, 1978); as a result, it becomes difficult to know the exact price associated with a particular transaction/contract and, thus, to undertake price comparisons with any degree of confidence.

Finally, there is the problem of 'price bundling', whereby a single price is quoted for a set (or 'bundle') of products/services; in 'pure' bundling the items involved can only be purchased as a set, while in 'mixed' bundling the items comprising the bundle are also available separately (Guiltinan, 1987).[1] Under such conditions, it may be difficult to identify the price of any one item in the bundle or to compare the total price of the bundle with the individual prices of its components (Simon, 1982).

From the above discussion, it becomes evident that the notion of price is far from being simple, in that both conceptual and practical problems have to be resolved in order to provide a meaningful description of 'the' price of a product/service. Thus the impression given in the majority of economic textbooks that 'the definition of exchange value or price offers no great difficulty and gives rise to no special ambiguity' (Wicksell, 1934, p. 16) does not appear to be justified.

THE FUNCTIONS AND IMPORTANCE OF PRICE

The importance of price cannot be overemphasized; price plays a central role in the functioning of the economic system and has wide-reaching implications for business firms and consumers alike.

At a macro-level, 'prices are the signals guiding the allocation of resources in a market economy. They are also a principal instrument determining the distribution of income among participants in the economic process' (Scherer, 1970, p. 1). Price performs both a stimulating and a rationing function, in that it influences what and how much will be produced and who will get the available supply of goods (Backman, 1965). The price system, which is the heart of any market economy, 'is a very complex network composed of the prices of all products bought and sold in the economy as well as those of a myriad of services, including labor, professional, transportation and public utility services, and others ranging from dry cleaning to lawn-mower repair . . . Each price is linked to a broad complicated system of prices in which everything seems to depend more or less upon everything else' (Harper, 1966, p. 1). At any given point in time, the price system reflects the evaluations of buyers and sellers and operates to keep the conflicts between the participants in the economic process in balance; the latter is achieved through the adjustment of the price of a good until the quantities demanded and the quantities supplied are equal, resulting in what in economic terminology is known as 'a state of equilibrium' (Staudt and Taylor, 1965).

In industries where prices are high in relation to costs, there is inducement for established firms to expand productive facilities and output and for new firms to set up production; conversely, output and productive facilities decline in industries in which prices have fallen relative to costs, thus adversely affecting profitability. Furthermore, prices 'move' productive factors from one employment to another and, therefore, help determine the type of goods that will be produced. Changes in the prices of raw materials, land, labour and investible funds shift productive factors to those uses and occupations which offer the greatest compensation.

The distribution of income and the total national output are also affected by price. A high unit price for a given quantity of goods transfers income from buyers to sellers, while price reductions enable buyers to obtain more goods for the same expenditure. The increase in volume as a result of lower prices may encourage investment to expand output further; however, if prices are so low as to result in losses, investment will suffer and output will be curtailed.

Needless to say, the above is a very brief and oversimplified description of the *ideal* functioning of the price mechanism; in reality, a number of imperfections and rigidities (e.g. non-price competition and government intervention) often prevent the price system from operating in the way that Adam Smith's (1776) 'invisible hand' was supposed to (Oxenfeldt, 1968; Samuelson, 1976). However, in spite of such complications, the price system is still the dominant influence on resource allocation, income distribution and size and composition of the national output; as Backman (1965) points out, 'although the price system may not be the sensitive regulator portrayed in theory, it does operate within broad limits, which producers cannot afford to ignore' (p. 25).

At a micro-level, 'prices are one of the main determinants of profits and of success or failure' (Haynes, 1962, p. 1). Price is the only element in the marketing mix that generates revenue; the remaining elements — product development, packaging, advertising, sales promotion and distribution — are cost-incurring activities aimed at generating or maintaining demand (Nimer, 1971). The pricing decision represents the 'moment of truth' for the company, for it sets the level of reward for all the designing, planning, financing and skills that have gone into the product (Marshall, 1979). Indeed, 'no matter how intelligently the product- distribution- and communication mixes are conceived, improper pricing of a product may nullify the effect of all other actions' (Staudt and Taylor, 1965, p. 450). It is for this reason that price has been described as a 'dangerously explosive variable' (Oxenfeldt, 1973, p. 48) which, if improperly manipulated, 'can cripple a business, no matter how otherwise efficient it may be' (Marshall, 1979, p. 1). In this context, the management literature offers a plethora of examples of pricing successes and failures (e.g. Plunkett, 1964; Harrison and Wilkes, 1973; *Business Week*, 1974, 1977; Moskal, 1978; Birnbaum, 1981; *Chief Executive*,

1981, 1982; Nagle, 1983), which indicate that 'a major reason for differences between the profit results of otherwise similar companies can be traced to their pricing methods and policy' (Marshall, 1979, p. 2).

Price is also the most flexible element in the marketing mix, in that price decisions can be implemented relatively quickly compared with other marketing decisions (Guiltinan and Paul, 1985). As a result, competition can normally respond to price changes within a short time period whereas responses in terms of product development or advertising require a longer time horizon due to the nature of the preparations involved (Simon, 1982). A related point is that competitors are altogether much more likely to react to price changes rather than changes in non-price variables such as advertising (Lambin, Naert and Bultez, 1975; Lambin, 1976). A major reason for this is that the impact of price changes on demand is felt much more quickly than the impact of advertising, where substantial time-lags are involved (Simon, 1980). Furthermore, demand is usually more sensitive to price than to non-price variables; for example, it has been shown empirically that, for a number of products, the price elasticity of demand is some 20 times higher than advertising elasticity (Lambin, 1976).

Price also plays a prominent role in strategic market planning, particularly in connection with the experience curve concept (Boston Consulting Group, 1968; Henderson, 1980); further, it is a critical element in market leader and market challenger strategies (Kotler, 1988) and a major variable affecting the probability of new product success or failure (Kraushar, 1970; Davidson, 1976; Cooper, 1979).

In the industrial market, the importance of price is highlighted by empirical evidence indicating that price is one of the three most important criteria governing supplier choice (Buckner, 1967; Wind, Green and Robinson, 1968; Kelly and Coaker, 1976; Dempsey, 1978; McGoldrick and Douglas, 1983; Shipley, 1985; Cameron and Shipley, 1985). In a major study of industrial buyers, 70% of respondents indicated that their ability to control prices was a prime criterion used by management to control their performance, 60% had cost constraints imposed upon them by management, and 54% of the respondents spent more than one-fifth of their time dealing with price increases alone (Farmer and Farrington, 1979). In 'make-or-buy' situations, the role of price becomes even more crucial, since 'a particular supplier may have the lowest price of all respected suppliers in an industry and yet lose an order if the price is higher than the cost to a prospective customer firm to produce the required product in-house' (Haas and Wotruba, 1976, p. 67).

Finally, from a public policy perspective, price has always been a major target of government legislation, not least because 'in the final analysis it is an industry's pricing behaviour which determines whether or not it is competitive' (Reekie, 1981, p. 52). Compared with other elements of the marketing mix price has received considerable attention, with monopoly and restrictive practices legislation, price controls and resale price maintenance providing examples of government intervention aimed at regulating prices. Against this background, Oxenfeldt (1951) points out that 'public policy regarding industrial activity is centered almost exclusively about prices and pricing practices' (p. 64), thus supporting the view that 'if business organization or practice is bad, the ill effects are seen on prices' (Nourse, 1944, p. 9).

In the light of the above, it would be expected that price would feature as a prominent factor in executive evaluations of the relative importance of alternative marketing mix elements for competitive success. Yet the empirical evidence on the issue is mixed. In some empirical studies, non-price factors — such as product development and sales efforts — were perceived by respondents as being considerably more important than price (Udell, 1964, 1968; Pass, 1971; Harris, 1978; Hooley, West and Lynch, 1984). In other studies, however, price was identified by respondents as being the number one or number two success factor (Banting and Ross, 1973; Robicheaux, 1975; Said, 1981; Coe, 1983; Fleming Associates, 1984, 1986; Samiee, 1987). One explanation that has been advanced in an attempt to reconcile the conflicting evidence is based on differences in self-reporting bias among studies and/or differences in methodology; for example, in comparing her findings with earlier studies, Said (1981) points out that 'this study is mainly concerned with pricing behaviour and our respondents probably are those who think that pricing is of more importance so they perceived it to be the most important area' (p. 411). A second and more general explanation is that price has become more important in recent years as a result of environmental pressures. In this context, Shipley (1986) states that 'the significance of price has been enhanced by the need to react to rising costs, sluggish domestic and world demand, intense home and foreign competition, fluctuating currency values and interest rates, product shortages, government regulations and widespread new product innovation' (p. 1). While most of these factors had been already identified in the 1960s as having an elevating influence on the importance of price (Dean, 1961; Hewitt, 1961; Backman, 1968), their impact since the mid-1970s has been particularly intense (Kniffin, 1974; *Business Week*, 1974; Moskal, 1978; Monroe, 1979; Wagner, 1981; Hatten, 1982; *Chief Executive*, 1982; Simon, 1982).

At this point, a word of caution is appropriate. Although a competitive price is undoubtedly a *necessary* condition for business success (especially in today's turbulent environment), it is not a *sufficient* condition (Baker, 1985). This is because 'price must be carefully meshed with the product, distribution and communication strategies of the firm . . . The interdependence of price and other strategy components must be recognized before the pricing function can be isolated for analysis' (Hutt and Speh, 1985, p. 360). While acknowledging such interdependence, price is, nevertheless, a sufficiently important and complex marketing variable to merit separate attention. From a managerial perspective, the study of price becomes of major importance, given that pricing is a thorny area of management decision-making. Table 3.2 provides a sample of expressed opinions (spanning a period of some 40 years) regarding pricing practices in industry; any further comment would appear to be unnecessary!

Table 3.2 Sample of opinions regarding industry pricing practices

. . . pricing policy is the last stronghold of medievalism in modern management. Frequently, pricing is still based on the theological notion of 'just' price. It is still largely intuitive and even mystical in the sense that the intuition is often the province of the big boss. It still has a large element of tradition. (Dean, 1947, p. 4)
. . . perhaps few ideas have wider currency than the mistaken impression that prices are or should be determined by costs of production. (Backman, 1953, p. 119)
. . . in spite of the importance of pricing decisions, the skills and analyses which are often used in practice do not approach the professional orientation used in the management of advertising, sales promotion or personal selling. (Staudt and Taylor, 1965, p. 450)
. . . for marketers of industrial goods and construction companies, pricing is the single judgment that translates potential business into reality. Yet pricing is the least rational of all decisions made in this specialised field. (Walker, 1967, p. 38)
. . . many businessmen deal with pricing as though it involved no more than a markup on costs, and remain quite unaware that with this attitude they may be doing serious damage to their and their companies' interests. (Nimer, 1971, p. 19)
. . . many managing directors do not concern themselves with pricing details; some are not even aware of how their products are priced. Yet pricing a product is one of the most critical decisions management is called upon to make. (Marshall, 1979, p. 4)
. . . pricing is approached in Britain like Russian roulette — to be indulged in mainly by those contemplating suicide. (*Chief Executive*, 1981, p. 16)
. . . in spite of the importance of the pricing decision, however, many firms do not thoroughly plan their pricing decisions. (Gultinan and Paul, 1985, p. 212)
. . . many companies fail to price effectively, even when they otherwise employ very effective marketing strategies. (Nagle, 1987, p. 1)

OVERVIEW OF THE PRICING LITERATURE

Given the importance of price, it is not surprising that 'it attracts independent study in whole areas of law, of economic theory, of the behavioral sciences, and of management science' (Wasson, 1974, p. 72). Table 3.3 provides an indication of the kind of pricing issues that have been addressed within the aforementioned disciplines. Needless to say, the list of topics presented is largely arbitrary and, most likely, incomplete. However, the sheer volume and diversity of the pricing literature make any attempt to objectively classify the subject matter into mutually exclusive and collectively exhaustive categories a rather futile exercise; alternative breakdowns of the pricing literature are provided by Laric (1980) and Lund, Monroe and Choudhury (1982).

Table 3.3 Classification of pricing topics by discipline

Topic	Discipline					
	Economics	Marketing	Law	Accountancy & finance	Psychology/ sociology	Manag. science
Price determination	X	X		X		X
Price and the marketing mix	X	X				
Price and buyer behaviour	X	X			X	
Price and industry structure	X		X			
Pricing and inflation	X	X		X		
Price differentials	X	X			X	

Price determination refers to the price-setting process at firm level. The main issues under this heading relate to the establishment of pricing objectives, the development of pricing strategy/tactics, the use of alternative pricing methods, the factors taken into account when setting/changing prices, and the allocation of price responsibility. In addition to general discussions of the above issues, a variety of deterministic and stochastic pricing models have been developed, reflecting alternative demand/cost/competitive conditions and different assumptions regarding the goal(s) of the firm. Notwithstanding their differences in terms of assumptions, model parameters and mathematical techniques utilized, the purpose of such models has been to derive optimal pricing policies under a given set of circumstances. Both static and dynamic models have been proposed and applied to the pricing of individual products or product lines; a related set of models is concerned with more specialized topics such as price deals, optimal discount structures and competitive bidding problems. This part of the literature is dominated by economic writings with respect to both theoretical and empirical contributions. In this context, given that 'questions of pricing and pricing strategy are among the most difficult problems marketing executives face' (Morton and Rys, 1987, p. 12), it is surprising that 'among all areas of marketing, pricing is one of the least researched areas' (Jain and Laric, 1979, p. 75).

The relationship of price to the other elements of the marketing mix has received attention in both the marketing and the economic literature. Two issues already touched upon in the previous section concern the relative importance of price *vis-à-vis* non-price elements as a determinant of competitive success and the flexibility/visibility of price as a marketing instrument. Other questions that have been addressed include the impact of advertising, product innovation and customer service on the level and elasticity of price and problems associated with pricing to the distribution channel (including such aspects as resale price maintenance, recommended prices and unit price implications).

The impact of price on buyer behaviour has been studied from a variety of angles. In the consumer market, relevant issues include the role of price in product/brand choice, the informational content of price (particularly its function as an indicator of product quality) and psychological aspects of pricing (e.g. odd *versus* even price endings, price thresholds and the '99' fixation). With the exception of rational (utility-based) models of consumer choice which form part of mainstream microeconomic theory, this part of the pricing literature owes a lot to the marketing discipline, particularly to researchers in the consumer behaviour field (which draws heavily from psychological/sociological sources); indeed, in marketing 'the majority of pricing articles deal with consumers' reactions to, or perceptions of, pricing' (Jain and Laric, 1979, p. 75). As far as the organizational market is concerned, economic researchers have focused primarily on the influence of dominant customers on the supplier's price policy, while in marketing the focus has been on the importance of price as a supplier selection criterion.

Under price and industry structure, the main issues concerned relate to the relationship between elements of market structure (e.g. concentration, product differentiation and barriers to entry) and the level/flexibility of prices, the structure of price–cost margins, the presence/effects of collusive arrangements, the exercise of various types of price leadership, predatory pricing and price discrimination, the nature of spatial (geographic) pricing practices and the level of profit rates. Problems of monopoly control, restrictive practices, price regulation and the question of price subsidies can also be included under this heading. These issues have traditionally been the subject matter of industrial economics, while their public policy implications have become part of the study of law.

With respect to inflation, at a macro-level, attention has been drawn to the nature of administrative prices and their relative inflexibility as a cause of inflationary pressure; this has been accompanied by debates on related public policy issues such as price controls and stabilization policies (these issues are analysed almost exclusively in the macroeconomic literature). On the other hand, at a micro-level, the focus has been on the adjustment of the firm's pricing policy in the presence of inflation, a problem which has been repeatedly addressed in both the marketing and the financial/accounting literature.

Regarding price differentials, the major concern has been with differences in the prices of similar/identical items sold in different geographical areas (neighbourhoods, cities, regions, or countries) or different types of outlet (e.g. department *vs* discount stores) and with comparisons between the price indices of different income categories or racial groups (e.g. affluent *vs* poor, black *vs* white). Studies on price differentials have appeared in the economic and marketing, as well as the sociological literature.

This brief excursion into the pricing literature indicates that a comprehensive review of all theoretical and empirical contributions on pricing would constitute a task of Herculean proportions. For present purposes, the most relevant part of the pricing literature is that dealing with the process of price determination by private firms and, in particular, manufacturing companies (excluding transfer pricing, export pricing and competitive bidding issues). The remainder of this chapter is devoted to an examination of this literature, involving (a) a critical presentation of the major theoretical contributions on price decision-making and (b) a review of empirical research focusing attention on both substantive and methodological issues.

PART 2. THEORIES OF PRICING

CONVENTIONAL PRICE THEORY

It can hardly be disputed that the theoretical approach which has dominated the study of business pricing is that of conventional (i.e. neoclassical) price theory. Historically, some of its basic tenets (e.g. the pursuit of maximum advantage) can be traced back to the writings of classical economists such as Smith (1776) and Ricardo (1817); however, it was the work (at the time largely unnoticed) of Cournot (1838) and Bertrand (1883), together with the explicit development of the theory of maximizing behaviour by Marshall (1890) and Edgeworth (1925), that provided the basis of the conventional theory of the firm as it is known today. By 1940 the theory, based on the principle of profit maximization and utilizing marginal analysis as its main expository vehicle, was more or less fully developed, following the contributions by Sraffa (1926), Hotelling (1929), Zeuthen (1932), Chamberlin (1933), Robinson (1933), Harrod (1934), Kaldor (1934, 1935), Hicks (1939) and Triffin (1940) among others.

This is not the place to embark on a detailed exposition of conventional price theory, given the extensive coverage it has received both in microeconomic texts (e.g. Horowitz, 1970; Krelle, 1976; Koutsoyiannis, 1979) and numerous state-of-the-art surveys (e.g. Brandt, 1953; Ott, 1962; Ranlett and Curry, 1968); doing so would result in unnecessary repetition of material with which the reader is undoubtedly familiar. Of more direct relevance is an examination of the extent to which conventional price theory constitutes an appropriate theoretical framework for analysing the process of price determination by individual firms and provides adequate conceptual guidance for the empirical study of pricing behaviour. Table 3.4 summarizes the major premises of conventional price theory relevant to price decision-making.

In conventional price theory, the firm is viewed as an input–output process, whereby certain inputs (factors of production) are transformed into saleable outputs (products). The value of inputs constitutes costs, the value of outputs constitutes revenues, and the excess of revenues over cost is net revenue or profit. Maximization of the latter is the single goal of the firm, which has to be achieved within certain constraints, namely, those posed by the production process (and reflected in the firm's cost function) and those posed by the market (and reflected in the firm's demand schedule). A single decision-maker, possessing full knowledge of such cost and demand conditions, uses the simple rule of equating marginal cost and marginal revenue to arrive at the price which achieves the firm's objective.

Table 3.4 Characteristics of conventional price theory

Theory element	Major assumptions	Implications
Decision-maker	Entrepreneur (owner/ manager)	Ownership and control coincide; no internal organization (thus no intrafirm conflicts regarding aims and/or means)
Firm's objective	Profit maximization	Single pecuniary motive guiding all activities of the firm
Decision horizon	Single period	Independence of decision periods; static decision-making
Type of product	Homogeneous, constantly divisible output	Single product
State of knowledge	Perfect	Decision environment characterized by complete certainty (deterministic environment)
Decision variables	Price (or output)	Only one variable open to manipulation at a time
Decision parameters	Own cost Own demand	No interdependence with competition*
Decision rule	Optimization	Optimal price/output combination obtained through the equation of marginal cost and marginal revenue

* In oligopolistic situations, further assumptions are needed to arrive at a determinate solution.

From the above, it would appear that conventional price theory offers a simple and elegant solution to the pricing problem of the firm. Yet the analysis of pricing behaviour along marginalist principles has sparked much controversy and heated discussion in the literature; indeed, 'perhaps nowhere in post-classical economic theory is there such a wide divergence in opinions as there is in the economic writings of pricing' (Fitzpatrick, 1964, p. 1). The 'marginalist controversy', as it came to be known, occupied a central place in the pricing literature for some 30 years, following Hall and Hitch's (1939) now classic study of pricing behaviour; although its chief protagonists have laid down their weapons and declared peace some time ago (see Machlup, 1967), the controversy does not appear to have been completely settled, as evidenced by some relatively recent empirical attempts explicitly aimed at verifying/infirming marginalist theory (e.g. Wied-Nebbeling, 1975; Said, 1981).

While a number of specific criticisms have been levelled at a conventional price theory (e.g. Boulding, 1942, 1960; Gordon, 1948; Papandreou, 1952; Von Mering, 1954; Haldi, 1958; Maxcy, 1968), in essence, dissatisfaction with the latter centres around three basic sets of issues: motivational issues, informational issues, and behavioural issues.

With regard to the former, the assumption of profit maximization has been challenged as (a) not being sufficiently specific both in terms of the precise operational definition of profit and in terms of the time horizon associated with its attainment; (b) providing a very narrow conception of the objective function of the firm, since profit may not be the only or even the most important objective relevant to price decision-making; and (c) presenting a false picture of the desired level of attainment, since firms are not necessarily concerned with maximization (of anything) but rather with the achievement of 'satisfactory' performance levels.

With regard to informational issues, it has been argued that the theory presents an oversimplified picture of the decision environment by (a) ignoring both the internal structure of the firm (multiple products, decentralization of authority, conflicts in objectives and desired courses of action among different stakeholders, etc.) and the complexity of the environment (competitor reaction, influence of intermediaries, government policy, etc.); (b) assuming that decisions are made under conditions of certainty, although uncertainty is the typical decision-making context facing the firm; and (c) treating information acquisition and interpretation as a non-issue.

Finally, as far as the behavioural dimension is concerned, the theory has been attacked as (a) being solely based on the principle of economic rationality and thus ignoring other very real aspects of human behaviour (e.g. social and moral dimensions); (b) reducing the complexity and creativity of management decision-making to a mechanistic stimulus–response type of behaviour centred around a single decision variable; and (c) failing to consider the implementation problems associated with a particular decision.

Thus, virtually no element of conventional price theory has been immune to criticism; it is, therefore, hardly surprising that its opponents contend that the theory 'is inadequate as descriptive and prescriptive tool of analysis' (Lieberman, 1969, p. 545).

But to what extent is the above conclusion *really* justified? In the author's opinion (and that of Krupp (1963), Langholm (1969) and Cyert and Hedrick (1972) among others), the attacks on conventional price theory have been largely misdirected, *not* because they are not accurate/legitimate, but because conventional price theory was never *intended* to serve as a descriptive/explanatory device for the analysis of the price decision-making process of the *individual* firm. In other words, the theory has been perceived by its critics (and some of its supporters) as purporting to do that which it was not designed to do in the first place; as a result, one is faced with the rather illogical (and somewhat amusing) situation whereby the theory's descriptive accuracy and explanatory power are questioned as applied to issues *other* than those for which it was developed to deal with! In this context, the birth of the marginalist controversy remains somewhat of a mystery, given that as early as 1946, one of the staunchest supporters of marginalist theory had this to say about it: 'The theory . . . is not as ambitious as is often believed . . . It does not attempt to give all the reasons why a firm . . . makes the output that it produces . . . or *why it charges the prices that it charges* . . . instead of giving a complete "determination" of output, prices and employment by the firm, marginal analysis really intends to explain the effects that changes in conditions may have upon the actions of the firm' (Machlup, 1946, pp. 520, 521, emphasis added). Unfortunately, the point that conventional price theory is not a theory of price determination at the individual firm level was not, at the time, sufficiently stressed by its supporters, who, instead, attempted to deal with the *substance* of the criticisms levelled at the theory (thus making the same conceptual error as the theory's critics); ergo the marginalist controversy.

More perplexing, however, is the continued preoccupation with conventional price theory, even *after* a number of writers pointed out the futility of attacking the theory on the grounds earlier described. For example, it has been stated that 'the concept of the maximizing firm on the level of microeconomic analysis does not attempt to describe the behavior of any unit . . . the firm in microeconomics is not part of a behavioral hypothesis which asks whether the businessman does or does not maximize and how he goes about his business' (Krupp, 1963, pp. 193, 194). A few years later, in his review of the marginalist controversy, Machlup was stating that 'the model of the firm in that (i.e. traditional) theory is not, as many writers believe, designed to explain and predict the behavior of real firms' (Machlup, 1967, pp. 9, 10); instead, conventional price theory 'is of a nature of an explanatory device of a much higher level of abstraction, permitting only broadly generalized deductions about the *aggregate* effects of entrepreneurial behaviour' (Langholm, 1969, p. 10, emphasis added). Viewed in this light, it can be argued that 'the controversy over the theory of the firm has arisen over a non-existent entity' (Cyert and Hedrick, 1972, p. 398).

Bearing the above in mind, it is evident that it would be unfruitful (and erroneous) to use conventional price theory as a unified framework to guide the theoretical and empirical study of price determination within real-world firms; as Harper observes, 'price theory has been primarily developed for use in the analysis of broad economic changes and the evaluation of social controls. It is too much to expect that the tools that are useful for social economics would also be useful in the same degree for the price maker' (1966, pp. 12, 13). At the same time, it would be equally wrong to conclude that conventional price theory has nothing to offer in this respect. The real contribution of price theory lies not in its accuracy/realism as a representation of the firm's pricing behaviour, but rather in some basic concepts to which it draws attention (Dean, 1951; Oxenfeldt, 1951, 1961; Harper, 1966; Horowitz, 1970; Monroe, 1979). Among the most important are elasticity concepts (e.g. price- and cross-elasticity of demand), cost concepts (e.g. fixed and opportunity costs) and competition concepts (e.g. reaction functions in oligopoly). From a pricing perspective, the usefulness of such concepts is not so much to be found in their precise theoretical meaning (e.g. price elasticity as an exact quantitative indicator of market response to price changes) but rather in their ability to highlight some important influences and relationships relevant to price decision-making (i.e. price elasticity as an impetus to understand and take account of buyer behaviour in pricing decisions).

The indirect contribution of conventional price theory should also not be ignored. It is largely as a result of dissatisfaction with conventional price theory that efforts have been made to (a) extend and enhance the traditional profit-maximizing model and (b) to construct alternative theoretical perspectives (such as industrial organization theory and managerial and behavioural theories of the firm). In this context, it has been pointed out that the development of the theory of industrial organization 'can partly be seen as a consequence of several inadequacies and faults of analysis in the [neoclassical] theory of the firm' (Hay and Morris, 1979, p. 26), while managerial and behavioural theories reflect 'the main strands of criticism of the neoclassical or traditional theory of the firm' (Howe, 1978, p. 26).

EXTENSIONS OF CONVENTIONAL PRICE THEORY

Efforts aimed at enhancing the basic profit maximization model have taken a variety of forms, with varying degrees of analytical complexity and mathematical sophistication. However, such efforts have two characteristics in common. First, they are all characterized by an emphasis on formal modelling, that is, on the development of optimal pricing rules geared at extending the scope of conventional price theory by selectively relaxing assumptions of the basic neoclassical model. Secondly, they all retain the assumption of profit maximization as the sole pricing objective of the firm. Thus these efforts do not represent radical theoretical departures but incremental contributions within a given theoretical domain.

RATE-OF-RETURN MAXIMIZATION

At a basic level, attention has been drawn to the definition of profit in general and the specific formulation of the profit motive in conventional price theory in particular. In this context, Knight (1934) points out that 'perhaps no other term in economic discussion is used with a more bewildering variety of well-established meanings than profit' (p. 480), while White (1960) highlights some of these interpretations by stating that 'the definition of profit varies from the gross margin concept in marketing to the residual return idea implicit in some economic interpretations . . . there is [also] the widely used accounting approach based on the income statement in which profit is the total net revenue per period of time. The financial idea of profit typically is expressed as a percentage return on total investment' (p. 182). The diversity of ways in which profit can be defined has raised the question whether maximization of money profits (i.e. the difference between total sales and total costs) as used in conventional price theory is the only or even the most appropriate specification of the profit motive consistent with rational behaviour. For example, Preiser (1934), Brovot (1955), Gutenberg (1958), Vormbaum (1959) and Gabor and Granger (1973) all maintain that the firm aims to maximize return on investment rather than money profits, while Wilson (1952) suggests that profit maximization takes different forms, depending on who controls the firm (i.e. shareholder-controlled firms seek to maximize dividend payments while management-controlled firms try to maximize undistributed profit). In response to these contentions, a number of authors have sought to derive formal solutions to maximization problems in which the profit goal has been specified differently, notably in terms of return on sales, return on capital employed or return on net worth.[2] Not surprisingly, the optimal price–output combinations generated by these efforts have generally been found to differ from that associated with the basic profit maximization model, although consistent results are obtainable under special circumstances (Pack, 1962).

While extensions of conventional price theory along the lines described above have been useful in terms of recognizing the fact that the profit motive can be modelled in different ways, their substantive contribution to the development of a more useful/comprehensive theory of price is rather limited; practically all criticisms levelled at the basic profit maximization model are equally applicable to these extensions as well.

PROFIT MAXIMIZATION IN THE MULTIPRODUCT FIRM

A second class of modelling efforts has attempted to deal with the issue of profit maximization in the context of a multiproduct firm. In general, a firm will produce and/or distribute multiple products 'either because (1) the demands for the various products are interrelated, (2) their costs of production and distribution are interrelated, (3) both costs and demand are interrelated, or (4) multiple products enable the firm to appeal simultaneously to several diverse market segments' (Monroe and Zoltners, 1979, p. 50). Multiple poduct pricing (or product line pricing as it is more commonly referred to in the marketing literature) presents no difficulty if there are no demand or cost interrelationships between the products concerned; in this case, maximization of total profits for the firm can be achieved by independently seeking the optimum price–output combination for each product (Palda, 1971). However, once interdependencies are assumed to exist (as is usually the case in reality), optimization of individual product prices is no longer sufficient (Reibstein and Gatignon, 1984). In this situation, 'if the firm is interested in *maximizing profits* it must consider not only the effects on revenues and costs of the particular product for which the price is being adjusted, but also the changes in revenues and costs for all other related products' (Monroe, 1979, p. 143, emphasis in the original). Specifically, the general theoretical solution for profit maximization requires that the adjusted marginal revenue and the adjusted marginal cost of each product should be equated, the adjustment reflecting the impact of a product's price and output changes on the revenues and costs of the other products in the line (Palda, 1969). Thus a number of pricing models have been developed in which interdependencies in terms of demand and/or cost are explicitly taken into account and which aim to identify the optimality conditions for the maximization of profits of the *entire* line;[3] in this context, demand interrelations indicate the extent of complementarity/substitutability among the products concerned (Oxenfeldt, 1966), while cost interrelations refer to the extent to which common resources are used in the production process of the products comprising the line (Dean, 1949).

Unfortunately, the inclusion of multiple products within the framework of conventional price theory appears to have created more problems than it has solved. The recognition of demand interdependencies has meant that cross-elasticities between products need to be estimated in order to operationalize the optimal pricing rules generated by product line pricing models. However, this is far from being a straightforward exercise, since 'the estimation techniques for measuring demand interrelationships have been severely lacking' (Monroe and Zoltners, 1979, p. 51). Compounding this problem are more subtle influences such as the psychological effect of a product line on buyers' perceptions of price and the impact of end prices (i.e. the highest and lowest prices) on total product line sales (Monroe, 1971, 1977). The commonly used expedient of ignoring the demand side and pricing products in the line in relation to their costs is not satisfactory either and can be 'fatal for sensible product line pricing' (Dean, 1950, p. 527); in addition, difficulties exist in identifying and correctly specifying cost interrelationships (Oxenfeldt, 1951) and, of course, the greater the number of products under consideration, the more complex the pricing problem (and thus the modelling task) becomes. Finally, there may be constraints that further complicate the product line pricing problem (e.g. competitive prices and resource constraints) and, thus, the search for an overall profit-maximizing solution. In short, 'deriving optimal prices is a complex optimization process requiring cost and demand information that is simply unavailable to the decision maker. Moreover, . . . the theoretical solutions have not been adequately specified, nor have the programming techniques been readily available' (Monroe and Zoltners, 1979, p. 51).

LONG-RUN PROFIT MAXIMIZATION

A third category of modelling efforts has concentrated on introducing a dynamic aspect to the problem of profit maximization. In its purest form, traditional price theory is static in nature, in that the firm is assumed to select that price which leads to maximum profits in each time period; as Robinson and Lakhani (1975) point out, 'one of the major shortcomings of conventional price theory is its focus on the short term. It assumes static market and production environments and uses the instantaneous profit flow as a key parameter for making value judgements' (p. 1113). The emphasis on maximizing short-term profitability has, however, been queried repeatedly in the literature in that it seems to present a rather distorted picture of the firm's profit-seeking behaviour, since 'if profit-maximisers are rational they will maximise long-run profits and not short-run profits as neoclassical models assumed' (Hawkins, 1973, p. 51); thus, 'there is no reason to assume that firms try to maximize their profits in the short-run, unless the policies accomplishing this happen to be those which also maximize long-run profits' (Fellner, 1949, p. 158). However, there is no guarantee that short-run maximizing behaviour (also known as 'myopic' behaviour) will automatically produce optimal results in the long run (Dolan, 1980). The reason for this is that 'a price set today may have considerable implications for future demand, cost and competition . . . prices today will affect prices tomorrow' (Dorward, 1987, p. 2) and, therefore, 'a firm's price or output policy must consider future effects as well as present profits' (Dolan and Jeuland, 1981, p. 54).

The attention drawn to the lack of dynamism in conventional price theory has led to the development of a large number of dynamic pricing models, which are scattered throughout the economic, management science and marketing literatures.[4] Such models depict demand, cost and/or competitive conditions in a dynamic manner, showing their development over time; for example, cost dynamics are typically modelled through the experience effect (Yelle, 1979; Day and Montgomery, 1983), demand dynamics through the diffusion process (Mahajan and Peterson, 1985) and competitive dynamics through assumptions regarding conditions of market entry (Simon, 1977). With regard to the specification of the firm's pricing objective, this usually takes the form of maximization of a discounted stream of profits over a given time horizon, the latter being treated in either a discrete (i.e. a set of individual periods) or a continuous fashion (Simon, 1982). Optimality conditions are then derived by the application of analytical techniques ranging from differential calculus to dynamic programming and optimal control theory.

As might be expected, there are a number of problems associated with attempts to model profit maximization behaviour in the long run which inevitably detract from their potential usefulness. First, in many cases, the dynamic approach to profit maximization results in the identification of an optimal price *strategy* rather than a specific long-run price; the optimal solution takes the form of a price path in which price rises or falls over time (Dorward, 1987). In such instances, one of the main attractions of the basic profit maximization model (i.e. the derivation of a *determinate* solution in the form of the optimal price) is lost and what is left in its place is of questionable utility, since 'very few of the models yield generalizable predictions and the price paths are varied' (Dorward, 1987, p. 125). Secondly, even in those cases in which a long-run base price can be determined, 'the complexity of the expression sometimes makes interpretation difficult' (Dolan and Jeuland, 1981, p. 55). The reason for this is that very advanced mathematical techniques are generally used to cope with the complexities of dynamic pricing models, so that 'while it is sometimes possible to write analytical expressions for optimal prices . . . these expressions are cumbersome enough to prevent analytical determination of optimal *vs* myopic behavior' (Dolan, 1980, p. 273). A third problem concerns the link between strategy and tactics, that is, the integration of short-term price decisions into a framework of long-run profit maximization. Rao (1984), for example, argues for a two-pronged approach to price determination, notably the setting of the product's base price based on long-run considerations and the implementation of pricing tactics (such as discounts and special offers) in specific time periods. However, 'the adoption of a pricing strategy in which the planned base price . . . would be *consistently* followed in the long-run requires a strategic *precommitment* which would preclude any opportunistic switching between alternative future pricing options . . . Consequently, the long-run profit-maximizing model . . . may not always be helpful in predicting an optimal tactical price for the short-run' (Dorward, 1987, pp. 125, 12, emphasis in the original). A fourth difficulty arises from the meaning attached to the term 'long run'. Heinen (1962, 1966), for example, maintains that the operational usefulness of the firm's objective function is adversely affected by the introduction of the time dimension, because a different profit-maximizing outcome will be obtained depending on the particular time horizon used by the firm for planning purposes. In the extreme, long-run profit maximization becomes rather tautological, since 'if the planning period is long enough, all actions of a firm could be justified on a profit basis' (White, 1960, p. 186). This is because *any* form of pricing behaviour (e.g. geared towards building market share and encouraging brand preference in the market) could be ultimately justified in terms of leading to profitability in the (unspecified) future (Papandreou, 1952; Krelle, 1961); as Machlup (1946) observed over 40 years ago, 'if whatever a businessman does is explained by the principle of profit maximization . . . the analysis acquires the character of a system of definitions and tautologies, and loses much of its value as an explanation of reality' (p. 526). Finally, and perhaps most importantly, there is the question of uncertainty. Bearing in mind that the future is by definition built into dynamic pricing models, in that future demand, cost and competitive conditions have to be taken into account as does the future impact of current decisions, difficulties arise in deriving optimal prices/ price paths because of the lack of perfect knowledge/foresight on the part of the firm. For reasons that will become clear shortly, in the presence of uncertainty, 'the long-run model is only usefully applicable to the selection of a rather generalized and somewhat subjectively based pricing strategy' (Dorward, 1987, p. 12).

PROFIT MAXIMIZATION UNDER RISK AND UNCERTAINTY

The incorporation of uncertainty within the traditional profit-maximizing model has been the focus of yet another stream of modelling work.[5] In its original formulation, conventional price theory is a theory of 'rational action under complete information' (Shubik, 1959, p. 165), because 'the decision-making unit knows exactly which goal it pursues and also foresees all consequences that may result from the choice of alternative actions' (Heinen, 1962, p. 29). It is obvious that, under conditions of perfect knowledge, the application of the profit-maximizing rule is problem-free, since the position and shape of the revenue and cost functions are uniquely and completely determined; however, it is equally obvious that this assumption is hardly tenable, because firms cannot know with certainty how their microenvironment (e.g. suppliers, buyers, competitors) will react to their decisions, nor are they completely informed about macroenvironmental (i.e. economic, social, political and technological) trends (Gutenberg, 1984). Once the assumption of perfect knowledge is dropped, the conventional profit maximization model becomes problematic, as a determinate solution (i.e. an optimal pricing rule) is no longer possible. Thus Enke (1951) observes that 'in the face of future uncertainty, the profit-maximizing motive does not provide the entrepreneur with a single and unequivocal criterion for selecting one policy from among the alternatives open to him' (p. 567), while Alchian (1950) goes as far as to say that 'where foresight is uncertain, "profit maximization" is *meaningless* as a guide to specifiable action' (p. 211, emphasis in the original). The reason for this is that each possible action by the firm can no longer be associated with one and *only* one outcome but with a *distribution* of outcomes; moreover, such distributions are typically overlapping. In other words, the introduction of uncertainty alters the decision-making environment from a deterministic to a stochastic one and, therefore, the traditional model has to be modified accordingly in order to cope with the increased complexity of the problem.

The way in which investigators have approached this task depends largely on the *type* of uncertainty involved. In this context, a distinction can be drawn between situations for which an objective or subjective probability distribution of potential outcomes can be constructed and situations for which it is not possible to attach any probabilities to the likelihood of occurrence of alternative outcomes/events (Heinen, 1962, 1966).

With respect to the former type of uncertainty, modelling efforts have utilized probability theory in reformulating the profit maximization model, the most common approach involving the use of 'expected values'; as Cyert and Hedrick (1972) observe, 'in general these models maximize expected profit . . . writers generally tend to view maximization of expected profit as the rational alternative under uncertainty' (p. 403). Unfortunately, the use of this criterion is hardly justifiable because it assumes that decision-makers are indifferent to risk, whereas, in reality, 'profit-seeking managements are very much aware of the risks to profits and these risks do significantly affect decisions' (Lintner, 1970, p. 241). In an attempt to incorporate risk preferences, some models have developed more complex decision rules which are based on multiple criteria (e.g. taking into account the variance and/or skewness of the profit distribution, in addition to the expected value). However, the benefits gained in terms of comprehensiveness are inevitably accompanied by drawbacks in the form of excessive information requirements bearing on the decision-making process (Heinen, 1966). A related approach to incorporating risk considerations involves the use of 'certainty equivalents'. This criterion is based on the assumption of risk aversion on the part of the decision-maker and involves the application of a 'risk-adjustment factor' to the expected profit values; this approach is also beset by problems, such as difficulties in specifying precisely the relationship between the risk adjustment factor and those indicators used to measure risk and the fact that risk aversion may not always be a reasonable assumption (Dorward, 1987).

As far as the second type of uncertainty is concerned, two approaches can be distinguished. The first involves the assignment of equal probabilities to all potential outcomes associated with a particular decision, the rationale being that, in the absence of further information, the decision-maker would perceive their occurrence as being equally likely; the same techniques as discussed above are then applied to find the 'best' alternative (i.e. that which maximizes profits). However, this approach appears to be rather arbitrary, since 'the lack of knowledge of probabilities should not lead to the conclusion that one would behave as if all outcomes were equally likely and definitely not that these outcomes are equally likely' (Krelle, 1961, p. 99). The second approach used to deal with the problem of uncertainty when probability distributions are unobtainable involves the use of decision criteria from game theory (Von Neumann and Morgenstern, 1944; Luce and Raiffa, 1957). Each of these criteria is based on different conceptions of the decision-maker's attitude to risk and thus the application of different criteria generally results in different optimal solutions (Heinen, 1966). For example, the 'minimax' criterion (Wald, 1945) assumes highly conservative behaviour on the part of the decision-maker, while the 'smallest risk' and 'minimax regret' criteria (Niehans, 1948; Savage,

1951) both assume that the decision-maker is primarily concerned with the costs of making a *wrong* decision. All these, as well as other criteria that have been proposed, have been subjected to criticism and none of them has emerged as unequivocally superior to the others (Oxenfeldt *et al.*, 1965).

By now it should be clear that the fundamental difficulty associated with *all* modelling efforts aiming to extend the profit-maximizing model to conditions of uncertainty concerns the incorporation of risk preferences; as Bradburd (1980) observers, 'in modelling pricing policy under uncertainty, the managerial attitude to risk will be a major determinant of behaviour' (p. 370). Given that risk preferences are not necessarily the same across different decision-makers, it is no longer possible to compare one solution with another and identify a clear optimum; what this implies is that 'if the certainty assumption is dropped, there will no longer be an objectively based unique price–output prediction, but many possible prices, each dependent on the subjective risk attitude of individual managers' (Dorward, 1987, p. 11). Thus one cannot but agree with Hamouda and Smithin's (1988) recent evaluation, that 'although the fact of uncertainty can hardly be denied, it seems to have been extraordinarily difficult to take this into account in formal economic theory. It remains . . . a troublesome theme' (p. 159).

In conclusion, it would appear that the collective contribution of modelling efforts aimed at extending conventional price theory to include alternative definitions of profit, multiple products, multiple time periods and conditions of uncertainty has been rather limited. While significant advances have undoubtedly been made from a *modelling* point of view, the theoretical insights generated by this work are of questionable value in terms of providing a theoretical framework for the empirical study of price decision-making by real-world firms.

INDUSTRIAL ORGANIZATION THEORY

The theory of industrial organization (or industrial structure) is concerned with 'the relationship between industry structure and firms' behaviour and with the implications of this behaviour for economic performance and aggregate satisfaction in the economy' (Needham, 1978, p. 1).

The central feature of industrial organization theory is the structure–conduct–performance (SCP) paradigm, emphasizing the existence of links between market structure, business conduct and market performance; Figure 3.2 summarizes this framework.

The SCP paradigm can be traced back to the writings of Mason (1939,

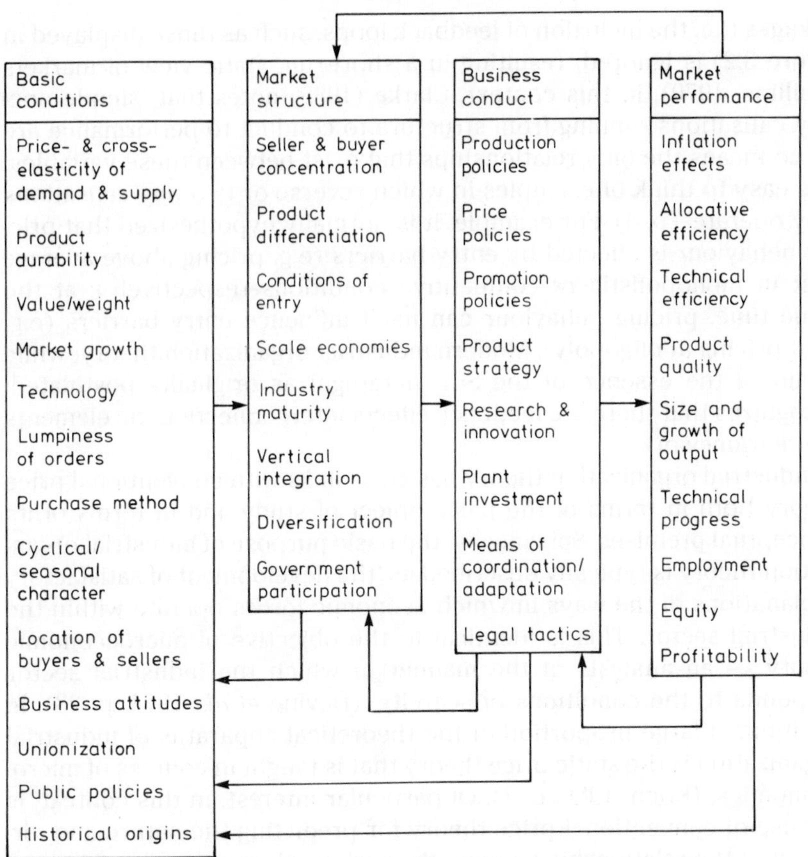

Figure 3.2 The SCP framework in industrial organization theory

1949) and in its basic form, 'it suggests that a causal link exists running from market structure to conduct and hence to performance' (Clarke, 1985, p. 2). In this scheme, market structure emerges as the central concept since, if conduct depends on structure and performance depends, in turn, on conduct, a deterministic link is established between structure and performance. The implications of assuming a one-way causation between structure and performance are twofold. First, the role of conduct as a determinant of performance is downgraded (Sawyer, 1981), the emphasis being on structure–performance and, to a lesser extent, structure–conduct relationships (McKie, 1970; Needham, 1978). However, it has been pointed out that 'we can neither predict performance from market structure, nor can we tell from structure alone how competitive the processes of the market are' (Kaysen and Turner, 1959, pp. 60, 61). Secondly, the possibility of two-way causal linkages (i.e. the inclusion of feedback loops, such as those displayed in Figure 3.2) is ignored, resulting in a short-run, static view of markets (Phillips, 1970); in this context, Clarke (1985) notes that 'simple one-way causations running from structure to conduct to performance are by no means the only relationships that exist between these variables. It is easy to think of examples in which reverse or two-way causations may operate' (p. 4). For example, it is normally hypothesized that pricing behaviour is affected by entry barriers (e.g. pricing above average cost in monopolistic *vs* competitive conditions respectively); at the same time, pricing behaviour can itself influence entry barriers (e.g. limit pricing in oligopoly). Modern industrial organization theory, while retaining the essence of the SCP paradigm as originally postulated, recognizes that there are feedback effects interconnecting the elements of the framework.

Industrial organization theory has close links with conventional price theory both in terms of the basic object of study and in terms of its conceptual premises. Specifically, the basic purpose of industrial organization theory is typically described as 'the development of satisfactory explanations of the ways in which economic forces operate within the industrial sector. This is identical to the objective of microeconomic theory — an analysis of the manner in which the industrial sector responds to the conditions of scarcity' (Devine *et al.*, 1974, p. 23). In addition, 'a large proportion of the theoretical apparatus of industrial organization is the static price theory that is taught in courses of micro-economics' (Koch, 1980, p. 2). Of particular interest, in this context, is the use of conventional price theory for predicting the nature and direction of the relationships among the various elements comprising the SCP framework; as Bain (1968) points out, 'a very significant . . . use of price theory is to predict the way in which market conduct and performance in different industries will vary because of differences in their market structures. It thus provides hypotheses concerning associations of market structure with market conduct and performance — hypotheses which are clearly relevant to the empirical study of industrial organization' (p. 25). For example, price policy is typically regarded as leading to higher profits if there are barriers to entry in the market (as in monopoly and oligopoly) than if there are no such barriers (such as in perfect and monopolistic competition); similarly, lack of product differentiation is reflected in the absence of brand advertising, and so forth.

The conceptual reliance of industrial organization theory on conventional price theory has two important implications as far as the analysis of pricing behaviour is concerned. First, with few exceptions, the conduct assumption which is made by industrial organization theorists is that of profit maximization (Sawyer, 1981). The focus on profit maximization is exemplified by Waterson (1984), who introduces his book *Economic Theory of the Industry* as follows: 'We view the firm as maximising profits subject to constraints imposed from without — actions of other firms which affect its marginal revenue or (to a lesser extent) its marginal cost and thus influence its profit maximising calculus' (p. 1). Second, and equally important, in analysing pricing behaviour (and indeed *any* form of behaviour) within the SCP framework, 'emphasis is placed on the nature of the industry rather than on the nature of the firms in the industry' (Sawyer, 1981, p. 18); Bain (1968), for example, in his classic text on industrial organization, states that 'my primary unit for analysis is the industry or competing group of firms, rather than the individual firm or the economy-wide aggregate of enterprises' (p. vii).

In the light of the above, it can be seen that industrial organization theory suffers from the same basic limitations as conventional price theory, in that it does not offer a comprehensive conceptual scheme for the analysis of price decision-making at the individual firm level; as Needham (1978) put it, 'neither the textbook literature of industrial organization nor price theory contains a satisfactory theoretical framework which includes all the determinants of a firm's optimal pricing behaviour' (p. vi). Be that as it may, there are at least three major areas bearing on the firm's price decision-making process in which the contribution of industrial organization theory is far from insignificant.

First, the SCP paradigm provides a more realistic and comprehensive specification of the firm's external environment than does conventional price theory (Scherer, 1980); reference to Figure 3.2 shows that a wide variety of basic conditions and market structure factors are used to characterize the environmental setting within which firms operate and which affect the firm's decisions in general and pricing decisions in particular. Thus, in addition to such factors as price- and cross-elasticity of demand and number of competitors, attention is drawn to buyer characteristics, product features and government intervention (to name but a few), all of which potentially affect the firm's pricing discretion.

Secondly, the SCP paradigm highlights the different forms in which price competition can be manifested in oligopolistic market situations (e.g. price leadership, collusion and price wars) and emphasizes the influence that potential entrants to the market may have on the pricing behaviour of existing competitors (e.g. the adoption of limit pricing strategies). From the individual firm's point of view, such considerations are of major importance as they reflect the strategic interdependencies between itself and its rivals and hence directly affect the deployment of price as a marketing weapon.

Finally, the SCP paradigm provides insights into the nature of competition within a particular market, highlighting both price and non-price dimensions; unlike conventional price theory, industrial organization theory 'recognizes the wider nature of competition in real-world markets in which product and process development, product design, advertising, investment strategies and so on all play a role (Clarke, 1985, p. 1). This implies that, in developing its price policy, the firm must take into account the interplay between price and non-price variables rather than limit its considerations to the former only.

In summary, while not providing a complete framework for the analysis of the pricing decision at the individual firm level, industrial organization theory makes a major contribution towards the construction of such a framework by highlighting the complex nature of the (external) pricing environment and, in particular, the potential influence of structural elements of the market and competitors' behaviour on price decision-making.

MANAGERIAL THEORIES

The theoretical contributions considered thus far were all based on profit maximization (in one form or another) being the sole pricing objective of the firm. Bearing in mind the conceptual and analytical difficulties associated with this motivational assumption, it is perhaps not surprising that 'disillusionment with profit maximisation has led to new models of firms being developed which concentrate on other aspects from which utility can be derived' (Hawkins, 1973, p. 62). Such models are known as 'managerial theories of the firm', the term encompassing a range of theoretical contributions in which the motives of *managers* are given prominence in the specification of the firm's objective function and the subsequent determination of its pricing (and other) behaviour; thus their emphasis contrasts sharply with that of conventional price theory, in which 'it is the ownership group which is determinative of firm behavior' (Phillips, 1967, p. 34).

The stimulus for managerial theories can be traced back to three interrelated developments, notably (a) the emergence of oligopoly as the predominant form of market organization, (b) theoretical efforts applying a utility maximization perspective to the analysis of the firm and (c) the separation of ownership and control characterizing modern large firms. A brief review of these developments is undertaken below, both in order to place managerial theories in a relevant context and because of the insights these developments themselves provide for the analysis of pricing behaviour.

With respect to the first development, the increasing incidence and importance of oligopolistic market structures in modern economies raised questions regarding the adequacy of conventional price theory in explaining the pricing behaviour of firms operating in oligopolistic markets. Although a number of attempts had been made to analyse oligopolistic behaviour within the traditional profit-maximizing framework,[6] the insights provided were less than satisfactory, not least because conventional price theory was originally aimed at the analysis of market structures characterized by relatively small-scale enterprises operating under competitive conditions (Rothschild, 1947). Thus, in reviewing the state of traditional oligopoly theory, Joskow (1975) concludes that 'the major problem with the conventional models of oligopoly arises from an approach which takes as given the neoclassical black box profit-maximizing firm embedded in a competitive market and then tacks on simple behavioral rules to turn it into an oligopoly model' (p. 274). Of particular importance in this context is the role assigned to profit maximization. Specifically, while profit maximization can (at least in principle) be defended on the grounds that it is a necessary condition for survival in competitive markets (since only 'normal' profits are earned by the firms concerned), 'in imperfectly competitive markets where barriers to entry are effective, the firm does not have to walk the tightrope of zero economic profits. Instead, the existence of monopoly power provides a certain latitude for error and inertia; the range of alternatives is much wider than under conditions of perfect competition' (Nordquist, 1965, p. 282). The implications of this are twofold. First, under conditions of oligopoly, the firm's long-term survival becomes dependent on earning *positive* but not necessarily maximum profits (Alchian, 1950; Enke, 1951; Drucker, 1954). Secondly, the oligopolistic firm has the freedom (and power) to pursue objectives *other* than profit maximization, such as security (Rothschild, 1947), market position (Heflebower, 1954; Knauth, 1956) and a 'quiet life' (Hicks, 1935). Thus, the attention drawn to oligopolistic forms of market organization resulted in a shifting of focus away from profit maximization and towards other potentially relevant pricing objectives; however, these contributions were purely qualitative/descriptive and did not result in any formal models of the firm's pricing behaviour based on other motives.

A parallel development to the discussion of the oligopoly issue took the form of modelling efforts aimed at expanding the traditional profit-maximizing framework by portraying the firm as a utility-maximizing entity and, thus, potentially allowing for the introduction of multiple goals in the firm's objective function; in this context, it is worth observing that 'the objectives of the firm are expressions of human decisions and, as such, non-unidimensional' (Bidlingmaier, 1964, p. 70). The utility maximization approach can be traced back to Higgins (1939), who proposed that the entrepreneur orders his preferences with respect to income and other rewards (e.g. leisure and prestige) in a way consistent with the axioms of rational choice; the implication of this formulation is that, under conditions of imperfect competition, price and output may be fully determinate but may differ from those associated with 'pure' profit maximization. The idea of an entrepreneurial preference (i.e. utility) function was subsequently used by Scitovsky (1943), who argued that the entrepreneur gains satisfaction both from income and from leisure, by Reder (1947), who postulated a trade-off between a greater profit and the entrepreneur's desire to retain control of his firm, and by Cooper (1949), who extended Reder's (1947) analysis by incorporating liquidity considerations; more recent contributions along similar lines include Heinen (1962), Ladd (1969), Ng (1969, 1974) and Olsen (1973).

The conception of the firm as a utility maximizer drew attention to the implications of multiple objectives, since the profit-maximizing and utility-maximizing solutions need not necessarily coincide to imply rational behaviour on the part of the firm; as Papandreou (1952) observed, 'profit maximization does imply rationality of course; but rationality is consistent with maximization of other things as well as profits' (p. 206). In addition, it provided a general framework within which the implications of almost *any* set of objectives could be formally analysed (Heinen, 1966). However, it should be noted that the utility maximization approach is not without problems. Thus, unless one specifies clearly the exact *content* of the utility function, utility maximization becomes 'a logically impeccable but meaningless concept' (Heflebower, 1952, p. 219); in these circumstances, utility maximization can be regarded 'simply as a more elaborate way of saying that it [the firm] does what it thinks best. This can hardly be untrue, but it is also not very helpful unless some content can be poured into the empty utility functions' (Boulding, 1960, p. 4). Secondly, even if the individual elements in the utility function are specified, there are still conceptual and measurement difficulties involved. Albach (1959), for example states that 'the disadvantage of a substitution of a profit-maximising function with utility maximisation lies particularly in the fact that the profit concept is more intelligible and interpretable than the concept of utility' (p. 132), while Cyert and March (1963) indicate that 'we can adopt the strategy of introducing subjective utility, but this does not help us until the util becomes a better behaved measure' (p. 9). Overall, from a pricing point of view, the major contribution of utility-based expositions of the entrepreneur's behaviour lies in the explicit recognition that a variety of monetary as well as non-monetary objectives may be potentially relevant in price decision-making and, consequently, a particular pricing decision may not be necessarily aimed at the optimization of any *one* of them but rather towards the simultaneous achievement of multiple goals.

The third, and arguably most important development relates to what has come to be known as the 'managerial revolution', reflecting the separation of ownership and control in the large corporation and the increasing role and power of managers (as opposed to owner-entrepreneurs) in decision-making. The pioneering work on the separation of ownership and control was undertaken by Berle and Means (1932) and was subsequently followed by a number of contributions, the most important of which are those by Burnham (1941), Gordon (1945), Florence (1961), Galbraith (1967) and Larner (1970).

Based on an analysis of the relationship between ownership and control of the 200 largest non-financial US corporations, Berle and Means (1932) drew attention to the dispersion and diffusion of ownership that had taken place as a result of the rise of the large joint stock corporation and the implications of such fragmentation for the control of the firm; in addition, they highlighted the increasing concentration of wealth (and thus economic power) with a small number of large corporations. There are three important points that emerge from their analysis. First, that the control of large firms is in the hands of managers who themselves have only small shareholdings (if any); as Wildsmith (1973) observes, 'the assets of large corporations are increasingly under the centralised control of small self-perpetuating groups of professional managers with small personal ownership of the assets they control' (p. 2). Secondly, that the motives and interests of managers are likely to be different from those of shareholders; while the latter are primarily concerned with high dividends and thus would favour profit-maximizing actions by the firm, 'managers may be more interested in the size of their offices, the number of employees who report to them, the absolute size of the firm and, in general, the perquisites that accompany their job. Those interests will usually not be consistent with profit maximization' (Koch, 1980, p. 45). The third and perhaps most important point is that not only may the interests of managers and owners not coincide, but managers may actually be *able* to pursue their own goals because the constraints on managerial discretion imposed by the capital market are not particularly effective. A major reason for this is that 'small shareholders rarely attend general meetings. Instead, the election of the board of directors is arranged by the existing board, assisted by the appointment of proxies (representatives of shareholders). The system of voting proxies is well manipulated by top management, which is often directly represented in the board of directors and thus can influence decisions of further appointments of top managers' (Koutsoyiannis, 1979, p. 324). In a nutshell, 'incorporation and limited liability, by facilitating the dispersal of shareholdings, has led not only to a separation but also to a divorce of ownership from control: not only were the shareholders no longer the main decision makers, but they had lost the capacity to control these decision makers' (Gilbert, 1972, p. 16).

However, it would be naive and incorrect to assume that managers are *completely* free from outside influences when making policy decisions; as Koutsoyiannis (1979) makes clear, 'the manager's discretion in defining the goals of the firm is not unlimited. A minimum level of profit is necessary for a dividend policy acceptable to the body of shareholders; for keeping a good reputation with banks so as to secure finance for current transactions; for avoiding a relative fall in the price of shares in the stock exchange and the risk of take-over. If these conditions are not satisfied the management runs the risk of mass dismissal; their job security is endangered' (p. 324). Further factors that may keep in check the extent of divergence between the interests of owners and managers include the fact that the latter may themselves own substantial shareholdings (Lewellen, 1969, 1971); the fact that part of the managerial compensation package may be profit-linked (Lewellen and Huntsman, 1970; Masson, 1971); and the fact that the two groups may have similar social backgrounds and thus share a common frame of reference with respect to the nature of business activity and practice (Nichols, 1969; Milliband, 1969). In addition, as noted previously, the nature of the market environment will also impinge upon the firm's ability to pursue goals other than profit maximization; indeed, 'market structure is a key factor in determining whether there is any scope for managerial discretion . . . or whether the competitive process can enforce profit-maximizing behaviour' (Gilbert, 1972, p. 27).

Bearing the above discussion in mind, the implications for managerial theories can be summarized as follows. The developments on the oligopoly front highlighted the *potential* for the pursuit of *alternative* objectives by the firm, profit maximization being no longer a necessary condition for survival; the models of owner-entrepreneur utility maximization demonstrated that objectives other than profit maximization can be consistent with *rational* behaviour and amenable to *formal* analysis; and the work on the separation of ownership from control showed *whose* objectives are likely to be given precedence in the large modern firm and *why* such objectives are likely to differ from the traditional profit maximization motive. It is upon these building blocks that *all* managerial theories are constructed; as Sawyer (1979) points out, managerial theories 'rely on the existence of barriers to entry into the industries in which their firms operate, so that potential supernormal profits are available to the firm . . . all the theories . . . assume that the controllers of the firm are maximizers, but differ in terms of which variables the controllers are thought to seek to maximize. In general, the controllers cannot maximize their utility regardless of what happens to profits, and so some constraint on profits or a profit-linked variable is introduced' (p. 90). Thus, the major difference between managerial theories and conventional price theory is that the former 'change the objective function. This modification can be made by substituting another entity . . . for profits and then proceeding to maximize the new entity. A second way is to substitute a utility function (which includes the effects of several entities) for profit and proceed to maximize utility' (Cyert and Hedrick, 1972, p. 402). A review of major managerial models follows.

SALES REVENUE MAXIMIZATION

The first formal managerial model can be attributed to Baumol (1958, 1959), who postulated that the firm aims to maximize its sales revenue subject to a profit constraint. According to Baumol (1958), the large oligopolist firm 'seeks to maximize not its profits but its total revenues which the businessman calls his sales. That is, *once his profits exceed some vaguely defined minimum level*, he is prepared to sacrifice further increases in profits if he can thereby obtain larger revenues . . . Profits must be high enough to provide the retained earnings to finance current expansion plans and dividends sufficient to make future issues of stock attractive to potential purchasers. In other words, the firm will aim for that stream of profits which allows for the financing of long-term sales' (pp. 253, 254, emphasis in the original).

It should be noted that Baumol (1958, 1959) did not consider constrained revenue maximization to be a universal objective applicable to *all* oligopolistic firms; rather, his main concern was to demonstrate that 'alternative hypotheses about business objectives were just as easily subjected to rigorous analysis as is the conventional profit maximization model' (1958, p. 242). Nevertheless, Baumol (1959) offers several justifications for his emphasis on sales revenue, in which the latter is portrayed both as a facilitator of other objectives (e.g. security and efficiency) and as an ultimate objective in its own right. In addition, he derives optimality conditions for price–output combinations, shows how these may differ from profit-maximizing solutions and explicitly incorporates advertising in his analysis. Thus, 'what is important about the basic Baumol model is that it suggests *why* firms should seek to maximise sales revenue, *how* the maximizing position is reached, and the *possible implications* of the imposition of a minimum profits parameter' (Howe, 1978, p. 28, emphasis in the original). It is worth noting that the revenue maximization model has generated a major debate in the microeconomic literature and has resulted in numerous criticisms, extensions and modifications of Baumol's (1958, 1959) original formulation;[7] the reason for this interest appears to be partly the fact that it was presented in the traditional mould of economic models and partly because of its '*prima facie* plausibility in this age of manager-dominated, advertising conscious giant corporations' (Hawkins, 1973, p. 68).

In subsequent work, Baumol (1962, 1967) extended his analysis to a dynamic context, by constructing a model in which the firm seeks to maximize sales growth; the rationale for this was that 'maximisation of the *rate of growth* of sales revenue seems to be a better approximation of the goals of many management groups in large firms than is maximisation of the current *level* of sales . . . A stationary optimum would doubtless be abhorrent to the captains of industry, whose main concern is surely not at what size their enterprises should finally settle down . . . but how rapidly to grow' (Baumol, 1962, pp. 324, 319, emphasis in the original). The relevance of sales growth as a managerial objective is justified on the basis that publicity materials of most companies seem to emphasize the 'progress' of the firm rather than its sheer size; that growth of other (competing) firms may jeopardize the firm's market share; and that 'orderly' growth is consistent with management's attitude to risk and shareholders' desires (Baumol, 1967). Furthermore, Baumol demonstrates that 'a very substantial rate of growth may be required even if growth is not among the company's objectives. Though the company may seek ultimately to maximise sales volume, current or future, or may be interested primarily in profits, a considerable rate of growth may plausibly be expected to serve its interests' (1967, pp. 100, 101).

From a pricing perspective, Baumol's (1958, 1959, 1962, 1967) work is of considerable importance in that it highlights the potential influence of revenue considerations in the firm's decision-making process, both from a short- and a long-term point of view. With respect to the latter, his analysis provided the springboard for subsequent efforts taking the form of dynamic pricing models, in which long-run revenue maximization features as the firm's primary objective (e.g. Sabel, 1973; Leland, 1972; Rao and Shakun, 1972).

OUTPUT MAXIMIZATION

In contrast to Baumol's (1958, 1959, 1962, 1967) emphasis on sales revenue, Lynn (1968) suggested that maximization of unit volume (i.e. physical output) subject to a profit constraint may be an appropriate managerial pricing goal; the sale of more product and the possible accompanying increase in market share may provide a broader basis for profits as well as enhance the security of the firm. In this context, 'unit-oriented pricing may be seen as a special case permitted where profit requirements are not high and where cost and demand combine to permit ample gross margins' (Lynn, 1968, p. 36); it may also be a legitimate goal for firms who are judged primarily by output but also told to break even (Kafoglis, 1969). It should be fairly obvious that the credibility of output maximization as a managerial objective depends crucially on the existence of a profit constraint, since, in the absence of the latter, output would be increased until total revenue was zero (i.e. the product would be given away free!). It should also be obvious that rather serious aggregation problems arise in the case of the multi-product firm; thus 'it is interesting to ponder how we can add a firm's output of refrigerators, biscuits and cars. Certainly, we could add up the *values* of the sales of each product, but the model would then merge indissolubly into a model of sales revenue maximisation' (Hawkins, 1973, p. 69, emphasis in the original). Since output maximization is proposed as an objective of large managerial firms (which are more than likely to produce a variety of products), this remains a rather troublesome theme.

GROWTH MAXIMIZATION

Another attempt to model formally the behaviour of the managerial enterprise can be found in the work of Marris (1963, 1964, 1971), in which growth is assumed to be the dominant objective guiding management decisions. Based on an impressive literature review of business motives, Marris (1963, 1964) highlights a number of linkages between the growth of the firm and managers' own psychological, sociological and economic needs, aims and ambitions (e.g. compensation, power, prestige, status, etc.). Such linkages would seem to imply that 'at first sight . . . rational managers should choose the fastest growth rate they can get away with, that is to say, the fastest growth rate permitted by the capital market on the one hand and their product market on the other' (Marris, 1963, p. 214). However, Marris also recognizes that managers are 'more than a little security conscious' (Marris, 1963, p. 213), not least because 'unlike the civil servant, the industrialist's immediate livelihood depends intimately on the continuity of his own organisation; if the organisation is disbanded there is no residual institution to guarantee him employment. And if a top executive is thrown on the market because his previous firm has failed, he himself will be tainted with the failure and the demand for his services correspondingly affected' (Marris, 1964, p. 64). The disutility attached by managers to the risk of dismissal suggests that they are likely to take measures to avoid financial failure of their enterprise, and discourage takeover raids (both of which are circumstances potentially leading to collective loss of employment). It is upon the twin considerations of growth and security that Marris (1963, 1964, 1971) builds a number of models of the managerial enterprise, all of which share the common premise that 'managers [seek] . . . to maximise the rate of the growth of the firm they are employed in subject to a constraint imposed by the security motive' (Marris, 1964, p. 47). In these models, the growth dimension is represented by the growth rate of gross assets and the security dimension by the valuation ratio (defined as the ratio of the market value of the firm to the book value of its assets). Optimality conditions are subsequently derived for two basic formulations. In the first, the growth rate is maximized subject to a minimum valuation ratio (the latter reflecting the level of security at which management feels safe from takeover). In the second formulation, the valuation ratio and the growth rate are both included in a managerial utility function (thus highlighting a continuous trade-off between the growth and security motives). In both formulations, a separate security-motivated constraint on leverage (gearing) is also included, reflecting management's concern with avoiding insolvency.

Marris's (1963, 1964, 1971) work precipitated an outpour of maximization models, in which growth features as the central variable.[8] Despite the fact that neither these models nor Marris's (1963, 1964, 1971) original contribution are directly concerned with the pricing decision (in that financial policy variables are given priority), they nevertheless provide important theoretical insights on price decision-making. In particular, they highlight the potential importance of growth considerations in the formulation of pricing policy *and* the risks associated with pursuing growth without due regard to safety factors; in addition, they help emphasize the dynamic nature of the firm's decision context and the interplay between short- and long-term requirements.

UTILITY MAXIMIZATION

The last managerial model to be considered is Williamson's (1963a, b, 1964) 'managerial discretion theory', which pioneered the use of a *managerial* preference function; this approach was subsequently adopted by other writers attempting to model the firm's behaviour (e.g. Kay and Diamantopoulos, 1987).

Williamson (1963a, b, 1964) attempted to follow Papandreou's (1952) suggestion that a more fruitful theoretical analysis of the firm could be obtained by replacing profit maximization with a more general preference function and also to demonstrate that it is *not* necessarily 'harder to derive operationally meaningful theorems concerning firm behavior from a construction which is directly based on preference-function maximization than to do so from the profit-maximization construction' (Papandreou, 1952, p. 211). The latter problem arises because 'most managerial motives are prevented from being directly incorporated into models of corporate behaviour because they canot be measured in monetary terms' (Dorward, 1987, p. 15). Williamson gets around this problem by suggesting that 'rather than attempt to introduce security, power, prestige and so forth into the theory directly, we ask instead: to what activities do these motives give rise? These activities, rather than the motives, are then made part of the model' (Williamson, 1963b, p. 240). In particular, he introduces the notion of 'expense preference', which is defined as the satisfaction which managers derive from certain kinds of expenditures, such as expenditures on staff (to increase their jurisdiction and sphere of authority), emoluments (i.e. 'slack' as reflected in managerial perquisites) and discrêtionary investment expenditure (i.e. investments beyond those required for the normal operation of the firm), all of which act as sources of security, power, prestige and professional achievement (as well as salary enhancement). It is these discretionary expenditures that are entered as arguments in a utility function (of which Williamson (1963a, b, 1964) examines a number of variants) which management seeks to maximize subject to a profit constraint. The latter is exogenously determined and plays the same kind of role as in Baumol's (1958, 1959) static sales revenue maximization model; in Williamson's own words, 'the existence of satisfactory profits is necessary to assure the interference-free operation of the firm to the management' (Williamson, 1963b, p. 242). However, unlike Baumol (1958, 1959), Williamson (1963a, b, 1964) maintains that management will always plan to *exceed* the profit constraint, as the excess profit provides the means for funding discretionary investment.

Although Williamson's (1963a, b, 1964) theory was not originally intended as a model of pricing behaviour, his analysis is not without relevance to the latter. In this context, the essence of his contribution lies in his explicit consideration of multiple *managerial* goals within a utility framework (much in the same sense that utility maximization approaches to the entrepreneurial firm recognize the pursuit of multiple objectives by owner-entrepreneurs); this framework could be appropriately adapted to the analysis of specific decision areas such as pricing (in other words, one could potentially formulate a utility function restricted to managerial *pricing* goals only).

The collective contribution of managerial theories to the analysis of the firm in general, and the pricing decision in particular, can be summarized as being the introduction of greater realism into the goal structure of the firm. Indeed, managerial theories are often referred to as 'realism-in-motivation' theories as distinguished from 'realism-in-process' (i.e. behavioural) theories (Williamson, 1964). Thus Wildsmith (1973) observes that 'managerial theories are . . . more realistic in their assumptions and as a consequence they predict responses which in most cases are different from those of profit maximisers and closer to those found in reality' (p. 125); moreover, managerial theories 'provide more plausible explanations of why and how decisions may be reached by business managers and seem to yield more realistic predictions about firms' likely responses to change' (Heidensohn and Robinson, 1974, p. 133). From an analytical perspective, 'the real advantage of these theories is that given the value of the paramaters and a knowledge of the cost and revenue functions we can trace the implications of the adoption of any of these newer objective functions . . . An additional advantage . . . is that changes in the business environment (such as a rise in the business's costs, or a rise in the rate of VAT) can be incorporated in the model' (Howe, 1978, p. 37).

However, managerial theories also suffer from a number of deficiencies. The first of these is that they do not pay sufficient attention to contextual influences in general and the market environment in particular. Thus, in contrasting managerial theories with industrial organization theory, Sawyer (1981) concludes that the former 'can be criticised for the opposite reason to that put forward . . . in respect to the structure–conduct–performance approach, that is for overemphasising the firm and neglecting the influence of industrial structure and the economic environment in general' (p. 152); in a similar fashion, Baldwin (1964) observes that 'the managerial literature, taken as a whole, has failed to recognize the full range and significance of internal and external constraints in limiting the ability of managers to translate their objectives into organisational purposes' (p. 44). Such criticisms are difficult to defend against, particularly because managerial models of the firm are supposed to be 'theories of oligopoly, in that potential supernormal profits are assumed; but the interdependence characteristic is largely ignored' (Sawyer, 1979, p. 89). The lack of attention to the role of competition in the market is, without doubt, a serious shortcoming of managerial theories as far as the analysis of the pricing decision is concerned (George and Joll, 1981).

A second problem of managerial theories relates to the specification of the firm's objective function, particularly when a utility formulation is employed. To make the model analytically tractable, one must avoid 'packing the kitchen sink in', which, in turn, raises the question of *how many* and *which* objectives to include. In this context, Machlup (1967) points out that 'in order to show how hopeless it is to construct a total-utility model . . . one merely has to visualize the large variety of possible "satisfactions" and the still larger variety of things that may contribute to their attainment . . . Total utility, which the manager by his decisions will try to maximize, will be a function of a large number of variables by virtue of the contribution they make to his pride, prestige, self-esteem, conscience, comfort, feeling of accomplishment, material consumption, and anticipation of future benefits and pleasures' (p. 19). Moreover, even if one somehow manages to confine the utility function to only a few carefully selected items, 'there is the nagging conceptual problem of whether or not it makes sense to speak of a well-ordered set of preferences for the firm in view of the size and complexity of most business operations' (Nordquist, 1965, p. 291).

A third problem area is that, as far as pricing is concerned, 'managerial theories are not more operational than entrepreneurial models . . . there are few conclusions to be drawn on the pricing policies implied in the models' (Wildsmith, 1973, p. 125) and, moreover, 'some of their predictions are ambiguous' (Dorward, 1987, p. 19); similar reservations are expressed by Silberston (1970) and George and Joll (1981) among others.

A fourth limitation of managerial models concerns their 'black-box' view of the firm in that, not unlike conventional price theory, they are based on an *a priori* specification of an objective function which reflects well-defined motives and a clear preference structure; given this objective function, the firm subsequently operates as a well-oiled machine (Horowitz, 1970). This black-box view has been attacked by Loasby (1987), according to whom 'though they [managerial theories] rely on the concept of firms as organisations run by managers to justify their objective functions they make no attempt to consider the firm as a system. They invoke group preference functions without enquiring how these may be formulated or why they may be relevant to decisions; they invoke complexity without considering how that might affect the definition of problems, the options considered or the choices made. They are managerial models without management' (p. 14).

Finally, one could question the emphasis (obsession?) on maximization which is a common characteristic of *all* theoretical contributions examined thus far; this is because 'despite the obvious theoretical and mathematical attractions of having the decision maker maximize *something*, from a practical standpoint the need, ability or indeed desire on the part of decision makers to exert the effort to maximize *anything* can be, and has been, cast in serious doubt' (Horowitz, 1970, p. 315, emphasis in the original).

The discussion of managerial theories concludes the examination of maximization approaches to the analysis of the firm; the next section completes the theoretical component of this literature review by discussing conceptual perspectives on price decision-making, in which the firm is depicted as a non-maximizing entity.

BEHAVIOURAL THEORIES

While the term 'behavioural theories' references a number of quite distinct theoretical strands, these 'have a great deal in common. First, they share the general premise that the objective function that enters into the firm's decisions is typically something less simple than profit. Second, because of the complex nature of the environment, the lack of information, uncertainty, or the inadequacy of the decision maker, these theories recognize implicitly or explicitly that maximizing is an unattainable procedure, and in its place substitute other guidelines or rules of thumb to determine what is "satisfactory"' (McGuire, 1964, p. 108).

Behavioural theories are also known as 'realism-in-process' theories (Williamson, 1964), in that they attempt to inject realism not only into the motives guiding business (and thus pricing) behaviour (as managerial theories do), but also into the decision-making process itself. In this context, they differ from the theoretical perspectives considered in the previous sections both in terms of emphasis and in terms of approach. With regard to the former, 'instead of attempting to derive from axioms and data the values which would be ascribed to the relevant variables by an optimal decision, attention is turned to the processes by which decisions might be made' (Loasby, 1985, p. 5). In other words, behavioural theories are not primarily concerned with deriving optimality conditions *given* a particular objective function, but rather with discovering *what* objectives are set in an organizational setting and *what* decisions are involved in their attainment. The different emphasis of behavioural theories is also reflected in their approach to theory construction; the latter is characterized by a focus on descriptive realism, in that it is considered important that '[a] theory should describe the way businessmen actually act and do it in terms of the type of real-world concepts and data that businessmen actually deal with in their day-to-day activities' (Koch, 1980, p. 50).

Behavioural theories can be broadly classified into four main groups, notably (a) contributions based upon the full- and normal-cost principles, (b) contributions using analogies from the physical sciences, (c) contributions drawing from organization theory, and (d) decision calculus contributions.

AVERAGE-COST THEORIES

Theoretical contributions based on the full-cost principle can be traced back to the work of the Oxford economists Hall and Hitch (1939) on the pricing behaviour of firms. Their study — which now enjoys 'classic' status — involved an empirical examination of pricing practices of British companies and produced results which could not be reconciled with the postulates of conventional price theory (which was the accepted theoretical doctrine of the time). Specifically, neither did the firms under investigation aim at profit maximization nor did they set their prices on the basis of marginal analysis. Instead, the firms aimed at a reasonable/conventional profit level and calculated their prices on the basis of average costs to which a profit margin was added. In Hall and Hitch's (1939) own words, 'the most striking feature of the answers was the number of firms which apparently do not aim, in their pricing policy, at what appeared to us to be the maximization of profits by the equation of marginal revenue and marginal cost . . . in pricing they try to apply a rule of thumb which we shall call "full cost", and that maximum profits, if they result at all from the application of this rule, do so as an accidental (or possibly evolutionary) by-product' (pp. 112, 113). To be fair, it should be noted that the full-cost principle was not an entirely new discovery, in that quite detailed discussions of various forms of it (such as target pricing and conversion cost pricing) had already appeared in the management literature of the time (see, in particular, Brown, 1924a, b, c; Bradley, 1927; Churchill, 1932). However, it was not until Hall and Hitch's (1939) exposition that full-cost pricing became part of the mainstream pricing literature, thus confirming that 'to the extent that economists were not aware of this pricing procedure . . . indicated their ignorance if not disdain of "business" literature' (Heflebower, 1955, p. 361).

There are two aspects of Hall and Hitch's (1939) analysis that merit closer attention. The first relates to firm's pricing objectives and the second to the methods used in calculating prices. With respect to the former, Hall and Hitch maintain that firms 'are thinking in altogether different terms' (p. 113) than a profit maximizer would, in that 'conventional' rather than maximum profits constitute the main pricing goal;

however, 'the conventional addition for profit varies from firm to firm and even within firms for different products' (p. 114). The size of the profit margin is considered to be dependent partly on tradition and partly on the influence of actual and potential competition. Moreover, there is a tendency for price stability, in that the firm typically expects that it would lose business if it raised its price (because competitors would not follow the increase) and would not gain business if it lowered its price (because competitors would also lower their prices); in other words, the firm faces a 'kinked' demand curve, which is elastic above the current price but inelastic below it.

It is important to note that Hall and Hitch (1939) *infer* the pricing goals of the firm from the *procedures* used in price-setting. In this context, they provide a number of reasons for why firms use full-cost pricing procedures which seem to reflect a common belief among firms that 'a price based on full average cost was the "right" price, the one which "ought" to be charged' (p. 113). They proceed to describe this procedure by stating that 'the formula used by the different firms in computing "full cost" differs in detail . . . but the procedure can be not unfairly generalized as follows: prime (or "direct") cost per unit is taken as the base, a percentage addition is made to cover overheads (or "oncost" or "indirect" cost) and a further conventional addition (frequently 10 per cent) is made for profit. Selling costs commonly and interest on capital rarely are included in overheads; when not so included they are allowed for in the addition for profits'. While this provides a summary description of price-setting under the full-cost principle, one must be aware that, in practice, the principle manifests itself in a *variety* of forms, depending upon (a) the assumed volume rate used in the calculation of average costs (e.g. historical *vs* forecast *vs* 'normal' output); (b) the kind of costs included in overheads (e.g. inclusion *vs* exclusion of administration and selling costs); (c) the method used to allocate overheads (e.g. as proportion of direct unit cost *vs* direct allocation to units of output); (d) the nature of the profit component (e.g. target profit per unit *vs* percentage on average total cost); (e) the rigidity of application of the full-cost principle, in terms of the variability of profit margins across products and/or over time; and (f) the adherence to the *same* basic cost calculation formula for all products in the business at all times (Oxenfeldt, 1951; Kuhlo, 1955; Heflebower, 1955; Wied-Nebbeling, 1975). Thus, it can be seen that a large number of outwardly similar but in reality quite different pricing methods can be potentially subsumed under the full-cost principle; indeed, 'the literature on pricing appears to have been caught up in an unusual amount of semantic confusion, with the use of the label "full-cost pricing" to cover a wide variety of behavior' (Haynes, 1962, p. 321).

While the study by Hall and Hitch (1939) highlighted the absence of marginalist principles in the pricing behaviour of real-world firms and drew attention to the prevalence of the full-cost principle, it was not until 10 years later that the latter became the core of a fully-fledged theory of price determination developed by Andrews (1949a, b). Commenting on the full-cost principle, Andrews (1949a) expressed his surprise that 'it has not yet emerged as a *postulate* of economic analysis . . . Scientific method would suggest that the right thing to do . . . would be at least to accept the principle as a basis for further theory in its own field — the analysis of price policy' (p. 82, emphasis in the original). He thus set out to develop a *general* theory of pricing, drawing partly from his experience as a consultant and partly from empirical research in the rayon and boot and shoe industries.

The central tenet of Andrews' thesis is that 'a business man producing an article with a given specification will normally base his price on his costs of production. He will be able to make fairly accurate estimates of his average direct costs, and, in order to get the quoted price, these will be grossed up by a definite amount which . . . we shall call the *average gross profit-margin* required per unit of product . . . the amount added will formally include an allowance *as for* profit, although . . . the actual earning of a profit will depend upon the sales actually achieved . . . This principle of pricing will be called the *Normal Cost Principle*, since the business man, in fixing his price in this way, appears to act on the idea that such a price will normally enable him to cover his costs' (Andrews, 1949a, p. 81, emphasis in the original). In a later work, Andrews (1949b) replaces the term 'average gross profit-margin' with 'costing-margin' and restates the normal-cost principle as follows: 'the price which a business will normally quote for a particular product will be the estimated average direct costs of production plus a costing-margin' (p. 184). Differences in terminology notwithstanding, the addition to direct costs is of crucial importance in Andrews' (1949a, b) theory, as it largely determines the height of the quoted price. Three important points are worth noting in this context.

The first is that 'the exact method by which the average required gross profit-margin is calculated will vary between businesses' (Andrews, 1949a, p. 81) and that 'the costing rules may well differ for different products within the same business or for the same sort of product between different businesses . . . but will tend to remain unchanged in any particular case' (Andrews, 1949b, p. 159). This implies — as was also the case with Hall and Hitch's (1939) full-cost principle — that, in practice, the normal-cost pricing principle is likely to be manifested in a variety of forms. Andrews, however, is not particularly concerned about this, since his theory 'is intended to have general application, and it will not be possible to go very far into the detailed modifications that are necessary when one is looking at a particular individual business producing given products at a given time' (Andrews, 1949a, p. 55).

A second point concerns the forces that determine the size of the margin. This is portrayed as being directly dependent upon competition in the *long run*, in that 'the right price in the long run cannot be higher than its [the firm's] competitors would quote' (Andrews, 1949b, p. 153); in other words, 'the businessman is thus seen as thinking of his long-run demand curve as being infinitely elastic for a certain level of price, in the sense that any attempt to maintain a higher price will mean the loss of his market, since other producers will find it profitable in the long run to continue to supply the market at that price' (Andrews, 1949a, p. 83). Thus Andrews (1949a, b) takes a broad view of competition, to include not only existing competitors but also potential entrants, the latter consisting both of entirely new firms setting up in the market and of existing firms currently producing different products but with the capability of entering the market if it becomes sufficiently attractive. The firm's concern with actual and potential competition implies that 'the normal costing-margin will tend to be at such a level as will cover the average direct costs in the long run and give a normal profit, in the sense of the margin at which new business will enter the market' (Andrews, 1949b, p. 174).

The third point relates to the applicability of the normal-cost principle in markets characterized by 'fixed' or 'conventional' prices or price ranges (e.g. retailing). According to Andrews (1949b), this case can be readily analysed on a normal-cost basis, in that a manufacturer will translate the retail price into an ex-works price (by subtracting the customary retail margins) and subsequently determine the specification of the product which can be sold at that price. This reduces to establishing the gross margin and thus the limits in the specification of the product that he can offer; specifically, 'the difference between the fixed price and the gross margin will be the amount which can be spent on direct costs, and these control the specification. Competition will ensure that this quality is at least as good as any rival would offer, and thus in the end determine the profit margin itself' (Andrews, 1949b, p. 163).

Thus, Andrews (1949a, b) considers his theory as giving an accurate description of pricing behaviour in most circumstances and indicates only two major exceptions in which the normal-cost principle breaks down (notably price-cutting in desperation by a firm unable to cover its paying-out overheads when demand is very depressed and price-cutting by a very small competitor wishing to grow and hoping to escape unnoticed because of its small size). He also proposes that conventional price theory should be revised, so that 'instead of the business man being thought of as restricting his *output* to the point where marginal revenue curves cut his marginal cost curves, he should be regarded *as quoting a price* which will bear a definite relationship to the average direct cost of the product' (Andrews, 1949b, p. 174, emphasis in the original) and that 'the theory of the gross profit-margin should be one of the central parts of economic analysis, and should be formulated in terms of competition' (Andrews, 1949a, p. 89).

One interesting feature of Andrew's normal-cost theory which seems to have passed largely unnoticed is that it can be seen as an early statement of the contribution approach to pricing;[9] as Dorward (1987) observes, 'Andrews seems to have inadvertently devised the first attempt at a contribution approach to full-cost pricing. As he did not find the distinction between overhead cost and the net profit margin to be useful for market price determination, his demand-determined costing margin can be thought of as transforming the conventional overhead allocation rate from a constant to a variable unit cost' (p. 101).

The analyses of Hall and Hitch (1939) and Andrews (1949a, b) were subsequently followed by a stream of contributions in which the main ideas of the full- and normal-cost (subsequently referred to jointly as average-cost) principles were further developed and modified, as well as — sometimes severely — criticised.[10] With regard to the latter, the main criticisms were directed towards the rather vague and imprecise character of average-cost theories (in terms of their ability to yield specific predictions regarding price and output levels/changes); the wide range of behaviour that is possible under the general heading of average-cost pricing which, in many cases, could be reduced to a description of profit-maximizing behaviour in a real-world environment (in that variation of profit margins over time and across products and further modifications before the final price is set can be seen as marginalist adjustments reflecting demand and competitive conditions); the irrationality of strict adherence to cost-based pricing rules (in that prices would be raised in times of declining demand); the presence of circular reasoning implicit in average-cost explanations (in that costs depend on volume which, in turn, depends — at least partly — on price); the fact that average-cost pricing procedures may be used not to set but to *justify* a price already decided upon by other means (in that costing systems can be easily manipulated so as to make a certain price *appear* that it has been set on the basis of cost); the fact that a particular average-cost pricing method can be consistent with different motivations on the part of the firm (in that the profit margin would depend on the firm's pricing goals and thus result in different price levels); and the fact that average-cost pricing may be merely a routine applied to situations in which information acquisition is difficult and costly (e.g. in multiproduct firms), having no explanatory power as far as the goals and the decision-making process of the firm are concerned.

Despite the above criticisms, it can hardly be denied that the full- and normal-cost principles constitute an important theoretical contribution to the study of pricing behaviour. For one thing, they were the first direct challenge to conventional wisdom in the field of price theory and a major instigator of the marginalist controversy. For another, they represent the first attempt at devising theoretical explanations of price determination based on observation of *actual* practices in industry and using concepts and terminology accessible to businesspeople. In short, the work of Hall and Hitch (1939) and Andrews (1949a, b) set a trend towards theories of pricing behaviour of real-world firms instead of 'theories of profit maximising firms for worlds where such firms logically would not exist; theories of firms that cannot also exist in a real world of incomplete information except "as if" approximations which may often be highly misleading' (Earl, 1980, p. 23).

BIOLOGICAL ANALOGIES

A second group of contributions within the behavioural tradition uses the method of analogy as its main expository vehicle and draws heavily from concepts traditionally associated with the physical sciences. There are two major analogies which have been employed in the theoretical analysis of the firm's behaviour, based on the concepts of homeostasis and viability respectively; the former emphasizes the short run and the latter the long run (Burns, 1959).

The term 'homeostasis' was coined by Cannon (1932) in a physiological context, to refer to the processes by which stability is maintained in an organism, and was applied by Boulding (1950, 1952) to the theory of the firm. In its broadest sense, the concept of homeostasis suggests that 'there is some state of the organism which it is organized to maintain and that any disturbance from this state sets in motion behavior on the part of the organism which tends to re-establish the desired state' (Boulding, 1950, pp. 26, 27). This forms the starting point of Boulding's analysis, according to which '[the] general theory of organization begins with the concept of homeostasis; that is, of a mechanism for stabilizing a variable or group of variables within certain limits of toleration . . . should any of the essential variables rise above the upper limit, machinery must be brought into play to reduce it; should it fall below the lower limit, machinery must be brought into play to raise it. An organization in this view consists of an aggregate of such governing mechanisms, sometimes called control or feedback mechanisms' (Boulding, 1952, p. 36).

Boulding applies the concept of homeostasis to the balance sheet, 'which is to a firm what is its "state" of the body: it describes the structure of the firm in terms of the various quantities of its parts. Anything that happens to a firm can be described in terms of a "dynamic" balance sheet — i.e. a movie of balance-sheet changes — for everything that affects the firm in any way will effect changes in the balance sheet' (Boulding, 1950, p. 27). This conception of the balance sheet is broader than the equivalent accountancy concept, since, in addition to incorporating tangible assets (e.g. cash and equipment), it takes account of such intangibles as market position and potential resources. The firm is thus portrayed as seeking to maintain an 'ideal' or 'optimum' balance reflecting a particular 'asset preference structure'. The latter indicates the preferences of the firm for different kinds of assets (i.e. balance sheet components) and is operationalized by means of 'preferred asset ratios', that is, the proportion of its total assets that a firm wishes to hold in a particular form. The decision-makers of the firm lay down rules for the operation of the firm which reflect some 'ideal' interrelationship among the parts of the firm (e.g. desired ratios of assets to liabilities, inventories to sales, and so on) and any deviation from the desired balance initiates a process to restore it; thus the balance sheet plays the role of a regulator of a firm's aggregate position and the firm's prime objective is stability. In short, Boulding's theory assumes 'that there is a "homeostasis of the balance sheet" — that there is some desired quantity of all the various items in the balance sheet, and that any disturbance of this structure immediately sets in motion forces which will restore the *status quo*' (Boulding, 1950, p. 27).

The homeostasis model is essentially a short-run model, in that 'it throws no light at all — nor does it claim to — on why and how the "ideal" relationships between the relevant variables which the firm is now attempting to maintain were originally established or on the conditions under which decisions may be made to alter them' (Penrose, 1952, p. 818). Nevertheless, Boulding (1952) provides some general insights regarding the 'ideal' balance-sheet structure. In particular, he contends that profit considerations are likely to be very important, given the role of profit for the firm's ultimate survival, but that profit maximization is only a special case of the homeostasis theory; the main reason for this is the presence of uncertainty in the firm's decision-making environment, which is likely to create preferences for liquidity, flexibility and security in addition to sheer profitability.

The notion of homeostasis is also implicit in the models of

Chamberlain (1955) and Knauth (1956). The former portrays the firm as aiming for a *specific* balance between inflows and outflows, which are defined respectively as 'all current receipts (from the sale of goods and services, from past investments, from gifts and from borrowing) plus any assets used . . . [and] all current disbursements (for the purchase of goods and services, for investment, for gifts, for repayment of debt) plus any money savings' (Chamberlain, 1955, p. 164). This *ex-ante* balance is termed the 'projected balance' (to distinguish it from the accounting balance that, by definition, exists between inflows and outflows at any particular moment in time) and reflects 'a combination of goals, a balance of satisfactions' (p. 231). The particular combination of goals that Chamberlain considers as being 'sufficiently dominant, prevalent, and persistent to be conceptually reliable' (p. 239) consists of a satisfactory profit, a satisfactory market share and a satisfactory growth (which may be equally or differentially weighted). These goals are described as being proximate objectives of management's *and* other stakeholders' individual aspirations, because, while management alone determines the projected balance, it nevertheless recognizes that it must 'meet in some measure the objectives of those on whom it relies upon in order to secure some measure of its own objectives' (p. 232). Thus management has a coordinating role in terms of balancing the aspirations of the various stakeholders so as to achieve a satisfactory norm, reflected in the projected balance. Failure to achieve the latter results in the firm revising its activity by manipulating its inflows or outflows and/or revising the projected balance to reflect 'a performance superior to that which is actually being realized even if inferior to that which was projected' (p. 176). This balance, resulting from the revision of aspirations, is termed the 'preferred balance' and becomes the new projected balance, which, again, may later give rise to another preferred balance, and so on. Thus Chamberlain (1955) describes the firm's behaviour as a process of continuous adjustment, with both past performance and future expectations affecting present decisions.

Knauth's analysis, on the other hand, is based on the notion of trade position, which is defined as 'the maintenace or increase of a proportionate share of the market of the industry' (Knauth, 1956, p. 163). Trade position is considered to be all-important because it provides a tangible expression of the *relative* role of the firm in the industry and, therefore, by analysing this position, management can determine objectively whether or not the firm is performing satisfactorily. In this context, trade position is the combined outcome of a balance of a variety of variables (price, volume, research and development, costs, etc.) and as such a concrete indicator of business performance. In short, Knauth (1956) contends that 'management concentrates on the maintenance of an equilibrium in motion among all its elements — not on profits alone. The dominant motive in setting prices is to induce a continuous and increasing flow of demand on the part of the customers. If this equilibrium can be obtained — especially an expanding equilibrium — profits result as part of the flow' (p. 169).

A second analogy, this time from biology, is based on the concept of 'viability', the latter referring to 'a firm's ability to live, grow, develop, and prosper' (Burns, 1959, p. 31). This analogy is largely derived from Darwin's principles of biological evolution and natural selection and looks at the firm as a 'creature of the environment'. It was first used by Alchian (1950), further developed by Enke (1951) and Winter (1964), and heavily criticized by Penrose (1952).

Alchian's (1950) aim was to provide a theoretical framework for analysing the firm's behaviour under uncertainty and thus overcome the logical difficulty that is associated with attempts to maximize profits in an uncertain world. This difficulty arises because 'each action that may be chosen is identified with a *distribution* of potential outcomes, not with a unique outcome . . . these distributions of potential outcomes are overlapping . . . [thus] the task is converted into making a decision (selecting an action) whose potential outcome *distribution* is preferable, that is, choosing the action with the *optimum distribution*, since there is no such thing as a *maximizing* distribution' (Alchian, 1950, p. 212, emphasis in the original). Consequently, 'there is no meaningful criterion for selecting the action that will "maximize profits" '. Thus Alchian (1950) proposes an alternative approach which 'embodies the principles of biological evolution and natural selection by interpreting the economic system as an adoptive mechanism which chooses among exploratory actions generated by the adaptive pursuit of "success" or "profits"' (p. 211).

The essence of Alchian's (1950) theory is that to survive a firm must earn profits. Positive rather than maximum profits thus become the criterion of natural selection; firms that earn profits are adopted (i.e. selected) by the environment while those which do not are rejected. This is taken to be the case *irrespective* of whether firms actually *aim* to make profits or not. Even if the firm's behaviour was dictated by chance, the surviving firms (i.e. those adopted by the environment) would be those that happened to act appropriately (i.e. those that were lucky), since 'even in a world of stupid men there would still be profits' (Alchian, 1950, p. 213). However, Alchian recognizes that purposive behaviour is likely to be exhibited by firms in that they will choose modes of action which enable them to adapt to their environment (and thus survive). Specifically, 'whenever successful enterprises are observed, the elements common to these observable successes will be associated with success and copied by others in their pursuit of profits or success' (p. 217). Thus, imitation of successful behaviour becomes the main vehicle through which firms attempt to ensure that they will be adopted by the environment. Alchian's (1950) argument was subsequently expanded by Enke (1951), who argued that if long-run competition was sufficiently intense to result in zero (economic) profits, then the profit maximization model and viability analysis would lead to identical predictions. However, Enke expressed a preference for the latter approach, because it is not based on the assumption of perfect knowledge on the part of the entrepreneur as is traditional marginal analysis. Some years later, another contribution was made by Winter (1964), who developed a complex mathematical model of economic 'natural selection' in an attempt to formalize and clarify the viability analogy.

The viability approach to the analysis of the firm has been strongly attacked by Penrose (1952), who felt that 'biological analogies contribute little either to the theory of price or to the theory of growth and development of firms and in general tend to confuse the nature of the important issues' (p. 804) and that 'in seeking the fundamental explanations of economic and social phenomena in human affairs the economist, and the social scientist in general, would be well advised to attack his problems directly and in their own terms rather than indirectly by imposing sweeping biological models upon them' (p. 819). These criticisms were partly based on the fact that viability analysis can, in principle, be undertaken without any assumptions relating to motivation or purposive behaviour and partly on the fact that the environment is depicted as the major deciding influence on the firm's 'destiny'. Penrose (1952) considered these features as being undesirable and unacceptable because, in reality, firms make decisions directed at achieving certain aims and, in so doing, they can influence (and thus modify) their environment. However, Penrose's criticisms are somewhat misguided in that she appears to have misunderstood Alchian's (1950) and Enke's (1951) use of the viability analogy. As Alchian pointed out in response to Penrose's (1952) comments, 'every reference to the biological analogy was purely expository, designed to clarify the ideas in the theory' (Alchian, 1953, p. 601) and 'it was not intended that businessmen's actions be explained by studying birds, plants, and flowers' (Burns, 1959, p. 31).

Taken collectively, contributions based on analogies from the physical sciences provide an interesting alternative conceptual perspective on the firm's behaviour. With specific reference to pricing decisions, they draw attention to the implications of multiple objectives and their attainment in a non-maximising context. Specifically, they highlight management's concern to achieve a balance among different aims which *in combination* determine the overall success of the firm. Moreover, they illustrate the dynamic nature of the price decision-making process as reflected in revision of objectives and imitation of courses of action that have been shown to produce successful outcomes; both these features inject a dosage of descriptive realism into the theoretical examination of pricing behaviour in that their main tenets are consistent with what is commonly observed in business practice.

ORGANIZATIONAL THEORIES

The third theoretical strand to be considered draws heavily from organization theory and is characterized by seven distinctive (and largely interrelated) features.

First, it places strong emphasis on induction as a vehicle for theory development, suggesting that 'instead of hypothesising about how rational men respond to various situations or say how they should respond, we should instead study how firms really do take decisions in practice. From this evidence it is hoped we can use logical argument to develop theories of behaviour relevant to a wide range of firms other than just the initial ones we have studied' (Hawkins, 1973, p. 70).

Secondly, it conceives the firm as a complex organization consisting of different participants with diverse and potentially conflicting goals and different amounts of bargaining power; this implies that 'people count in the decision-making process both individually and collectively and . . . therefore the internal organisational characteristics of a company must be investigated' (Pickering, 1974, p. 107).

Thirdly, it replaces the 'objective' (i.e. perfect) rationality attributed to the decision-maker in maximization models with the more realistic notion of 'bounded rationality'; the latter reflects the fact that 'the capacity of the human mind for formulating and solving complex problems is very small compared with the size of problems whose solution is required for objectively rational behavior in the real world — or even for a reasonable approximation to such objective rationality' (Simon, 1957a, p. 198).

Fourthly, it accepts the presence of uncertainty in decision-making as the normal state of affairs, since 'there is no evidence that . . . managers have knowledge of all alternatives or the functions underlying their alternatives or of a ranking of possible outcomes' (Margolis, 1958, p. 190).

Fifthly, it recognizes that 'search processes and information-gathering processes constitute significant parts of decision-making'

(Cyert, Simon and Trow, 1956, p. 248) and that 'the obtaining of information is not a costless activity' (Silberston, 1970, p. 535).

Sixthly, it formally introduces the notion of satiation, which suggests that 'the motive to act stems from *drives*, and action is terminated when the drive is satisfied . . . the conditions for satisfying a drive are not necessarily fixed, but may be specified by an aspiration level that itself adjusts upwards or downwards on the basis of experience' (Simon, 1959, p. 25, emphasis in the original).

Finally, and largely as a result of the previous points, it conceives the firm as a 'satisficing' entity, with satisficing consisting of 'ascertaining a course of action that is "good enough" — that is satisfactory although it is not optimal' (McGuire, 1964, p. 182).

Undoubtedly, the most comprehensive theoretical model under the organizational tradition is Cyert and March's (1963) *A Behavioral Theory of the Firm*, although earlier efforts along similar lines were made by Alt (1949), Margolis (1958) and Clelland (1960). This work attempts to integrate into a cohesive theory several ideas that the authors had previously exposed in a number of publications[11] and is strongly influenced by the writings of Simon (1955, 1956, 1957a, b, 1958, 1959) on organization theory and decision-making. Specifically, Cyert and March (1963) attempt to construct a theory that takes '(1) the firm as its basic unit, (2) the prediction of firm behavior with respect to such decisions as price, output, and resource allocation as its objective, and (3) an explicit emphasis on the actual process of organizational decision making as its basic research commitment' (p. 19) and apply it to 'the large multi-product firm operating under uncertainty in an imperfect market' (p. 115). In this context, the focus on specific type of decisions (primarily price and output decisions) 'was intended to constrain the tendency of theories of decision making to become excessively general' (p. 2), while the approach adopted was to 'study the actual making of decisions and reproducing the behavior as fully as possible within the confines of theoretical manageability' (p. 2). This orientation is clearly reflected both in the material used by the authors as a basis for theory development (comprising a number of case studies and laboratory experiments) and in the method used to trace the implications of the models developed (notably computer simulation).

Cyert and March (1963) conceive the firm as an 'organisational coalition' consisting of individuals and groups (i.e. managers, workers, customers, shareholders, governmental agencies, etc.) which have some interest in the firm's activity. Each coalition member (or member group) has its own set of goals and demands which may be in conflict with the goals of other members. The demands of each group are too many to be totally satisfied at any one point in time, given the limited resources of the firm, and, therefore, each member 'attends to only a rather small subset of his demands, the number and variety depending . . . on the extent of his involvement in the organization and on the demands of the other commitments on his attention' (p. 35). Demands by coalition members take the form of aspiration levels which are not static but change over time depending on past aspiration levels, future expectations, available information, past achievement of demands previously pursued, achievement of demands of other groups in the firm and achievement of demands of similar groups in other firms. Given the goals of individual coalition members and their degree of involvement in the firm (e.g. employees *vs* 'passive' shareholders), the firm's overall objectives are defined through a process of bargaining. Such objectives have the following characteristics: (a) they are imperfectly rationalized (that is, new demands may be inconsistent with existing policies but this inconsistency may escape detection); (b) some objectives are stated in the form of aspiration-level constraints rather than maximands (the aspiration level being a weighted function of the firm's past goal, the firm's past performance and the past performance of other 'comparable' firms); and (c) some objectives are stated in non-operational form (thus making them consistent with virtually any set of objectives).

While recognizing the potential relevance of a wide range of pecuniary and non-pecuniary goals, Cyert and March (1963) suggest that, for purposes of analysing price and output decisions, 'we can represent organizational goals reasonably well by using about five different goals (p. 40), notably (a) a production goal, (b) an inventory goal, (c) a sales goal, (d) a market share goal and (e) a profit goal. Some of these goals may be desirable (and thus acceptable) to all members of the coalition and others to only some of the groups; as a result, there may be potential conflict among these goals which may never be fully resolved. In pursuing these goals, the firm operates as a satisficing rather than a maximizing entity, satisficing being considered as rational behaviour in the light of the internal (limited resources and lack of omniscient decision-makers) and external (environmental uncertainty) constraints on the operation of the firm. In this context, the decision-making process of the firm is characterized by sequential attention to goals (i.e. attending to different goals at different times, depending upon pressing needs); limited search for information for alternative courses of action which is terminated once a 'satisfactory' solution (i.e. one that achieves the set of relevant aspiration levels) has been found; use of standard operating procedures and rules of thumb (e.g. mark-up pricing) as uncertainty-reducing devices; and the employment of organizational slack (that is, payments to coalition members over and above those required to maintain the organization) as a stabilizing mechanism on the performance of the firm (i.e. reducing slack if the environment is adverse and increasing slack when business is flourishing).

On the basis of the above conceptualization of the firm's behaviour, Cyert and March (1963) subsequently formulate a number of highly detailed models of price and output determination in which they formalize the premises of their theory and illustrate the pursuit of specific pricing objectives (stated in aspiration-level form) through the use of particular rules of thumb (e.g. mark-up and mark-down pricing rules). The implications of these modelling efforts are threefold. First, they highlight that it is possible to construct formal theoretical representations of the firm's pricing behaviour without recourse to the assumption of a well-specified and internally consistent system of preferences on the one hand and the use of constrained optimization techniques on the other. Secondly, they show that close investigation of actual decision-making processes of *specific* firms can be a most useful starting point for the development of more *general* models of price determination. Thirdly, they indicate that the inclusion of institutional detail and realism (e.g. imperfect information, conflict, bounded rationality) does not necessarily conflict with the aim to generate theoretical propositions of the firm's behaviour. As a result, the basic theoretical apparatus developed by Cyert and March (1963) has since been used by a number of authors to develop models of the firm's pricing behaviour.[12]

Despite the insights provided by Cyert and March's (1963) analysis, a number of doubts and criticisms have been expressed regarding the ultimate usefulness of their approach. One such criticism is that 'non-maximising models may offer useful insights but they will ultimately be unsatisfactory if they fail to yield identifiable equilibrium conditions. Satisficing, mark-up pricing, adaptive systems, all run the risk of being no more than descriptions of business behaviour masquerading as economic analysis. Realism may be destructive of logic and of understanding alike' (Wildsmith, 1973, p. 30). A second criticism is that the organizational approach 'has . . . provided no theory of the determination of the rules of thumb themselves. It has not suggested how these rules will vary with changes in the values of exogenous economic variables as, say the price level of interest rates' (Baumol and Stewart, 1971, p. 119). A third criticism is along the lines of using 'a sledgehammer to crack a walnut. Do we really need to construct mirror-images of companies, virtually assembling the decision-making process brick by brick, in order to predict their behaviour? Would not simpler models suffice for the limited purposes we have in mind?' (Hawkins, 1973, p. 72). A fourth criticism is that the organizational approach 'gives rise to ambiguities not present in more conventional theories, since it allows for different responses by different firms, in similar circumstances, to the same stimuli' (Silberston, 1970, p. 536). Finally, it has been argued that 'the acceptance of satisficing behaviour renders practically the theory into a tautological structure: whatever the firms are observed to do can be rationalised on the lines of satisficing' (Koutsoyiannis, 1979, p. 401).

DECISION CALCULUS CONTRIBUTIONS

The final theoretical framework to be examined has its origins in Little's (1970) seminal work on the integration of models and managerial judgement. His major concern was that formal models are not used widely by managers because of their complexity, data requirements, assumptions and inability to incorporate variables and issues that are considered relevant and important by management; in other words, 'much of the difficulty lies in implementation and an especially critical aspect of this is the meeting between manager and model' (Little, 1970, p. 466). In an attempt to overcome this problem, Little proposes a new approach to model-building, whereby 'a manager's implicit model of a situation is formalised into an explicit model which is then used to evaluate alternative decisions' (Chakravarti, Mitchell and Staelin, 1979, p. 251). Specifically, according to Little (1970), 'if we want a manager to use a model, we should make it his, an extension of his ability to think about and analyze his operation . . . A *decision calculus* will be defined as a model-based set of procedures for processing data and judgements to assist a manager in his decision-making' (pp. 469, 470, emphasis in the original).

Under the decision calculus approach, managers express their understanding of the marketplace by responding to a set of questions regarding the impact of a particular marketing mix variable (e.g. price) on a performance variable (e.g. market share). Their replies, which reflect their judgement and experience, are subsequently used to derive the parameters of a response function (e.g. market share response to price). Finally, different response functions can be interrelated by the introduction of an overall model structure so as to optimize some objective function (e.g. profit). It can be seen that this approach explicitly allows for the incorporation of managerial judgement in model-building as well as for the inclusion of new informational inputs into a basic model as they become available; thus, when comparing alternative courses of action, the standard of comparison is not perfection 'but rather what the manager has available to him now' (Little, 1970, p. 482).

It can hardly be disputed that 'by all indications, decision calculus has had a major impact on model building especially in marketing. Models based on this approach have been implemented in industry and are also used extensively in graduate business programs' (Chakravarti, Mitchell and Staelin, 1979, p. 251). While most applications of the approach have been in areas like advertising and sales management, decision calculus models have also been applied to the pricing decision, particularly in competitive bidding situations (e.g. Sewall, 1976). In this context, the major contribution of the decision calculus approach can be summarized as being the removal of the barrier separating quantitative models of pricing and qualitative approaches. Thus, it is the integrative power of decision calculus which, by combining *both* descriptive realism (as reflected in the incorporation of managerial judgement) *and* technical rigour (as reflected in the derivation of formal model structures), provides a fresh perspective for the study of the pricing decision.

In spite of the appealing nature of decision calculus as a modelling device, there are some potential problems associated with this approach, most of which are a direct result of the inclusion of the human input in the modelling process. Specifically, it has been pointed out that successful application of decision calculus models requires that 'the manager must have the cognitive skills to (a) provide a good description of the functional form of the process generating the data and (b) accurately specify the parameters . . . These two assumptions rely heavily on a manager's cognitive abilities and current behavioral evidence raises some doubt regarding these abilities' (Chakravarti, Mitchell and Staelin, 1979, pp. 252, 253). In reviewing such evidence in the context of decision calculus models, McIntyre and Currim (1982) report that managers may be subject to anchoring bias to past operating levels; that if managers are asked to estimate parameters relating to outcomes outside their range of experience, substantial estimation errors may occur; that use of a decision calculus model does not appear to improve ability to estimate response functions; and that the use of such a model does not provide a marked improvement in the perception that better decisions are being made. These difficulties suggest that, in adopting a decision calculus approach, one 'must consider the cognitive abilities of managers in the model-building and implementation process . . . model builders should develop models and implementation procedures that build upon a manager's strength and compensate for his weaknesses' (Chakravarti, Mitchell and Staelin, 1979, p. 261).

THEORIES OF PRICING: CONCLUSIONS

In the light of the previous discussion, it should be obvious by now that there is no one universally accepted theory of pricing behaviour, but rather 'a seemingly endless array of theories, individually persuasive but often mutually contradictory' (Hawkins, 1973, p. 8). This, however, is not necessarily a bad thing because 'each theory is of value in its own right if it contributes to answering a particular limited set of questions, or if it gives a useful emphasis to one issue in business behaviour' (Howe, 1978, p. 43); indeed, 'logical consistency between one theory . . . and another is a luxury and not a necessity' (Shubik, 1970, p. 412).

The diversity of theoretical approaches can partly be attributed to the shortcomings of conventional price theory but also, more importantly, to the complexity of the problem under investigation, as Hawkins (1973) argues, 'recognising the wide range of types of firms now in existence, allowing for the enormous size range that our concept of a firm must now cover . . . and considering the whole gamut of motivations which can be and are being followed by the several hundred thousand owners, directors, managers and workers all involved in one large bureaucratic organisation, it would be surprising — not to say miraculous — if any simple formula existed, even for one firm, which remained invariant over time. And even if it did, it is surely almost beyond belief that such a formula could also hold without modification for every other firm in the economy as well' (pp. 81, 82).

The divergence in terms of aims and focus of the various theoretical perspectives considered in the previous sections makes it difficult to undertake a direct comparison between them and declare a 'winner'; given that different theories perform different tasks, a comparison in relevant terms is not easy (Machlup, 1967). However, one can provide a rough indication of their respective contributions/limitations with regard to the study of pricing behaviour by using the two general evaluative criteria of tractability and realism. In this context, it should be noted that 'ideally any theory of business behavior should be both realistic and tractable. It should be compatible with the factual evidence as provided by business activities, but yet should contain a relatively small number of variables that can be easily manipulated and that are inclusive of a wide range of business situations . . . If the theory is too realistic it loses its universality. If it is too tractable . . . it becomes too abstract, and is unrealistic. The line between realism and tractability, therefore, is a narrow one in any theory, and often a work may be criticized as being too oriented to one side, to the neglect of the other . . . The choice often, therefore, seems to be between a theory that is elegant but empty, and one that is too full of detail to be elegant' (McGuire, 1964, p. 244).

Figure 3.3 utilizes the twin dimensions of tractability and realism to indicate the relative positioning of the various theoretical approaches previously discussed; needless to say, this is merely intended to illustrate the differential 'performance' of the theories according to the two evaluative criteria and, given the absence of specific values on either axis, the picture drawn is suggestive rather than conclusive.

As might be expected, different theories score differently on the two dimensions; the diagonal line splits the graph into two sections, roughly corresponding to the two broad theoretical streams of maximization (emphasizing tractability) and satisficing (emphasizing realism) respectively. Viewed in this light, it is evident that the choice of theoretical approach should depend upon the problem under investigation and the desire of the analyst to achieve tractability *vs* realism, and *vice versa*. For example, formal modelling of pricing behaviour at industry-wide level under competitive conditions may be best done by employing the framework of conventional price theory. On the other hand, managerial theories may be more appropriate for devising elegant models of the behaviour of large firms which are largely sheltered from the pressure of competitive forces and which enjoy a degree of managerial discretion. Finally, behavioural approaches would appear to be best suited for analysing intrafirm decision-making processes and providing realistic descriptions of the operation of real firms, albeit at the expense of some generality.

It is also important to realize that, as Table 3.5 shows, there is a degree of complementarity among the various theoretical perspectives,

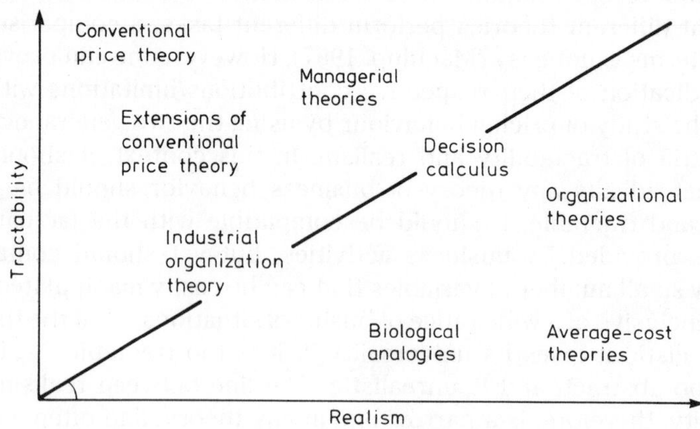

Figure 3.3 Realism and tractability of theoretical perspectives on pricing

in that they tend to focus on and emphasize different aspects of price decision-making. Such complementarity would appear to suggest that empirical efforts would benefit from being guided by conceptual frameworks that reflect a *combination* of selected elements of the various approaches. Unfortunately, as will be discussed later, the potential of such integration has not been recognized in empirical work, with most studies being characterized either by an over-reliance on conventional price theory or by the total absence of *any* conceptual framework whatsoever!

Table 3.5 Focus of different theoretical perspectives on pricing

Main focus	Theoretical perspective			
	Conventional price theory & its extensions	Industrial organization theory	Managerial theories	Behavioural theories
Pricing objectives				
Profit	X	X	X	X
Other			X	X
Pricing methods				
Optimal rules	X		X	
Rules of thumb				X
Pricing environment				
Internal			X	X
External	X	X		X

As a parting shot regarding the theoretical component of this literature review, it is interesting to mention that despite the conceptual shortcomings of conventional price theory, despite the absence of a concrete body of evidence in its favour and despite the range of theoretical alternatives currently available, students of pricing are still primarily (if not overwhelmingly) exposed to profit maximization as the appropriate theoretical framework. This is not only the case for students of microeconomics and industrial organization, with which the profit-maximizing paradigm is traditionally associated, but also for students of more business-related disciplines as well. For example, the first sentence of the latest edition of a leading text in managerial economics reads as follows: 'Throughout this book we assume that the objective of the firm is to maximise profits' (Reekie and Crook, 1987, p. 1). Similarly, in a recent review of pricing strategies in the *Journal of Marketing*, the author states that 'the article describes a set of ideal options one may choose and outcomes that result from such choices, assuming profit maximization by the strategist' (Tellis, 1986, p. 147). Lastly, in the most recent book on pricing by a UK author, 'profit maximization will be retained . . . as the basic assumption in the analysis of pricing behaviour' (Dorward, 1987, p. 20). In this context, it is worth recalling Chamberlain's statement, made some 30 years ago, that 'for many years the argument has raged whether maximum profit constitutes the businessman's objective. It now appears that this argument is fairly well resolved, and its prolongation involves only the flogging of a dead horse' (Chamberlain, 1955, p. 240). In the light of the above, it seems that Chamberlain was wrong. The horse is far from dead — a little tired perhaps, but still alive and kicking!

PART 3. PRICING IN PRACTICE

OVERVIEW OF EMPIRICAL RESEARCH

Having discussed in some detail the main theoretical perspectives on pricing, we shall now turn our attention to an examination of empirical efforts. As can be seen from Figure 3.4, the present review of empirical work is restricted to supply-side studies in the manufacturing sector of the economy concerned with the process of list price determination by private firms in the domestic market. Moreover, its scope is limited to studies utilizing data obtained directly from firms (i.e. through surveys and case studies), to the exclusion of econometric investigations based on secondary data (at either industry- or economy-wide level) and investigations instigated by government departments.

The reason for excluding econometric studies is that these are typically concerned with the *collective* behaviour of an industry rather than that of the individual firm or with the consequences of price determination at a macroeconomic level (e.g. inflation and price inflexibility). The reliance of econometric studies on published material, coupled with the high level of data aggregation, considerably limits their ability to make detailed inferences regarding the process of price decision-making in the *individual* firm. As Bain (1949) points out, 'in such studies, the view of behavior is often excessively synoptic, and frequently little more can be done than to establish the general correspondence of a particular industry with some theoretical model, to carry out a rough and usually unsatisfactory statistical analysis of conditions of industry demand and cost, and to attempt a sketchy mensuration of significant results' (p. 148). The exclusion of econometric studies should *not* be interpreted as implying that they have nothing to contribute towards a better understanding of pricing behaviour *in general*; it merely indicates that econometric investigations are designed to address *different* research questions, notably those relating to aggregate patterns of behaviour.

As far as government investigations into the pricing practices of firms are concerned (such as those undertaken by the Sub-Committee on Anti-Trust and Monopoly in the USA and the Monopolies Commission in the UK), their exclusion can be justified on three grounds. First, the relevant material is not readily obtainable, as it has not been disseminated through mainstream academic research channels but rather through a diversity of government reports. Secondly, even if accessibility did not pose a problem, the sheer volume of the material concerned makes it impossible to summarize and evaluate within the confines of the present work. Thirdly, and most important, governmental investigations have been primarily concerned with questions of

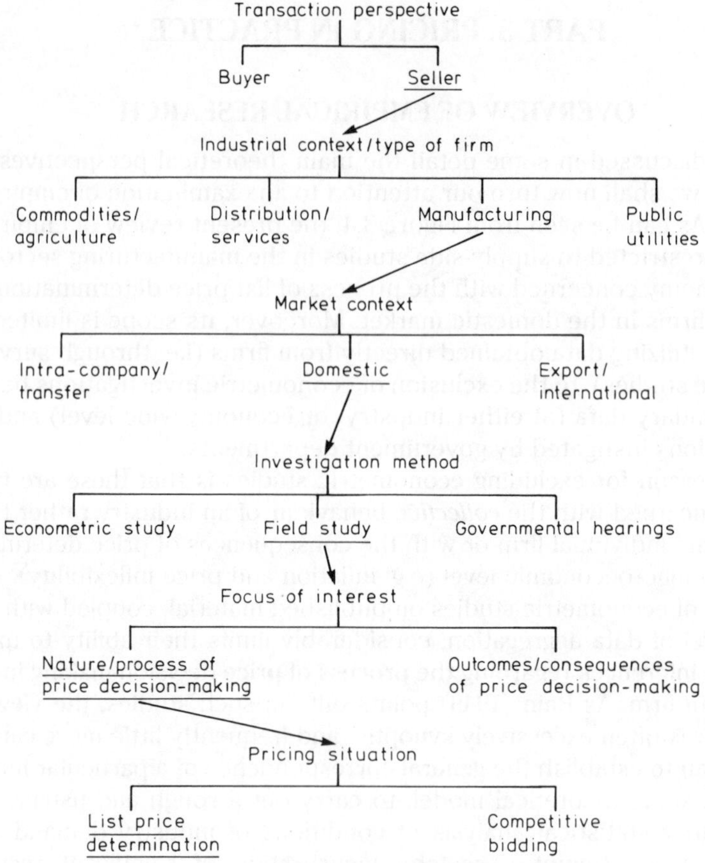

Figure 3.4 Scope of review of empirical pricing studies

public interest and, as a result, the testimonies of company officials in such inquiries are largely aimed at defending and justifying pricing practices rather than merely describing/explaining them (as is the case when executives participate voluntarily in academic research projects, in which anonymity and confidentiality are normally preserved).

Appendix 1 provides a listing of empirical studies which satisfy the criteria for inclusion in the present review. The studies are listed in chronological order (spanning some 65 years of research) except where the results of the same investigation have been disclosed in more than one publication, in which case the relevant publications are grouped together. In addition to providing some background information on each study, Appendix 1 also indicates the broad topic areas and the study covered by adopting the threefold classification used earlier to indicate the contribution of alternative theoretical perspectives on pricing; methodological details are also summarized where available.

The literature search unearthed no fewer than 97 publications in which the results of 86 empirical studies were reported. Table 3.6 provides a simple breakdown of this material by time period, country and academic discipline, respectively.

Table 3.6 Classification of empirical efforts (column percentages)

Time period	No. of studies	Country of origin	No. of studies	Academic discipline	No. of studies
1924–1939	4 (4.7%)	USA	36 (41.9%)	Economics	38 (44.8%)
1940–1949	6 (6.9%)	UK	34 (39.5%)	Management	20 (23.2%)
1950–1959	19 (22.1%)	Germany	6 (6.9%)	Marketing	13 (15.1%)
1960–1969	26 (30.2%)	Denmark	2 (2.3%)	Finance/ accounting	15 (17.4%)
1970–1979	14 (16.3%)	Switzerland	2 (2.3%)		
1980–1988	17 (19.8%)	Australia	2 (2.3%)		
		Canada	2 (2.3%)		
		Austria	1 (1.2%)		
		S. Africa	1 (1.2%)		
Total	86 (100%)		86 (100%)		86 (100%)

From Appendix 1 and Table 3.6 it can be seen that a considerable amount of empirical research into the pricing practices of firms has been undertaken since 1939, when Hall and Hitch's famous study was published. It seems, therefore, that the repeated claims (complaints?) of previous workers in the field about the lack of empirical studies on pricing are not particularly well founded. To illustrate this point, back in 1960, Fog was stating that 'it is surprising that so few empirical investigations have been undertaken' (p. 5), a sentiment echoed a couple of years later by Haynes (1962), according to whom 'hundreds of pamphlets, bulletins, and textbooks specify how pricing should be done, but only a few examine how it actually is done' (p. 3). Yet by the time that Fog's (1960) study was published, there had already been some 29 empirical investigations in five countries, and another five studies had been published by the time Haynes (1962) disclosed the results of his investigation. Similar concerns were voiced a number of years later by Sonkondi (1969) and Silberston (1970), by which time, however, the number of empirical investigations that had been conducted had risen to 55!

There are a number of reasons that explain the inconsistency between the claims of researchers regarding the paucity of empirical work and the actual situation in this matter. To begin with, it is practically impossible to detect all empirical studies on pricing practice by relying on the study's title alone. In some cases, empirical evidence has been obtained largely as a by-product of a wider investigation and thus not even the word 'price' or 'pricing' appears in the title (e.g. Lydall, 1958; Udell, 1972; Hooley, West and Lynch, 1984). In other cases, the title may contain the relevant keyword(s) but it may give no indication as to whether empirical material is included (e.g. Kellogg, 1958; Hapgood, 1965; Wentz, 1966) or, even if it does, it may still be positively misleading (e.g. Foxall, 1972). A second factor which may contribute towards the impression of lack of empirical evidence is the diversity of disciplines (and even greater diversity of publication outlets) in which empirical pricing studies are encountered; economists in particular, who account for the majority of empirical research in the field, are often guilty of confining their literature reviews to the economic literature only and thus frequently by-pass relevant material originating from other disciplines. Finally, there is also a language problem, in that all empirical studies that have been conducted in Germany and Switzerland have (perhaps not surprisingly!) been published in German and, as a result, the English-speaking pricing literature is practically unaware of their existence; this is most unfortunate, since some of these efforts (particularly those by Wied-Nebbeling, 1975, 1985) are among the better ones in this field, in terms both of research design and execution.

In the light of the above, it is evident that merely identifying/locating relevant studies (let alone summarizing/evaluating them) for the purposes of a truly comprehensive empirical review is likely to be a lengthy process, involving a lot of checking and cross-checking, a bit of detective work as well as an element of luck (the author is speaking from experience!). It should also be noted that, while this process will certainly be facilitated/accelerated by referring to previous state-of-the-art reviews (notably those by Bain, 1949; Heflebower, 1955; Silberston, 1970; Wied-Nebbeling, 1975; Said, 1981; Dorward, 1987), there are many studies of pricing practice that are not covered by any of them, which implies that search of original sources remains an inescapable activity.

In addition to highlighting the sheer number of studies undertaken, Table 3.6 is informative as to the development of empirical work in the area. On a longitudinal basis, it appears that the 1950s and, even more so, the 1960s have been the most productive decades in terms of the number of studies conducted, accounting for over 50% of the total. In contrast, the pre-war period (i.e. pre-1939) accounts for only about 2% of the total number of studies, while the 1970s and 1980s account for about 36% split almost equally among the two decades. This pattern is quite interesting in that it seems to reflect (a) a period of growth, following the stir caused by Hall and Hitch (1939), and (b) a settling-down period, following the (partial) resolution of the marginal controversy offered by Machlup (1967). On a country basis, the US and the UK together account for over 80% of the total number of studies and the division between them is approximately equal. A somewhat disturbing pattern emerges from looking at the classification according to academic discipline, which is heavily skewed towards economics, the latter accounting for almost half the total number of contributions. Marketing, on the other hand, is represented in only 13 studies, which seems to reflect partly the preoccupation of the discipline with demand-side studies of pricing (i.e. price as a determinant/influence of consumer behaviour and, to a lesser extent, of organizational buying behaviour) and partly its rather late entry in the mainstream pricing literature; indeed, as can be seen from Appendix 1, marketing was not represented in supply-side empirical studies until the mid-1960s. Although in recent years marketing has made important inroads in the empirical study of the firm's pricing behaviour (as evidenced by the fact that over a third of the studies conducted since 1980 have a marketing origin), it is still fair to say that marketing's interest in this area has not been commensurate with the importance of price as an element of the marketing mix and its role in the firm's successful operation.

METHODOLOGICAL ASSESSMENT OF EMPIRICAL PRICING STUDIES

Now that the general background to the empirical literature has been given, a final issue that needs to be addressed before embarking on a substantive discussion of the empirical evidence concerns the methodological characteristics of previous research. This is important for two main reasons. First, unless one is aware of any major methodological weaknesses of previous efforts, it becomes very difficult to assess effectively their results and the conclusions drawn. Secondly, awareness of the virtue and shortcomings of past studies can be of immense help in designing future studies, learning from the experiences (good and bad) of other workers in the area.

From Appendix 1, it can be seen that not all studies are equally comprehensive in terms of the methodological details they disclose. Some studies provide virtually no information on methodology (e.g. Churchill, 1932; Friday, 1955; Wray, 1956), while others omit important methodological details such as the number of firms examined, the sampling procedures employed and/or the data collection method(s) utilized (e.g. Fog, 1948; Karger and Thompson, 1957; Howe, 1962). On the other hand, a number of studies provide very detailed accounts of their methodology, frequently extending to disclosing the actual test instrument (i.e. the questionnaire and/or interview schedule) used in the research (e.g. Fitzpatrick, 1964; Lanzillotti and Parrish, 1964; Wied-Nebbeling, 1975, 1985).

The research designs employed in empirical research on pricing practices are invariably of the case study and survey variety (in practically equal proportions), with only one exception (notably Schackle's (1955) quasi-experimental investigation). The former can be subdivided into single-firm case studies (18 in all) and more extensive investigations of two or more firms using the case approach (22 studies). Survey-type investigations, on the other hand, have largely been based on personal interviews (five studies), mail questionnaires (17 studies) or a combination of both approaches (seven studies); only in three instances have telephone interviews been employed and always in connection with other methods (i.e. mail questionnaires and/or personal interviews).

Regarding sampling plans and data collection methods, as Table 3.7 indicates, the former appear to be dominated by non-probabilistic samples and the latter by face-to-face interviewing. These patterns are not surprising, bearing in mind the case study nature of a substantial number of investigations; one also needs to bear in mind that multiple sampling plans and/or data collection methods may be utilized within a single study.

Table 3.7 Sampling plans and data collection methods in previous studies

Sample type	No. of studies	Data collection method	No. of studies
Convenience	7	Executive's self-report	9
Purposive	16	Document analysis	15
Simple random	4	Personal interviews	38
Stratified random	8	Telephone interviews	3
Systematic random	2	Mail questionnaires	28
Population	4	Self-administered questionnaires	2

As far as data analysis is concerned, a large proportion of past studies are characterized by a qualitative rather than a quantitative orientation. Excluding four studies which could not be located despite repeated attempts (notably National Association of Cost Accountants, 1953b; Cook and Jones, 1954; Hatzold and Helmschrott, 1961; Zimmermann, 1971), 34 (41.4%) of the remaining studies contain no statistical analysis whatsoever; moreover, of those studies in which some statistical analysis is undertaken, the vast majority (68.8%) is limited to very basic statistical description (i.e. percentages, cross-tabulations, etc.). Only 11 studies use inferential statistics (i.e. significance tests) and in no instance are multivariate techniques employed.

Undoubtedly, however, the above picture is distorted by the inclusion of research designs which cannot be reasonably expected to produce data amenable to quantitative analysis. Still, the exclusion of single-firm case studies and studies with a small sample size appears to make little difference. For example, excluding *all* studies with a sample size less than 20 and ignoring studies with undisclosed sample sizes reduces the number of studies potentially offering scope for (at least non-parametric) statistical analysis to 45; of these nine are purely qualitative and a further 21 are limited to statistical description only. Nevertheless, it is encouraging to see that the statistical sophistication of empirical pricing studies has improved in recent years, as evidenced by the fact that out of 14 surveys of pricing practices reported between 1980 and 1988, nine contain not only a descriptive but also an inferential analytical component.

Shifting attention to the methodological *quality* of previous research, a number of doubts and criticisms have been expressed through the years relating both to particular empirical approaches and to individual investigations. With respect to the former, one line of criticism questions the utility of *all* approaches relying on information obtained through questioning decision-makers, irrespective of the specific method employed. Baumol (1977), for example, in discussing price objectives, argues that 'there is no simple way of determining the goals of the firm (or of its executives). One thing, however, is clear. Very often the last person to ask about any individual's motivation is the person himself . . . In fact it is common experience when interviewing executives that they will agree to every plausible goal about which they are asked' (p. 377). However, Baumol (1977) provides no evidence whatsoever in support of his position, nor does he make any suggestions regarding better methods of investigation. Instead, he places the researcher in a 'catch-22' situation by subsequently stating that 'the nature of the firm's objectives cannot be assumed in advance. It is important to determine the nature of the firm's objectives before proceeding with formal modeling and the computations based on it' (p. 378). Given that from secondary (i.e. published) material 'it is impossible . . . to get an insight into the motives underlying the setting of prices' (Fog, 1960, p. 7), Baumol (1977) leaves the researcher with no alternative (short of divine guidance, that is). Thus his kind of criticism is hardly constructive.

A more realistic concern that has been expressed questions the sole reliance on information provided by executives without checking their actual pricing behaviour; as Heflebower (1955) observes, 'that businessmen's responses to questions about their policies without definite checking as to their conduct is disconcerting' (p. 375). The rationale behind this criticism is that 'it is certainly debatable whether firms would act in a real situation as they indicated they would in answering the hypothetical question' (Fog, 1960, p. 4). While this is certainly true, in many instances the necessary access to the relevant company material is simply unobtainable; indeed, 'the reluctance of businessmen to confide to economists their methods of price calculation and the character of their associations with rival firms . . . has been a serious barrier to close investigation of price policy as seen by the price maker' (Bain, 1949, p. 149). It should also be noted that some attempts *are* made by researchers to cross-validate responses obtained from executives, as indicated by the use of document analysis in many intensive investigations of pricing practices (see Appendix 1).

A third strand of criticism relates to the appropriateness of the mail questionnaire in eliciting information about pricing behaviour. According to Simon (1962), 'for studies of pricing decisions, interviewing has many advantages over less intensive techniques using questionnaires . . . respondents provide less deliberate misinformation in a face-to-fact interview than in a mail questionnaire, and when they consciously warp the facts, they are more easily found out. The interview need not rely on general statements of practice but can probe these by applying them in detail to concrete examples . . . Finally, the interviewer need not rely on a single respondent but can usually get access to a number of executives and functionaries who participate in different aspects of the pricing decision' (p. 10). There is a lot of truth in this statement, particularly in the light of the confidential nature of price information. In this context, as Appendix 1 shows, the response rates achieved in mail surveys of pricing practices have, in many cases, been rather disappointing; coupled with the tendency of many researchers to 'forget' to disclose the response rates obtained, this cannot but create suspicion as to the representativeness of the samples obtained. While it is readily admitted that mail response rates depend on a multitude of factors, of which confidentiality of the topic examined is only one, this picture is broadly consistent with the view that a mail survey may not be the best way to gather empirical information on pricing decisions (Bain, 1949).

A fourth line of criticism questions the use of standardized instruments (in the form of self-administered questionnaires or predetermined interview schedules) in empirical pricing studies. This is largely based on the fact that 'it is impossible to regard the conception "business men's terminology" as being univocal. What such words as "costs", "unproductive wages", "price discrimination", "sales effort" etc. cover, varies not only from one industry to another but also from firm to firm' (Fog, 1960, p. 4). Accordingly, Machlup (1946) argues that 'a set formulation of questions will hardly fit any large number of business men in different fields . . . Only through detailed discussions of different situations and decisions, actual as well as hypothetical, will an investigator succeed in bringing out true patterns of conduct of the individual business man' (pp. 537, 538). Indeed, a number of authors have warned that the use of standardized instruments may result in a partial and often erroneous view of pricing behaviour. For example, in one study, the author warns future researchers that 'what is especially interesting from the methodological point of view is the fact that all the officers of the company approached were in the first instance unanimous in saying that prices were fixed according to cost. The investigator who confined himself to the straightforward questioning method would almost certainly have concluded that full-cost pricing was the rule in this company' (Pearce, 1956, p. 445); a similar warning was sounded a number of years later by Foxall (1972). Be that as it may, one must also bear in mind that 'the costs of intensive studies and the degree of cooperation required of the firms usually limit such studies to small and unrepresentative samples of firms. Hence there are major difficulties in extrapolating the findings to . . . business as a whole' (Simon, 1962, p. 7). However, the conflict between the desire to generalize and the need to obtain valid information is not impossible to resolve. As early as 1949, Bain was arguing for a *combination* of data collection methods in order to ensure quality of information as well as provide scope for generalization; his suggestion was that 'appropriate employment of interview and questionnaire methods might assist considerably in gaining a knowledge of those managerial motivations and price calculating processes which logically bridge the gap between observed environment and observed price and output results' (Bain, 1949, p. 166).

The origins of the above criticisms can be traced back to the dissatisfaction of many writers with the methodological quality of early pricing studies, particularly those based on questionnaire data. Thus Bain (1949) points out that 'the Oxford game of Twenty Questions, as played by Hall and Hitch and by Saxton with a random sample of thirty or forty businessmen, is not a promising pursuit . . . The questionnaire technique *per se* has been disappointing in this field mainly because of the way in which it has been applied' (pp. 165, 166). Similarly, Boulding (1942) voices the opinion that 'the Oxford inquiry, for all the interest of its results, shows marks of the gentleman-amateur' (p. 124).

It is difficult to defend against the substance (if not the tone) of such criticism, as even a casual inspection of the methodologies of Hall and Hitch (1939) and Saxton (1942) reveals that they leave a lot to be desired. In the former study, the non-disclosure of the actual questionnaire meant that 'gnawing doubts as to its tendentiousness in its presentation find easy prey' (Kahn, 1952, p. 126); coupled with an absence of statistical tests and a rather imprecise discussion of the research findings, this has resulted in the study being used to *support* conventional price theory by marginalist thinkers (e.g. Machlup, 1946)! In the Saxton (1942) study, on the other hand, the disclosure of the questionnaire served primarily to highlight the frailty rather than the robustness of the empirical material obtained. Leaving aside the actual questionnaire (which, almost in its entirety, provides a textbook example of poor questionnaire design), the way in which Saxton utilizes the empirical data is frequently astonishing. To illustrate the point, he has no hesitation in concluding that 'in general it cannot be doubted that entrepreneurs do make attempts to maximize their profits by every method which is open to them' (p. 5), despite the fact that no question on pricing objectives was included in his questionnaire!

To be fair, the weaknesses of early pricing studies must be seen in context. Thus it should be appreciated that it is almost inevitable that pioneering efforts are likely to be fraught with methodological difficulties and also to attract most of the flak. In addition, it is hardly a coincidence that the staunchest critics of early empirical efforts also happen to be the staunchest opponents of their theoretical implications (as is the case, for example, with the critiques by Machlup (1946, 1952) and Kahn (1952)). It is also a curious fact that these same critics are not empiricists but theorists who find it perfectly acceptable to complain about the poor quality of other people's studies without, however, making any attempt to generate empirical evidence themselves! This is unfortunate, since taking 'a back seat' and criticizing the empirical efforts of others would seem to be a rather soft option compared with the frustrations, practical difficulties and analytical problems that empirical workers have to deal with in their daily endeavours. As Lieberman (1969) aptly put it, 'the marginalists, even though occasionally referring to empirical findings, have established their case mostly on pure and simple logical reasoning, on deductions from a set of unverified principles, drawing at times challengeable inferences from the empirical evidence to support their views' (p. 547).

Bearing the above in mind, a few more points are worth noting in relation to the methodological soundness of previous studies.

First, there are instances of *ad hoc* approaches masquerading as empirical research. In one study, for example, the author states: 'For some time, I have tried to make observations which were not too comprehensive and did not proceed according to a definite plan. By cross-examining Danish businessmen I have met I simply tried to find their motivations. It is by no means certain that my impressions are correct, but since the results turned out to be surprisingly uniform from firm to firm, I shall venture to propound the more important generalizations' (Fog, 1948, p. 90). It remains a mystery how a study with such a shaky methodological base was ever accepted for publication; as far as the 'surprising uniformity of results' is concerned, this is not at all surprising given the 'flexibility' offered by the data collection technique!

Secondly, there are instances of failing to fully appreciate the potential dangers associated with the employment of unstructured interviews as a data collection device and, thus, to take the necessary steps to guard against them. An example is the study by Haynes (1962, 1964), in which more than one interviewer was employed to gather the desired information but no guidelines were given to minimize the effects of interviewer variability. The following passages from the study's methodology illustrate this problem: 'It was necessary to have *complete* freedom in directing the questioning to the particular situation. The interviewers did of course have *a* list of questions *in mind*, and *usually* had these jotted down on slips of paper, but these were used as suggestions for useful lines of thought that might be developed rather than rigid outlines of the direction the interviews might take . . . The analysis consists *largely* of the *subjective interpretations of the research workers*' (Haynes, 1962, pp. 5, 6, emphasis added).

Thirdly, there are instances of poor question formulation and wording in interview schedules and survey questionnaires. These are manifested in the form of (a) leading questions (e.g. Lydall, 1958), (b) ambiguous questions (e.g. Schackle, 1955), (c) double-barrelled questions (e.g. Earley, 1956), (d) biasing questions (e.g. Fitzpatrick, 1964), (e) implicit assumptions (e.g. Fog, 1960), (f) potentially unfamiliar terminology (e.g. Nimer, 1971), (g) implicit alternatives (e.g. Hooley, West and Lynch, 1984) and (h) lengthy questions (e.g. Udell, 1972). Related to question-wording problems are response format and measurement weaknesses. In particular, there has been a tendency towards nominal and ordinal scaling at the expense of higher levels of measurement, despite the advantages of the latter (i.e. interval and ratio scales) in terms of measurement sensitivity and analytical manipulation. This tendency is manifested in varying degrees, ranging from studies in which *all* questions have response formats that produce nominal-level data (e.g. Nimer, 1971), through studies with a mixture of nominal and ordinal response formats (e.g. Fitzpatrick, 1964), to studies the questionnaires of which generate overwhelmingly ordinal-level data (e.g. Wied-Nebbeling, 1975, 1985). Moreover, even in those cases in which it is evident that a conscious effort was made to secure interval-level data (e.g. Said, 1981), the statistical advantages of better measurement are not fully capitalized upon at the data analysis stage.

Fourthly, there are instances of failing to separate quite distinct issues from one another with the result that they end up lumped together under a single question. For example, Samiee (1987) used a constant-sum scale to determine the relative importance of nine pricing objectives, one of which read: 'Prices are set at a high level and subsequently lowered after a certain period has elapsed'; it is evident that this is not an objective but a *strategy* associated with new product pricing (notably market skimming). In some cases, failure to define precisely the issue about which information is sought has resulted in a complete breakdown of the logical connection between question and answer; for example, Fitzpatrick (1964) asks the respondent 'what is your price policy?' and among the alternatives he lists 'maximize profits for the entire product line' (a pricing objective) and 'a set and systematic method of pricing new products' (an empty statement)!

Fifthly, there are instances of failing to specify adequately the terms of reference within which an answer to a particular question/series of questions is expected. For example, with regard to pricing objectives, some studies provide no indication whatsoever as to the time horizon relating to their attainment (e.g. Abratt and Pitt, 1985), other studies merely distinguish between short- and long-run objectives without any further specification as to the time frames involved (e.g. Fog, 1960), while still others specify the time horizon for some objectives but not for others (e.g. Fitzpatrick, 1964). A similar pattern is observed with respect to the desired level of attainment. In some studies only the nature of the objective is given (e.g. profit) without clarifying whether maximization or satisficing (i.e. a target level) is aimed at (e.g. Abratt and Pitt, 1985), in other studies quantifiable objectives are cast *either* in maximization *or* satisficing terms (e.g. Said (1981) and Shipley (1981) respectively), and in yet another set of studies some pricing objectives are presented as maximands and others as target levels (e.g. Wied-Nebbeling, 1975, 1985). To make matters worse, there are also instances in which the precise nature of the objective itself is not adequately specified; for example, 'sales' as a pricing objective can refer to both physical volume (i.e. output) or revenue and a similar confusion arises for the 'growth' objective (growth of what?). Quite apart from introducing ambiguity in the questioning process (and thus in the answers obtained), failure to adequately specify the terms of reference generates formidable comparability problems across studies which have an adverse effect on the ease with which *meaningful* conclusions based upon the *collective* evidence can be drawn.

Sixthly, largely as a result of the qualitative orientation of much of previous research and the descriptive focus of most quantitative studies, relatively few studies utilize statistical testing to identify/verify relationships and patterns in the data and support the inferences made (see Appendix 1). As a result, doubts can be raised about the extent to which many of the conclusions drawn are actually justified and solidly based on empirical fact rather than an 'impressionistic' interpretation of the data by the researcher.

Lastly, mention should be made of the lack of conceptual diversity in the theoretical frameworks that have guided empirical research; this has important implications, since 'in this field as in many others, the answers depend a good deal on the questions, and the questions themselves depend on the theoretical approach of the questioner' (Silberston, 1970, p. 514). In this context, conventional price theory and the full/normal-cost theory have almost completely dominated past empirical efforts; this is true of virtually all studies with an economics and accountancy/finance background, which is not very surprising given the importance of conventional price theory in the economic discipline and the fact that costs and costing systems are a major area of study in finance and accounting.

The influence of alternative theoretical perspectives is much less prevalent; a few studies have been influenced by the organizational approach (e.g. Weston, 1970) and a few others by managerial theories (e.g. Richardson and Leyland, 1964). What is most surprising, however, is the number of studies in which *no* conceptual framework is (either explicitly or implicitly) employed; most of the studies published in the management literature and quite a few marketing studies fall in this category, which is unfortunate as 'little can be accomplished by gathering data for their own sake — that is, without some purpose or plan' (Cassady, 1963, p. 47).

Two notable exceptions in terms of conceptual framework are the studies by Gordon *et al.* (1980) and Said (1981), both of which appear to have passed largely unnoticed in the mainstream pricing literature. This is probably because the former has appeared in the trade rather than the academic literature, while the latter has not been published at all. The major contribution of these studies is the explicit introduction of contextual factors (such as firm size, type of product and production/distribution methods) in an attempt to identify and explain *variations* in pricing practices. Said (1981) went a step further and developed a model of pricing behaviour based upon statistically verified relationships between contextual factors and pricing variables and among the latter variables themselves. Thus her work laid the foundation for a contingency approach to the study of pricing behaviour, although it was not explicitly acknowledged as such by Said.

What follows next is an attempt to summarize the empirical evidence produced by the studies listed in Appendix 1. In the light of the large number of studies involved, it is clearly not possible to refer to the findings of each and every study without ending up with a hopelessly lengthy and tedious discussion. Instead, the *essence* of the empirical evidence will be presented under the three headings of pricing objectives, pricing methods and pricing environment respectively, drawing from the *collective* results of relevant studies; the interested reader is referred to Appendix 1 for a listing of original sources.

THE EMPIRICAL EVIDENCE

PRICING OBJECTIVES

For exposition purposes, the insights provided by empirical research on pricing objectives can be conveniently considered under four interrelated issues, notably (i) the number of objectives pursued, (ii) the type of pricing objectives, (iii) the interconnections/linkages between objectives and (iv) the factors that have been found to be related to pricing objectives.

Number of Pricing Objectives

Regarding the number of objectives, virtually all empirical studies indicate that firms formulate their pricing policies with a variety of pricing objectives in mind. In other words, the objective functions of real-world firms are multifaceted rather than singular, which implies that any theoretical representation of pricing behaviour based on a single goal (whatever that goal might be) involves a substantial (and potentially unacceptable) degree of abstraction from reality. The specific number of pricing objectives varies from firm to firm and so does the particular combination of objectives that is pursued; some objectives enter the objective functions of virtually all firms, while others are more or less unique to the individual firm. Moreover, the exact content of the objective function *within* a firm is not constant over time but subject to change and different objectives may apply to different markets, products or distribution channels. What the collective evidence shows quite categorically is that there is no *one* objective which serves as a universal and unequivocal guide for pricing decisions.

The multiplicity of pricing objectives has a number of important implications. The first of these is that complexity rather than simplicity characterizes the objective function of the firm; such complexity is manifested in complementary as well as conflicting relationships among objectives (a point further discussed below) and varying degrees of importance attached to different goals. Secondly, empirical comparisons of pricing policies, strategies, etc., across firms are not in themselves very instructive, unless differences in the specific objectives pursued are taken into account. Thirdly, the effectiveness of a particular pricing method cannot, in general, be judged with reference to a single outcome (such as profit) if a number of objectives are considered relevant at the price-setting stage. Fourthly, any attempt to interpret empirical evidence in constrained maximization terms runs into difficulties when multiple objectives are involved; these difficulties, even when only two goals are considered, are aptly illustrated by Boulding (1960), who asks 'Do we maximize profit subject to the constraints of morality, or do we maximize virtue subject to the constraints of satisfactory profits?' (p. 17). Finally, there is the methodological question of where to draw the line when examining pricing objectives so as to avoid generating an endless list of possible aims while at the same time ensuring that no important objectives are left out; in other words, care must be exercised not to allow the quest for comprehensiveness to degenerate into an unmanageable number of objectives defying classification and offering little opportunity for interfirm comparison and generalization.

Types of Pricing Objectives

With respect to the types of pricing objectives uncovered in empirical studies, the evidence falls under three main headings relating to the content (i.e. nature) of pricing objectives, the desired level of attainment and the associated time horizon; these headings reflect the dimensions of objectives as proposed by Heinen (1966).

Regarding the nature of pricing objectives, the empirical evidence indicates that both quantifiable and non-quantifiable objectives enter the objective functions of real-world firms; the former can be expressed in terms of some metric (such as money, physical quantities or percentages) while the latter can only be described qualitatively.

Focusing initially on quantifiable pricing objectives, there is a consensus in the empirical literature that some sort of profit goal is common to all firms; this is hardly surprising, considering the role of profit as a 'bottom line' performance indicator in modern economies. However, the exact specification of the profit objective is by no means uniform across firms. In some cases it is expressed in money terms, while in others it takes the form of a ratio (i.e. return on sales, return on costs, return on capital employed or return on net worth). Moreover, in addition to 'global' formulations of the profit objective, the latter is often related to individual products/product lines and expressed on a per unit basis (i.e. as a profit margin based on unit cost or price). Further variations among firms arise from the specific cost components which are subtracted from sales revenue (or price), resulting in gross profit, net profit (before or after tax) and contribution formulations of the profit goal. Finally, there is evidence to suggest that firms do not necessarily focus on a single type of profit goal but may set a combination of profit objectives (e.g. a target return on investment for the firm as a whole, coupled with specific profit margins for individual products/ product lines). Thus profit, as a pricing objective, is much more complex than may initially appear, in that while one can conclude that a profit *orientation* is a common motivational characteristic of all firms, one cannot conclude that the *specification* of profit objectives is uniform. The implication of this is that, for purposes of empirical research, one must differentiate among alternative formulations of profit goals in order to obtain a clear picture of the similarities/differences between firms.

A second set of quantifiable pricing objectives repeatedly observed in empirical studies is composed of what can be loosely termed 'volume' or 'output' goals. Such goals can be formulated from a demand (i.e. market) or, albeit less frequently, a supply (i.e. production) angle. The former usually take the form of sales revenue, sales volume and market share objectives, while the latter are typically expressed in terms of capacity utilization levels, production rates and inventory levels. In addition, some firms set objectives relating to the scale of distribution and market coverage that is desired; these are usually expressed in terms of the number (or percentage) of distribution outlets in which the firm aims to establish/maintain a presence. As was the case with profit goals, there are differences among firms in terms of the output goals they consider relevant for pricing purposes. However, according to the empirical evidence, sales revenue and market share objectives seem to be the most common output goals adopted by firms in practice; this appears to reflect the former's role as a summary indicator of market performance and the latter's significance as a *relative* success criterion.

Finally, a third set of quantifiable pricing objectives that has been identified in past studies relates to the firm's financial position and capital-raising ability. Such 'financial' objectives include liquidity/cash flow goals, dividend goals, earnings per share and price–earnings ratios.

Shifting attention to non-quantifiable pricing objectives, a wide range of goals have been encountered in empirical studies with various degrees of popularity. First, there are objectives specifying a firm's desired relationship with competition; these include price positioning objectives (e.g. matching/undercutting competition), stability objectives (e.g. avoidance of price wars) and defensive objectives (e.g. discouraging potential competitors from entering the market). Secondly, there are objectives relating to the firm's orientation and attitudes towards the marketplace; these include the desire to charge prices that are fair to resellers and/or final customers, to maintain goodwill, to provide a full range of prices so as to appeal to a variety of market segments, to ensure prices will be maintained in the distribution channel and to provide value for money to actual and potential buyers. Thirdly, there are objectives describing the firm's philosophy regarding its obligation to the public at large; these include the desire to be seen as a socially responsible corporation, to attain/maintain prestige through the projection of a high-quality image and/or technological advances, to avoid accusations of exploitation/indifference/negligence towards the buying public and to earn/maintain respect for moral conduct. Fourthly, there are objectives with internal significance to the firm; these include survival objectives (e.g. as reflected in the avoidance of loss), security objectives (e.g. the desire to remain an independent company) and employee welfare objectives (e.g. the desire to safeguard employment and enjoy healthy industrial relations). Finally, there are objectives transcending all previous categories; these include the avoidance of frequent price changes (which may upset competitors and customers alike and also prove costly for the firm itself) and the desire to avoid government attention as a result of an overly aggressive price policy (which may tarnish the firm's image among the trade and the public and also result in unwanted share price movements).

From the above, it should be evident that many non-quantifiable objectives are hardly operational, in that it is very difficult to compare a *specific* outcome with the pre-specified target and establish the degree to which the latter has been met. To illustrate this point, consider the objective of 'fair prices' (which has been repeatedly found in empirical studies as a common pricing objective among many firms). The questions that inevitably arise include (a) fair to whom? (a price fair to a distributor may not be necessarily fair for the final buyer and *vice versa*) and (b) who decides what is fair? (if it is the price-setter that decides, the fairness of the price will naturally depend on the firm's own conception of fairness, which may or may not coincide with that of the distributor and/or final customer). To the extent that these questions remain unanswered, then *any* price could be considered as being fair (or unfair), which implies that the objective 'fair prices' has little operational significance.

The non-operational nature of an objective may also be due to another reason. This is the inability to establish a sufficiently *direct* and *explicit* connection between an objective and the price-setting process to enable the former to serve as a clear guide for action. A good example in this context is the 'safeguard employment' objective (again an often-mentioned pricing goal in empirical studies). How can an individual pricing decision be directly guided (and subsequently evaluated) in terms of this goal? The simple answer is that, in most cases, it cannot.

With respect to non-quantifiable pricing objectives which *are* operational, only *broad* (i.e. yes/no) conclusions can normally be drawn regarding their attainment; this contrasts sharply with quantifiable objectives, the attainment of which can be measured in *degrees*, thus enabling inferences to be made about *how much* the actual outcome fell short of or exceeded the target initially set. For example, the extent to which a prudent pricing policy aimed at providing no incentive for government intervention is successful can only be judged with reference to whether or not a governmental investigation has been initiated (i.e. there are no in-between outcomes).

At this point, a word of caution is warranted regarding the two-way classification into quantifiable and non-quantifiable pricing goals. Strictly speaking, most objectives can be potentially expressed in terms of some metric, i.e. quantitatively. For example, the price similarity objective can be translated into a specific percentage that the firm's price should exceed/fall short of that charged by the competition (as reflected in the major competitor's price or some average price calculated over a number of competitors); similarly, the entry prevention objective may be quantified in terms of the number of new firms entering the market over a given period, and so on. While such quantification may be possible *in principle*, the empirical evidence provides no indication that any such attempt is made by firms *in practice*. In addition, for some objectives, it is very doubtful whether quantification serves any useful purpose; for example, attempting to quantify the image of the firm in terms of, say, the ratio of favourable *versus* unfavourable mentions in the media is of little use to a decision-maker contemplating the setting/changing of a product's price. Finally, there *are* objectives the very nature of which defies quantification and any attempt to the contrary is bound to fail; for example, trying to cast the objectives of 'morality' and 'social responsibility' in strict quantitative terms is as fruitful as trying to gauge a mother's love for her child by counting the number of times she kisses it! On the whole, therefore, the distinction between quantifiable and non-quantifiable pricing objectives appears to be justified on a mixture of empirical, practical and commonsense grounds.

The preceding discussion has indicated that a wide variety of pricing objectives have been reported in empirical research. So far, however, only the possible *nature* of objectives has been examined; neither the desired level of attainment relating to these objectives nor the relevant time horizon has yet been considered. The former manifests itself in different forms, depending on whether a quantifiable or non-quantifiable objective is involved. For quantifiable objectives, one can initially distinguish between aiming for no change (i.e. maintaining the current level) and aiming for change (i.e. increasing/decreasing the current level); to the extent that change is contemplated, a further distinction can be drawn between optimization (i.e. aiming for a maximum/minimum level) and satisficing (i.e. aiming for a target level). In the case of non-quantifiable objectives, the level of attainment typically takes a binary form (i.e. 'achieve *X*' or 'avoid *Y*', where *X* and *Y* are non-cardinal magnitudes). As far as the relevant time horizon is concerned, a basic distinction can be drawn between short-run and long-run pricing objectives, which can be further refined by introducing specific time frames (i.e. *X* months or *Y* years); such a refinement increases the scope for making detailed comparisons between firms and/or different pricing objectives.

The incorporation of the desired level of attainment and time horizon in a description of pricing objectives serves to highlight subtle differences between firms initially appearing to pursue the *same* basic objective(s). For example, it has been reported in a number of studies that sales revenue is a common pricing objective in practice. This, however, should not be interpreted as implying that the *formulation* of the sales revenue goal is the same for all firms; stating the objective as 'to achieve a 35% increase in sales revenue over the next three years' is very different from, say, 'maximize sales revenue in the immediate future'. Failure to appreciate the potential existence of these sorts of variation can result (and has resulted) in a false picture of uniformity being gained from empirical research whereas the reality may be very different indeed.

Bearing the above in mind and concentrating on those studies in which the level of attainment and/or time horizon has been considered, the available empirical evidence can be summarized as follows. First, there is little support for short-run profit maximization as postulated by conventional price theory. Although there have been instances of firms claiming that their pricing policy is geared towards producing the highest possible profit in the immediate future, these appear to be exceptions. On the other hand, there is more evidence suggesting that firms attempt to maximize profits in the long run. However, in interpreting this finding, one has to bear in mind the conceptual difficulties associated with long-run profit maximization, and also note that, in practice, the notion of maximization is expressed somewhat differently than is assumed in theoretical modelling. Rather than stating that the objective is the attainment of the maximum profit position, the aim is usually cast as trying to achieve the greatest possible increase from the current level over a given period; put differently, firms claiming profit maximization aim to improve as much as possible their profit performance rather than attain a specific value/level which is *a priori* recognized as representing the optimal (i.e. equilibrium) position.

While profit maximization has found some support in empirical studies, the bulk of the available evidence shows that, overwhelmingly, firms seek a satisfactory or target level of profitability in either the short or the long run and do not think in maximization terms; indeed, if firms are asked explicitly whether they could increase profits by changing their existing prices, most say yes. In practice, firms either aim to maintain their current profit position (if deemed satisfactory) or improve upon it (in relation to their historical performance and/or that of other comparable firms). In other words, profit objectives are typically specified in satisficing rather than maximization terms, and in most instances in which maximization is alleged it is further qualified by reference to the distant rather than immediate future.

A similar pattern to that relating to profit goals has also been observed for other quantifiable pricing objectives, notably output/volume and financial goals. With respect to market share objectives, the empirical evidence shows that firms usually aim to *at least* maintain their position in the short run and improve it in the long run. The targets set may take either a discrete or a continuous form, for example 'achieve *X* share in the next *Y* years' or 'attain an *X*% annual increase in share over the next *Y* years'. In a few instances, it has also been noted that an *upper* limit may be placed on market share, beyond which the firm perceives that problems may be encountered (e.g. government intervention to investigate allegations of monopolizing the market); should this limit be exceeded, the firm may actually take steps to achieve a planned reduction in market share to a 'safer' level. Market share maximization is not often adopted as a *permanent* pricing objective by firms, not least because attainment of this goal implies a complete monopoly; it can also prove to be very costly given that diminishing returns are likely to set in once a certain (critical) share of the market has been achieved. To the extent that market share maximization is mentioned as a pricing objective, it is usually qualified as being applicable to the introduction of a new product or to breaking into a market already served by established suppliers. Alternatively, market share maximization may be a legitimate objective for relatively small firms wishing to improve their position (in the sense of attempting to gain the greatest possible increase from their current (usually low) market share level). Regarding sales volume and sales revenue goals, the evidence indicates that firms normally aim at short- as well as long-run increases for both magnitudes so as to facilitate growth and ensure capacity utilization. Financial objectives, on the other hand, usually take the form of minimum target levels, the attainment of which is considered essential so as not to endanger the short- and long-run stability of the firm.

With regard to non-quantifiable pricing objectives, here only the issue of the time horizon is relevant, since notions of maximization or satisficing are clearly no longer applicable. Overall, no consistent pattern can be discerned from the empirical evidence. Some non-quantifiable objectives (e.g. price similarity with competition and fair prices) are usually perceived by firms as being essentially related to the short run, others (e.g. goodwill and entry deterrence) are perceived primarily as reflecting long-run considerations and still others (e.g. survival and social responsibility) have both short- and long-run dimensions.

At this point it should be noted that not all firms attach *specific* time frames to their pricing objectives, particularly as far as non-quantifiable objectives are concerned. This is not altogether surprising given that the latter are less amenable to being expressed in operational form than are quantifiable pricing goals. Moreover, even in those cases where time horizons are explicitly stated, these are by no means uniform across firms. What is considered to be a short-run period for one firm may well be a long-run period for another and, consequently, unless specific time frames are introduced to distinguish between the short- and long-run concepts, these terms are devoid of empirical content.

The examination of the empirical evidence relating to the kinds of pricing objectives that have been observed in empirical studies highlights the complexity that characterizes the objective functions of real-world firms; this is illustrated in Figure 3.5, which shows a taxonomy of pricing objectives based on the collective evidence furnished by empirical research.

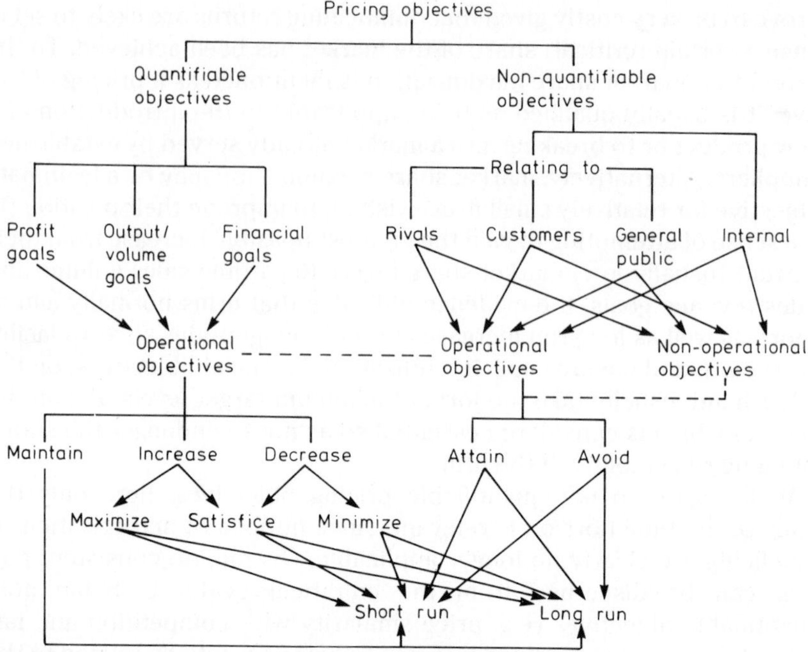

Figure 3.5 A taxonomy of pricing objectives

Linkages among Pricing Objectives

The fact that firms pursue multiple pricing objectives of various kinds inevitably raises questions about the existence and nature of potential interrelationships between them. In the light of the large number of pricing objectives that have been reported in the literature, it is clearly not possible to discuss all possible interrelationships among pricing goals. What can be done, however, is to draw attention to the different *types* of interrelationships that have been identified in empirical research and refer to specific objectives for illustration purposes only.

First, and most obvious, there are definitional interrelationships among pricing objectives, that is, interrelationships that arise automatically once a particular objective is specified. For example, money profit is, by definition, related to revenue and cost, since it is calculated as the difference between the latter two magnitudes; a particular level of attainment of the money profit goal is, therefore, associated with particular levels of attainment of the sales revenue and cost efficiency goals.

There are two contexts in which a definitional interrelationship assumes substantive significance. In a control context, it plays an accounting role by enabling the computation of the degree of fulfilment of the objectives under consideration (i.e. the specific revenues and costs associated with the profit level attained). In a decision-making context, it plays a coordinating role by ensuring that the objectives set are consistent with one another and no 'irrational' targets are specified; for example, it would make little sense to set a target revenue of X and a money profit target of $2X$. A more subtle form of definitional interrelationship is manifested when the specification of a particular objective in a given situation has explicit and direct implications for the specification of another objective; for example, the *maintenance* of market share in a *growing* market requires an *increase* (i.e. growth) in sales revenue. It can be seen that definitional interrelationships reflect a formal logical structure among different elements in the firm's objective function and, because of their very nature, are much easier to identify for quantifiable than non-quantifiable pricing goals. It is also evident that such interrelationships are of limited empirical interest since they are largely invariant across firms.

A second type of interrelationship reflects the extent to which the pursuit of a particular objective facilitates or hinders the attainment of another. Empirical research indicates that firms are very sensitive to potential complementarities and conflicts between pricing objectives and that these can take a variety of specific forms. First, conflicts/complementarities can be identified between pricing objectives within the same time horizon (i.e. short *or* long run); for example, the objective of increasing market share in the short run will normally facilitate capacity utilization but may only be achievable at the expense of short-run profitability (due to the price reduction necessary). Secondly, conflicts/complementarities can exist between the attainment of a given goal in the short run and the attainment of the *same* goal in the long run; for example, aiming for the greatest possible profit in the short run may jeopardize long-run profitability if it induces customers to start searching for other (more competitive) sources of supply. Thirdly, the pursuit of a given objective in the short-run may affect the attainment of *another* objective in the long run; for example, emphasis on short-run profitability may result in the long-run erosion of the firm's market share if other (outside) firms decide to break into the market attracted by the high profits that existing suppliers enjoy. Fourthly, there may be a 'chain reaction' of complementarities/conflicts between objectives over time; for example, emphasis on increasing market share in the short run, even at the expense of short-run profitability, may eventually result in a considerable degree of market power which, in turn, may facilitate the firm's profit-making ability in the long run. Finally, it is worth noting that both complementary *and* competing linkages can exist between the *same* pricing objectives, a fact which further complicates the structure of the objective function of the firm. For example, the objective of increasing market share may be in principle complementary to the objective of providing a 'good deal' to customers; this complementarity, however, may eventually be transformed into conflict if the firm's prices are set at such a (low) level that doubts are raised in the minds of buyers regarding the quality of the firm's product *vis-à-vis* competitive offerings.

A third type of interrelationship arises from the relative importance that firms attach to different pricing objectives. Given the multiplicity of pricing objectives pursued and the complementarities/conflicts that can exist between objectives, it is obvious that not all objectives can be given equal consideration at any one time; this implies that *choices* have to be made as to the priority/importance of alternative pricing goals. Such choices define the emphasis that is given to objectives of different kinds (e.g. market share *vs* profitability) and the desired balance between short- and long-run considerations. Unfortunately, the evidence on this issue is extremely difficult to summarize because of the variety of measurement schemes that have been applied in empirical studies; these range from simple 'popularity' counts of the frequency with which a particular objective crops up, through ordinal ranking of a specified set of objectives (which is, of course, different from study to study!), to conventional rating scales of the monadic or comparative variety; the ensuing comparability problems are further exacerbated by the methodological deficiencies relating to the operationalization of pricing objectives as discussed earlier.

With this caveat in mind, the overall impression that emerges from the empirical evidence is that profitability and volume/output goals are generally perceived as constituting the most important pricing objectives, with the former being the number one priority in a greater number of instances than the latter. Financial goals and the various non-quantifiable objectives appear to play a supplementary role in the sense of exerting important moderating influences on the specific *targets* that are set with respect to profitability, sales revenue, market share, etc. To illustrate this point, consider a firm that has as its main objective to increase its market share; while this may be its ultimate goal, the *rate* at which it will attempt to achieve it will depend upon the importance attached to, among other things, the avoidance of a price war and the maintenance of price stability. Thus the latter two (secondary) objectives play the role of moderating factors on the main (primary) pricing goal.

The empirical evidence also indicates quite clearly that firms, in general, are not willing to direct their pricing policies towards the attainment of short-run objectives which may adversely affect the long-run welfare of the firm; thus, in most cases, firms place greater importance on long-run objectives. Having said that, there are circumstances in which the emphasis is reversed; for example, a recession is likely to force a firm to direct its policies towards ensuring its short-term survival even if that has negative implications for its market share position and profitability in the long run. It is also important to appreciate, as some studies have clearly shown, that the relative importance attached to different objectives is not invariant over time; priorities may change depending upon the state of the market environment and the extent to which the objectives set in the past were actually attained. Moreover, the specific weights/priorities given to individual pricing objectives vary from firm to firm as well as within firms which produce a variety of products and/or sell to a variety of different markets.

Influences on Pricing Objectives

The final issue to be addressed concerns the factors that have been found to have an impact on pricing objectives. Both internal (i.e. organizational) and external (i.e. environmental) factors have been identified, which may impinge upon pricing objectives in two main ways, notably (a) by influencing the formulation of individual objectives and (b) by influencing the emphasis/importance attached to different objectives. An example of the former kind of influence is company size; thus, it has been observed that larger firms are more likely to specify their profitability objectives as return on investment rather than money profit, to focus more on the long rather than the short run and to adopt a maximization rather than satisficing perspective. The latter kind of influence is illustrated by the fact that interfirm variations in terms of pricing objectives have been found to be systematically linked to such factors as the type of industry and product involved, the stage of market evolution, the nature of competition and the allocation of price responsibility. It should be noted that *rigorous* investigation of the internal and external influences impinging upon pricing objectives has only recently become a topic of interest in empirical studies (in that most of the relevant evidence is the product of research conducted in the last decade) and a lot more needs to be done in this direction.

In conclusion, perhaps the most important point that emerges from the discussion of the empirical evidence on pricing objectives is the variety of ways in which firms may potentially differ in terms of their pricing aims. A methodological implication of this is that great care must be exercised when operationalizing pricing objectives in empirical research to enable valid interfirm (and interstudy) comparisons to take place; sadly, as already mentioned, many empirical studies tend to be deficient on this point.

PRICING METHODS

The picture of wide diversity painted by empirical research with respect to pricing objectives is also obtained when considering the evidence relating to pricing methods; this supports the view that 'the problem of price is far too difficult for one formula to suffice in all markets, for all products and at all times' (Davies and Hughes, 1975, p. 73). A number of pricing methods have been found to be used by firms to set their prices and, in many instances, more than one method may be in use within the same firm; for example, a particular method may be used for routine pricing decisions while a different method may be applied in one-off situations (e.g. to gain a large order or dispose of surplus stock). Before examining in detail the individual methods used in practice, it is useful to draw attention to some more general points regarding pricing methods.

To begin with, not all pricing methods are equally clear/informative as to exactly *how* a price is built through their application; they range from highly sophisticated formulae providing an explicit statement of the computation of prices (e.g. return on investment formulae) to rather basic and somewhat vague methods indicating only the broad approach adopted in price determination with little, if any, operational detail (e.g. pricing according to, say, the manager's 'gut feeling' of the market).

Secondly, firms differ from one another in terms of the extent to which their methods of price calculation are formalized, as reflected, for example, in the existence of documents (i.e. pricing guides or manuals) describing the steps/components of the price-setting process; indeed, what little evidence there is on this issue indicates that written-down pricing procedures are the exception rather than the rule.

Thirdly, there are differences between firms in terms of their adherence to prices arrived at through the application of a particular pricing method; in other words, firms differ in terms of the degree to which initial prices are subsequently modified through the use of discounts, allowances or negotiation with individual customers.

Finally, a number of organizational and environmental factors have been identified which may impinge upon the pricing method(s) used by the firm. Specifically, it has been established that the more sophisticated pricing formulae are typically used by large firms, the latter being more likely to decompose their costs into fixed/variable and direct/indirect elements, undertake return-on-investment calculations and tailor mark-ups to different products and/or market conditions. It has also been observed that pricing methods vary across different industry sectors, product types, and production and distribution methods. Moreover, links have been identified between the types of information used in making pricing decisions and the choice of pricing method.

While a number of individual pricing methods have been uncovered by empirical research, these can be seen as falling into six basic types (Figure 3.6) according to (a) the firm's basic perspective on price determination (i.e. proactive *vs* reactive) and (b) the primary focus during price calculation (i.e. cost, demand or competition). The former dimension indicates whether the firm actually *builds* a price rather than *adjusts* to a price initially established by forces outside its direct control, while the latter dimension specifies the *principal* factor around which price determination is centred. Note that the use of the terms 'proactive' and 'reactive' to describe the basic pricing perspective of the firm should not be interpreted as implying that proactive approaches are inherently superior to reactive ones (or *vice versa*); these terms are used in a descriptive sense alone and carry no evaluative connotations.

Proactive Cost-based Pricing

Two pricing methods fall in this category, notably cost-plus and contribution pricing (the latter is also known as 'marginal cost', 'variable cost' or 'direct cost' pricing). Both methods share the common feature that the starting point in price determination is the calculation of the firm's costs; however, they differ from one another in terms of the specific cost elements that are considered relevant for pricing purposes and the way in which the profit mark-up is specified.

The cost-plus method of pricing has already been extensively discussed in connection with the full-cost and normal-cost principles and, consequently, only a few additional points will be raised here. The distinguishing characteristic of this pricing method is that it involves the calculation of unit cost for the product under consideration, incorporating both direct cost elements and an allocation of indirect costs; a profit mark-up is subsequently added to unit cost to arrive at the selling price. The rationale behind this method is that each product should carry a 'fair' share of the firm's total costs, which should be covered by the selling price and also yield a profit. As mentioned earlier, cost-plus

Primary focus		Basic perspective: Proactive	Basic perspective: Reactive
	Cost	Cost-plus pricing Contribution pricing	Price-minus pricing
	Demand	Marginal analysis Trial-&-error pricing Intuitive pricing	What the market will bear Monopsonistic pricing
	Competition	Product analysis pricing Value pricing	Imitative pricing

Figure 3.6 A taxonomy of pricing methods

pricing can be manifested in a variety of forms, since firms differ in terms of the volume rates used to arrive at unit costs, the specific cost elements considered as overheads, the overhead recovery rates and the calculation of the profit mark-up. With respect to the latter, this may be established as a proportion of total unit costs, as a unit profit to achieve a target profit level, as a percentage to yield a predetermined return on sales/investment, or as a proportion of conversion cost (i.e. total manufacturing cost less material cost); as far as the *level* of the mark-up is concerned, this will reflect the particular specification of the firm's profit objectives.

According to the empirical evidence, cost-plus pricing (in its various forms) is by far the most widely used pricing method in industry. The evidence also shows that firms differ from one another not only in terms of the components that constitute their pricing formulae (in the sense discussed above) but also in terms of the way in which such formulae are actually applied. Three distinct variations of the cost-plus pricing approach have been identified in empirical studies, reflecting different degrees of flexibility in price-setting. First, cost-plus pricing can take a rigid form, whereby a single predetermined mark-up is applied to all products in the range and held stable for a considerable length of time. Secondly, cross-sectional flexibility may be introduced in cost-plus pricing by applying different mark-ups to different products and/or sectors of the business but keeping such mark-ups stable over time. Thirdly, in addition to the cross-sectional flexibility of mark-ups, the latter may be varied over time to take into account changes in market conditions. In this context, empirical research shows quite conclusively that flexible cost-plus pricing approaches predominate in practice as opposed to rigid applications of the method. What this implies is that most firms, by varying their mark-ups across products and/or over time, actively consider the market environment in their price calculations and do not simply rely on a mechanistic application of a formula. Having said this, there are many instances (particularly among smaller firms) of rigid application of the cost-plus approach. It is also worth noting that, in industries characterized by similarity in the cost structures of suppliers, cost-plus pricing is considered as promoting price stability and 'fair play' among competitors and its use is frequently encouraged by trade associations (e.g. through the publication of 'typical' costs, 'industry' mark-ups, etc.).

The other pricing method in this category, contribution pricing, is also a cost-based approach but differs from cost-plus pricing in that only variable costs are considered relevant for pricing decisions. Specifically, only those costs that can be attributed directly to the production/distribution of a particular product and which are influenced by variations in output are used to build a cost estimate, to which a further addition is made to arrive at the selling price. The difference between price and average variable cost is known as the contribution margin and the firm decides on its production and sales plans for different products in such a way as to generate the highest possible total contribution. The rationale behind this method is that in multiproduct and/or multimarket situations, allocation and absorption of fixed costs to individual products is both absurd and virtually impossible to carry out effectively in practice. Rather than expecting each individual unit of each individual product to generate a specific amount of profit, attention should be paid to the total product mix and the extent to which the *total* contribution generated is sufficient to cover the firm's fixed costs and also show a profit commensurate with the profit goals that have been set.

The empirical evidence on the prevalence of the contribution method of pricing is rather mixed. Some studies show that many firms (particularly large ones) make use of the distinction between fixed and variable costs in pricing decisions and establish different contribution margins for different products in their range. In other studies, however, only a small proportion of the firms examined were found to rely on this approach. Bearing in mind the conflicting results, the overall picture that emerges from the empirical evidence is that, while cost-plus pricing is undoubtedly a more frequently used method than contribution pricing, the latter is also used quite extensively, albeit primarily in 'special' rather routine pricing situations (e.g. to decide on whether or not to take on a large order at a pre-specified price or to adjust prices for products which are being phased out from the range). Thus cost-plus and contribution methods can coexist within the same firm, as some studies have clearly shown. A final point to note in connection with the contribution approach is that, since it is the *total* contribution (i.e. aggregate contribution of all individual products sold) which determines the extent to which fixed costs have been covered and a profit earned, the firm is actively encouraged to consider the volumes attainable at different prices for each product; this, in turn, necessitates that market considerations enter the pricing process at an early stage.

Reactive Cost-based Pricing

This pricing method is commonly referred to in empirical studies as 'backward cost pricing', 'price-minus pricing' or 'product tailoring'. It is usually discussed in the context of market situations in which traditional/conventional prices or price ranges exist and to which the firm must broadly conform if it wishes to supply the market in question. Essentially, this approach involves the firm taking the 'traditional' price as practically fixed and subsequently deciding on the specification of the product which it can offer at that price. By making such adjustments, the firm aims to equate the full cost of the product (including an allowance for profit) to the given price. It can be seen that a cost-plus rationale underlies this approach in that all costs are expected to be recovered on a product basis (and also yield a profit). The only difference is that the order of the steps taken to establish a price is reversed (i.e. from full cost to price in cost plus *vs* from 'given' price to full cost in price minus). Indeed, in many studies no distinction is made between the two approaches, a fact which makes it difficult to state accurately how widely the price-minus approach is used in practice; nevertheless, the evidence seems to suggest that, for long-established types of product (e.g. certain clothing categories) with customary retail prices, price-minus pricing may be the rule rather than the exception.

Proactive Demand-based Pricing

The pricing methods in this category share the common feature that demand rather than cost considerations are used as the focal point in price-setting. This does not, of course, mean that costs are unimportant but rather that price determination based mainly on costs is not deemed to be desirable or feasible.

The first method in this category is the familiar marginal pricing approach, which has its origins in conventional price theory. It involves the estimation of total revenues and total costs at different price–volume combinations and the selection of that combination at which marginal revenue and marginal cost are equal; whenever either costs or demand conditions change, the process is repeated and a new combination selected. The use of this method in practice is, according to the empirical evidence, not very widespread and lags substantially behind cost-plus pricing methods in popularity. However, some firms do attempt to calculate marginal costs and marginal revenues for at least part of their product range and tend to apply this method in a manner similar to that associated with the contribution approach, i.e. for non-routine pricing decisions. Use of marginal analysis appears to be most prevalent among large firms operating in markets with a few competitors, a finding which is not surprising given the substantial computational demands involved in the estimation of marginal magnitudes.

A second demand-oriented method is the trial-and-error or 'experimental' method of pricing, which is characterized by an explicit attempt to obtain information about the likely market reaction to different prices. This may be done informally by consulting salespeople and by obtaining management's expert opinion on the effects of alternative prices on volume and profit or, albeit less frequently, by undertaking formal investigations in the form of customer surveys, market experiments, field tests, and the like. By experimenting with a set of different prices, the firm can analyse their implications in the light of its pricing objectives and select the price which is most likely to achieve them. With specific reference to profit goals, trial-and-error pricing can be seen as a somewhat cruder version of the marginal approach, in that it involves a comparison of alternatives from which the one offering the greatest profit potential is selected. The trial-and-error method has been frequently observed to be associated with the pricing of new products, a finding which makes intuitive sense given that the uncertainty regarding market reaction is usually higher than with established or 'run-of-the-mill' items. It is also evident that the time and cost implications of price experimentation (particularly when market surveys, etc., are used) are quite considerable and thus likely to impose constraints on the firm's ability to employ this method on an everyday basis (especially when a large number of products and/or markets are involved).

The final method in this category is intuitive pricing, which, according to empirical studies, is frequently encountered in industry, particularly among smaller firms. It is rather difficult to be precise about exactly what intuitive pricing entails other than a 'hunch' on the part of the decision-maker regarding the 'right price'; it is thus debatable whether it can be legitimately considered as constituting a pricing *method*. At best, intuitive pricing can be seen as the establishment of a price which reflects the decision-maker's knowledge and experience of the market in general and his perceptions of current and future market conditions in particular. In other words, the decision-maker's subjective evaluation of the environment is somehow translated into a specific price which is thought to be the 'right' one. Note that in firms where intuitive pricing is used, pricing objectives are rarely stated explicitly or, if they are, they tend to be non-operational; this, of course, severely restricts the scope for assessing the outcomes produced by the intuitive approach since it is not clear *how* the price is established and *what* the price is intended to achieve. The author's overall impression from the empirical evidence on intuitive pricing is that it is often given as a justification for the lack of any systematic pricing procedure, that is, in order to cover up a situation where pricing is simply a 'hit'n'miss' affair!

Reactive Demand-based Pricing

The most widely known demand-based pricing method is the 'what the market (or traffic) will bear' approach, which, according to the empirical evidence, is the second most popular pricing method used in practice (after cost-plus pricing). It is usually encountered in market situations characterized by intense competition and involves setting a price at the 'market' level. Firms using this method invariably describe themselves as having little price discretion, since the price they can charge is already established by the market (or by 'supply and demand' as is commonly stated). In a sense, the use of the 'what the market will bear' approach can be seen as the real-life equivalent of the perfect competition model in microeconomic theory; operating in a highly competitive industry, the firm acts as a price-taker rather than a price-maker in that it has to accept the market price and adjust its output plans accordingly. As was the case with the proactive demand-based methods, there is a broad consensus among firms employing the 'what the market will bear' approach that costs do not constitute an appropriate basis for determining prices. Instead, it is the customer that has the final say, as he can choose among competitive offerings. The importance placed upon the customer is further reflected by the fact that some firms actually attempt to measure formally the degree of customer acceptance of price, particularly if a departure from the established market price is considered by the firm (e.g. in the case of a new/improved product).

The second method in this category, monopsonistic pricing, is encountered in markets characterized by a bargaining power asymmetry between supplier and customer, with the latter occupying the more powerful position. Under such conditions, the (typically large) customer virtually dictates the price at which he is willing to buy from a (typically small) supplier. The price may be set on a 'take-it-or-leave-it' basis or may be subject to negotiation between the two parties until a mutually acceptable price is agreed upon.

There are a number of circumstances in which a firm may find itself with little option but to accept a price set by this 'method'. For example, the firm may be trying to get a foothold into a market which is dominated by a small number of retailers, or it may be dealing with a customer facing a make-or-buy decision (i.e. with the potential of producing the product(s) in question in-house). Alternatively, the firm may be dependent upon a particular customer for the absorption of a major proportion of its output and thus be 'locked in' a trading relationship which, if terminated, may have dire consequences for the firm's survival. It is interesting to note that monopsonistic pricing is not frequently mentioned in the empirical literature as being a widespread practice. However, its incidence may well be under-reported because firms are, understandably, reluctant to admit that their pricing decisions are practically made for them by a customer firm; in this context, it has been observed that, in most cases, firms prefer to describe their price-setting decisions under the 'what the market will bear' approach, although closer examination often reveals that the true situation is one of monopsonistic pricing.

Proactive Competition-based Pricing

The distinguishing characteristic of this approach is that an explicit attempt is made by the firm to translate differences in its product offering from competitive products into a price differential. The rationale behind this is that a customer is normally faced with a range of product options from which to choose and he is willing to pay different prices for products possessing different combinations of relevant (i.e. need- or want-satisfying) characteristics.

One version of this approach is the product analysis pricing method developed by the Glacier Metal Company (Brown and Jacques, 1964; Simons, 1967). This involves the decomposition of a product into its constituents, the latter reflecting both objective (e.g. weight, size, finish) and subjective (e.g. style and brand image) attributes. Next, standard values are established for the various product attributes (or 'product properties' as they are sometimes referred to) and an algorithm is applied to arrive at a total product value which reflects a specific combination of attributes. Finally, an adjustment factor (which reflects current market conditions) is applied to arrive at the target price; the latter may be accepted as the final price or further adjusted in the light of exceptional circumstances (e.g in order to retain an important customer). It can be seen that the importance attached to competition is reflected in (a) the identification of product attributes, variations among which can constitute a source of competitive advantage, and (b) the market adjustment factor, which reflects temporary changes in the market.

The second method in this category is the value-pricing procedure proposed by McKinsey consultants (Forbis and Mehta, 1979; Garda, 1984). This is based on the concept of economic value to the customer (EVC), the latter representing the value a given products offers to a specific customer in a particular application. The starting point in value pricing is the selection of a 'reference' product (i.e. the one the customer is currently using or views as the best substitute for the product being evaluated) and the calculation of its life-cycle costs; the latter include the purchase price as well as start-up (e.g. installation) and post-purchase (e.g. maintenance) costs. Next, the product to be priced is examined to identify whether it possesses differentiating features which provide additional customer benefits (e.g. superior performance); the value of such features represents incremental (or differentiation) value. Finally, EVC is calculated as the reference product's life-cycle costs less start-up and post-purchase costs of the product under consideration plus any incremental value offered by the latter. Given the EVC expresses a product's relative value, it can be viewed as representing the *maximum* price that an informed customer should be willing to pay for it. It is also evident that if the product is offered to different customer groups and/or has different applications, its EVC will vary across different market segments. This allows the setting of price to be tailored to the characteristics of each segment, capitalizing on EVC differences. Note that the actual price set is likely to be lower than the product's EVC, so as to provide 'customer savings' and thus making the product a more attractive proposition than the reference product (otherwise the customer would have no incentive for choosing it over the product he is currently using).

The main benefit of value pricing is that it encourages the firm to analyse its product offering against competition in terms of attributes that are relevant and important from the *customer's* point of view and, as such, it can be viewed as being the most marketing-oriented pricing procedure. Its main drawback is that it requires considerable effort to identify key buying factors and relevant differentiating characteristics and is more difficult to apply in the case of consumer products (because the greater portion of EVC may be due to intangible values — e.g. prestige — which are hard to quantify). It also goes without saying that, in applying value pricing, it is important that the customer is encouraged to think in terms of *all* elements affecting EVC (i.e. life-cycle costs and differentiating features), since a 'product's market value is not only determined by the product's economic value, but also by the accuracy with which buyers perceive that value'(Nagle, 1987, p. 110).

It is interesting to note that empirical studies have revealed only a few isolated instances in which product analysis pricing and value pricing are used in practice. While this may be due to methodological limitations of previous efforts, in that researchers have not even looked for this method (e.g. making no provision in their questionnaires for attribute pricing under the response alternatives for 'which of the following methods do you use?' type of questions), it may also be the case that the time and costs associated with the development of a comprehensive attribute pricing system are, for many firms, rather prohibitive. Alternatively, it is also possible that firms using this approach may not wish to disclose it for confidentiality reasons, preferring instead to describe their pricing method as being of the 'what the market will bear' variety.

Reactive Competition-based Pricing

This pricing method is described in the empirical literature as 'imitative pricing', 'competitive parity' or 'price leadership' and has been found to be a widespread approach in industry. Its distinguishing characteristic is that price calculation is based mainly on the prices offered by competition, which are either matched exactly or exceeded/undercut by some (usually small) fraction. Firms practising imitative pricing typically perceive themselves either as being unable to develop an independent (i.e. more aggressive) pricing policy due to the presence of larger and more powerful competitors or as being less well equipped to make correct price decisions than are their rivals. The latter case may arise if the firm is new to the market and is still trying to obtain a 'feel' about the market's reaction to price or simply because the firm is a small supplier, lacking the resources to engage in sophisticated price-building as do (or, at least, are supposed to) larger firms; it may also arise if the firm has as one of its main pricing objectives to match competition on price, in which case the obvious way of doing this is to peg its own price at the competitive level.

In its purest form, as its name implies, imitative pricing involves little else other than adopting the price set by the market leader, the latter being usually (although not always) the dominant firm in the market; every time the leader undertakes a price change, this is mirrored in corresponding price changes by the price followers, i.e. by the competitors practising price imitation. This form of imitative pricing has also been observed in markets in which cost variations among firms are not great, in which case the price leader plays a coordinating role in the market and his actions are acknowledged by other suppliers as promoting the collective welfare of the industry.

A more flexible form of imitative pricing involves using the price set by the market leader as a basic guide but setting the price somewhat above or below it to reflect differences in product quality, features, etc. The degree of divergence (particularly in a downward direction) from the 'market price' as established by the leader will depend on the firm's perception of 'what it can get away with' without upsetting the leading firm through market share encroachment (and thus potentially incurring its wrath in the form of a price war). A further variation of imitative pricing involves the firm calculating a 'typical' market price by averaging the prices of its major competitors and subsequently setting its own price at, below or above the 'market average'. As might be expected, imitative pricing has been found in empirical studies as being usually associated with smaller firms operating in oligopolistic markets dominated by a small number of established suppliers. It has also been observed that, while price imitation may be the approach used to set list/published prices, the latter may be subsequently lowered through the use of hidden allowances and concessions.

PRICING ENVIRONMENT

The term 'pricing environment' is used here in a broad sense to collectively reference the multitude of elements that constitute the setting within which price decision-making takes place. Aspects of the pricing environment have already been discussed throughout this literature review, both as part of introducing the subject matter and during the review of the theoretical and empirical contributions on pricing. For example, in considering the nature and importance of price, reference was made to the various factors that influence the 'true' price of a product and the relationship between price and other marketing mix elements. Similarly, issues relating to the internal (i.e. organizational) and external (i.e. market) environment were repeatedly raised during the examination of the various conceptual perspectives on pricing.

Finally, in the presentation of the empirical evidence on pricing objectives and pricing methods, attention was drawn to the various factors that empirical research has shown to be related to the aims and methods of price determination and which help explain variations in pricing practices among firms.

In the light of the above and in the interest of avoiding repetition, what will be attempted in this section is to structure the empirical evidence on the pricing environment in such a way as to (a) highlight the potential complexity of the overall setting within which price decisions are made, and (b) illustrate the different roles played by different elements of the environment in shaping the pricing decisions of the individual firm.

An examination of empirical studies making reference to the pricing environment (see Appendix 1) resulted in the identification of more than 100 individual elements representing potentially relevant organizational and market influences on pricing. These, however, can be reduced to a more manageable number of distinct groupings, each comprising a set of influences of a particular kind; a suggested decomposition of the pricing environment based on these is shown in Figure 3.7, while a complete listing of empirically observed environmental influences is provided in Appendix 2.

As an inspection of Appendix 2 will readily confirm, a considerable number of diverse influences may constitute the pricing environment of the individual firm. However, the frequency with which different types of environmental influences crop up in empirical studies varies

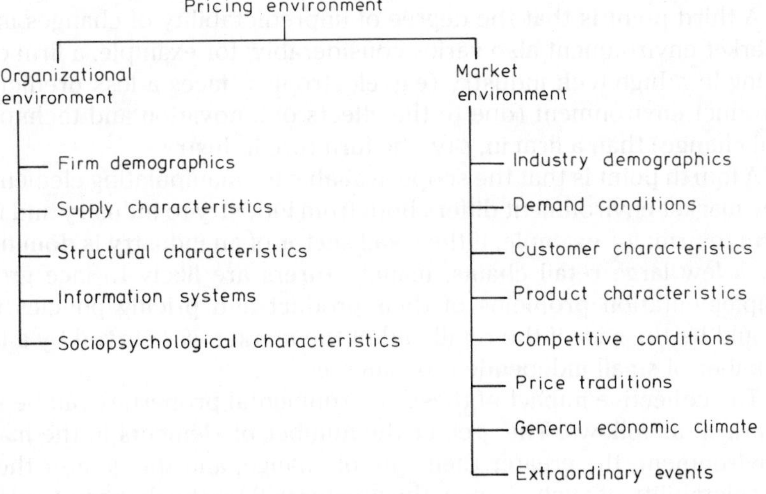

Figure 3.7 Overview of the pricing environment

considerably. For example, virtually all studies make some reference to competitive conditions and customer characteristics; in contrast, reference to, say, structural characteristics is much more rare. A similar pattern is observed at a more detailed level, notably *within* each broad type; thus, for example, with respect to customer characteristics, much more frequent reference is made to buyers' sensitivity to price than, say, their price negotiation tactics. In spite of such imbalances, a number of important points emerge from the evidence furnished by empirical studies; these can be usefully discussed under two main headings, relating to the nature and the role of the pricing environment respectively.

The Nature of the Pricing Environment

The first point to note relates to the composition of the external pricing environment and indicates that the latter is not invariant across firms; in other words, not all factors listed in Appendix 2 are relevant in every case. For example, in the case of a frozen food manufacturer, considerations of a second-hand market are irrelevant in pricing decisions and so are the prices of products in other (i.e. non-food) industries.

A second point is that firms operating in different industries face different rates of change in their market environment; for example, in the clothing industry, the dictates of fashion result in a much greater rate of product modification (and thus price adjustment) than is the case in, say, the detergent industry.

A third point is that the degree of unpredictability of changes in the market environment also varies considerably; for example, a firm operating in a high-tech industry (e.g. electronics) faces a less predictable product environment (due to the effects of innovation and technological change) than a firm in, say, the furniture industry.

A fourth point is that the scope available for manipulating elements of the market environment differs both from industry to industry and from firm to firm; for example, if the retail sector of an industry is dominated by a few large retail chains, manufacturers are likely to face greater implementation problems of their product and pricing policies than would be the case if the retail end of the market was served by a large number of small independent businesses.

The collective impact of these environmental properties can be summarized as follows. The greater the number of elements in the market environment, the greater their rate of change, and the greater the unpredictability of such change, the greater will be the degree of environmental complexity and uncertainty and, thus, the more difficult the pricing task. To complicate matters further, a firm may be facing multiple market environments if it operates in more than one product market; bearing in mind that most firms nowadays fall in this category, one cannot but conclude that the demands placed upon the decision-maker are grave indeed.

The nature of the internal (i.e. organizational) environment also has important consequences for price decision-making. Specifically, the capacity of the firm to cope with the complexity and uncertainty of the market and make effective pricing decisions depends directly upon its organizational characteristics. For example, a large firm with considerable experience in the industry is likely to be better equipped to predict and, where possible, manipulate its external environment (e.g. through superior information systems, financial strength and technical/managerial resources) than would a small newcomer to the market. What this suggests is that, even within the *same* product market, behavioural differences may be observed among firms with respect to pricing. Moreover, such differences may arise not only because of firm differences in terms of their 'objective' features (i.e. firm demographics, supply characteristics and structural characteristics) but also because of differences in sociopsychological characteristics, resulting in different *perceptions* of the same market environment.

Curiously, the fact that subjective perceptions may colour the firm's pricing decision has not been fully recognized by researchers in the past, who, on occasion, have been at a loss when faced with what appeared to be gross inconsistencies in respondents' replies. In one instance, for example, in being asked to indicate the number of their competitors, firms clearly operating in the same (oligopolistic) market gave different answers; this was subsequently interpreted as reflecting simply 'respondent error'. While this might well have been the case, an alternative explanation is that different firms have different perceptions as to the exact constituents of their competitive environment (e.g. some may have taken a broader view and included competitors in other industries, while others may have concentrated on their immediate major rivals). It is also worth noting that different firms attach different importance to the various elements in their internal and external environment; on this point, the findings of empirical research suggest that competitive and customer considerations are generally considered as being the most important environmental elements.

A final point to note regarding the nature of the pricing environment is that its various elements are not independent but interconnected through a complex set of linkages. As a result, changes in one environmental component set off changes in others which, in turn, create further repercussions, and so on. For example, changes in competitive conditions (e.g. a new firm enters the market) will be reflected in changes in industry demographics (i.e. increased supply), which will call for adjustments in existing firms (e.g. product/price improvements to regain lost business). The interconnectedness in the pricing environment implies that the firm has to take into consideration a complex chain of cause–effect relationships when reaching its price decisions; in this context, the multiplicity of pricing objectives noted earlier can be seen as an attempt by the firm to deal with the complexity of the pricing environment, a point further elaborated below.

The Role of the Pricing Environment

In discussing the role of the pricing environment, the aim is to highlight, on the basis of the available empirical evidence, the different ways in which market and organizational factors may impinge upon price decision-making. Given the length of the list of environmental elements in Appendix 2, it is clearly not possible to discuss each and every one of them; instead, the tactic adopted when discussing the interrelationships among pricing objectives will be employed, that is, the different *types* of roles/functions of the environment will be highlighted, together with illustrative examples.

To begin with, a major function of the pricing environment is to provide a point of reference for the formulation of pricing objectives. For example, market share objectives can be seen as reflecting a desired relationship between total market size (an element of demand conditions) and that proportion of the market supplied by competitors (an element of competitive conditions); indeed, many of the pricing objectives earlier discussed can be seen in this way.

A second function of the pricing environment is to provide a basis for price calculation; the reactive pricing methods considered previously illustrate this function very clearly and no further elaboration is necessary.

Thirdly, the pricing environment plays a comparative/evaluative role in that it gives clues as to the relative appropriateness of alternative pricing strategies and tactics; for example, if the firm develops a new product which is superior to those offered by competition, is protected by a patent and is of importance to the buyer, then a skimming pricing strategy is likely to be more appropriate than would a market penetration approach.

Fourthly, the pricing environment has a constraining or limiting function, that is, it places limits on the pricing discretion of the firm; for example, the existence of 'traditional' or 'customary' prices in the market implies that the firm is constrained as to the price it can charge and, therefore, should it need to increase profitability, it would have to attain it through cost reduction rather than a price rise.

Fifthly, the pricing environment plays an important warning role, by providing signals regarding the need for price adjustments; for example, changes in the prices of raw materials and their impact on product cost may be capitalized upon by the firm by undertaking appropriate price revisions.

Sixthly, another function of the pricing environment is to highlight opportunities that can be potentially exploited by the firm through intelligent pricing; for example, a buyer's expectations regarding price rises can be dealt with by increasing prices by a smaller fraction than competition but at the same time increasing the minimum order quantity sufficiently to compensate.

Seventhly, the pricing environment has a regulatory role, that is, it specifies the 'rules of the game' and the norms of 'acceptable' pricing behaviour; for example, trade association pricing guidelines, if repeatedly violated by the firm, may have adverse effects for the firm's reputation in the industry which, in turn, may eventually tarnish the firm's image as perceived by customers.

Finally, the pricing environment plays a technical role, in the sense that it determines the price decision-making capability of the firm; for example, the quality of the firm's sales forecasting system and the sophistication of its demand estimation procedures will largely determine the degree of 'fine-tuning' that can be attained when setting prices.

Thus, it can be seen that the role of the pricing environment is manifested in a variety of forms. However, not all elements of the environment perform all the above-mentioned functions. Some aspects of the environment, such as competition, may impinge upon pricing decisions in more than one way, while others (e.g. general economic conditions and extraordinary events) have a more limited impact. Thus, the pricing environment of real-world firms is a complex structure of diverse but interrelated influences which may affect pricing decisions in a number of ways. As a result, unless one has at least a rudimentary knowledge of the major elements constituting the pricing environment under consideration, any attempt to explain/predict pricing behaviour is doomed to fail; pricing objectives and pricing methods lack substantive meaning in the absence of information about the setting to which they are applied.

PRICING IN PRACTICE: CONCLUSIONS

The excursion into the empirical pricing literature undertaken above gives rise to a number of implications bearing upon theoretical analysis and empirical research alike.

From a conceptual point of view, it is interesting to note that *all* theoretical perspectives on pricing considered earlier find *some* support in the empirical evidence, albeit in varying degrees. For example, partial support for conventional price theory is found in the prevalence and importance attached to profit goals as well as the (albeit limited) use of marginal pricing. Similarly, the evidence relating to the external pricing environment is broadly consistent with industrial organization theory, which emphasizes the impact that the market environment has on price decision-making. Managerial theories find support in the evidence relating to non-profit goals (particularly output/volume objectives), while behavioural theories are supported by the prevalence of non-maximizing pricing objectives and the popularity of cost-plus pricing methods in practice. On the whole, it is fair to say that behavioural theories are most consistent with the findings of empirical research, a fact which is not surprising given the inductive nature of most behavioural models (i.e. average-cost and organizational theories).

While some degree of correspondence can be established between the various theoretical perspectives and the evidence on pricing behaviour generated by empirical studies, the latter show quite conclusively that pricing in the real world is *much* more complex than *any* theoretical perspective suggests. Firms operate within a multifaceted and variable pricing environment, have multidimensional objective functions and employ a variety of pricing methods. Their pricing objectives are often imperfectly formulated and rationalized, their pricing methods sometimes crude and their view of the pricing environment reflects decision-makers' perceptions as well as objective characteristics. Of particular significance is the fact that the typical firm usually faces a variety of potentially distinct environments for its various product markets and has a different set of pricing objectives and/or pricing methods for each; none of the established theoretical perspectives on pricing appears to explicitly recognize and incorporate this fact into its conceptual scheme. For purposes of theoretical analysis, this suggests that it would be closer to reality to conceive the firm as a collection of smaller entities, i.e. as comprising a *set of vectors* of pricing objectives, methods and environmental influences, as illustrated in Figure 3.8. In short, it appears from the empirical evidence that theorizing must become *richer*, taking into account intrafirm differences (in addition to interfirm variations) and placing emphasis on identifying the factors responsible for variations in pricing behaviour rather than on generating universalist explanations; indeed, as was pointed out more than two decades ago by Barback (1964), 'what is needed is not one universal

	Product market						
	1	2	3		i		n
Pricing objectives ($j = 1, \ldots, x$)	(O_{1j})	(O_{2j})	(O_{3j})		(O_{ij})		(O_{nj})
Pricing methods ($k = 1, \ldots, y$)	(M_{1k})	(M_{2k})	(M_{3k})		(M_{ik})		(M_{nk})
Pricing environment ($r = 1, \ldots, z$)	(E_{1r})	(E_{2r})	(E_{3r})		(E_{ir})		(E_{nr})

Figure 3.8 Proposed conceptualization of the firm for purposes of price analysis

generalization alone, but along with it a complementary series of hypotheses each appropriate for its purpose and for the type of situation and level of abstraction with which it deals' (p. 170).

From an empirical point of view, two major points emerge from the current state of research on pricing practices. First, bearing in mind the methodological limitations of previous efforts, it is clear that a lot can be done to improve research design and execution. Given the complexity of the subject area, great care must be exercised in the development of questionnaires/interview schedules and the measurement of the variables involved. The second issue concerns analysis. This needs to become much more rigorous and focus on an examination of associations/differences in addition to simple description. Without wishing to undermine the value of qualitative studies (which have produced valuable insights into pricing behaviour), it is nevertheless strange that in some 86 pricing studies (see Appendix 1) one cannot find a *single* correlation analysis of short- *vs* long-run pricing objectives, or an analysis of variance of factors bearing upon the choice of pricing method. A major priority in this context is the *systematic* examination of the impact of the environment on price determination and the linkages between different aspects of price decision-making; as was stated in the discussion of the empirical evidence, very little rigorous testing of this kind has been undertaken so far. Increased attention to methodological issues and increased sophistication in analysis strategies would go a long way towards providing a solid empirical basis from which existing theories could be tested and new ones developed.

NOTES

1–12. A listing of relevant studies is available upon request from the author.

REFERENCES

Abratt, R., and Pitt, L.F. (1985) Pricing practices in two industries. *Industrial Marketing Management*, **24**, 301–306.

Albach, H. (1959) *Wirtschaftlichkeitsrechnumg bei unsicheren Erwartungen*. Westdeutscher Verlag, Koeln and Opladen.

Alchian, A.A. (1950) Uncertainty, evolution and economic theory. *Journal of Political Economy*, **58**, 211–221.

Alchian, A.A. (1953) Comment: Biological analogies in the theory of management of the firm. *American Economic Review*, **43**, 600–603.

Allen, B.H., Tatham, R.L., and Lambert, D.R. (1976) Flexible pricing systems during high inflation. *Industrial Marketing Management*, **5**, 234–249.

Alpert, M.I. *Pricing Decisions*. Scott, Foresman, Glenview, Illinois.

Alt, R.M. (1949) The internal organization of the firm and price formation: An illustrative case. *Quarterly Journal of Economics*, **63**, 92–110.

Andrews, P.W.S. (1949a) A reconsideration of the theory of the individual business. *Oxford Economic Papers*, **1**, 54–89.

Andrews, P.W.S. (1949b) *Manufacturing Business*. Macmillan, London.

Atkin, B., and Skinner, R. (1975) *How British Industry Prices*. Industrial Market Research Ltd, London.

Backman, J. (1953) *Price Practices and Price Policies*. Ronald Press, New York.

Backman, J. (1965) Pricing. In Schwartz, G. (ed.) *Science in Marketing*. Wiley, New York.

Backman, J. (1968) The new framework for pricing. In Marting, E. (ed.) *Creative Pricing*. American Management Association, New York.

Bain, J.S. (1949) Price and production policies. In Ellis, H.S. (1949) *A Survey of Contemporary Economics*. Blackiston, Berkeley, California.

Bain, J.S. (1968) *Industrial Organization*, 2nd edn. Wiley, New York.

Baker, M.J. (1985) *Marketing — An Introductory Text*, 4th edn. Macmillan, London.

Baldwin, W.L. (1964) The motives of managers, environmental restraints, and the theory of managerial enterprise. *Quarterly Journal of Economics*, **78**, 238–256; reprinted in Needham, M., ed. (1970) *Readings in The Economics of Industrial Organization*. Holt Rinhart and Winston, New York, pp. 32–47.

Balkin, N. (1956) Pricing in the clothing industry. *Journal of Industrial Economics*, **5**, 1–16.

Banting, P.M., and Ross, R.E. (1973) The marketing mix: A Canadian perspective. *Journal of the Academy of Marketing Science*, **1**, 29–36.

Barback, R.H. (1964) *The Pricing of Manufactures*. Macmillan, London.

Bartholomew, J. (1987) The marginalist controversy. Honours Dissertation, Department of Business Studies, University of Edinburgh.

Baumol, W.J. (1958) On the theory of oligopoly. *Economica*, **25**, 187–198; reprinted in Archibald, G.C., ed. (1971) *The Theory of the Firm*. Penguin, Harmondsworth, Middlesex, pp. 253–269.

Baumol, W.J. (1959) *Business Behaviour, Value and Growth*. Macmillan, New York.

Baumol, W.J. (1962) On the theory of expansion of the firm. *American Economic Review*, **52**, 1078–1987; reprinted in Archibald, G.C., ed. (1971) *The Theory of the Firm*. Penguin, Harmondsworth, Middlesex, pp. 318–327.

Baumol, W.J. (1967) *Business Behaviour, Value and Growth*, revised edition. Harcourt Brace and World, New York.

Baumol, W.J. (1968) Sales maximization vs profit maximization: Are they consistent? *Western Economic Journal*, **6**, 242.

Baumol, W.J. (1977) *Economic Theory and Operations Analysis*, 4th edn., Prentice-Hall, Englewood Cliffs, NJ.

Baumol, W.J., and Stewart, M. (1971) On the behavioural theory of the firm. In Marris, R.L., and Wood, A. (eds) *The Corporate Economy*. Macmillan, London.

Berle, A.A., and Means, G.C. (1932) *The Modern Corporation and Private Property*. Macmillan, New York.

Bertrand, J. (1883) Theorie mathematique de la richesse sociale. *Journales Savants*, Paris. September, 499–508.

Bidlingmaier, J. (1964) *Unternehmerziele und Unternehmerstrategien*. Gabler, Wiesbaden.

Birnbaum, J.H. (1981) Pricing of products is still an art, often having little link to costs. *The Wall Street Journal*, November 25, p. 16.

Boston Consulting Group (1968) *Perspectives on Experience*. Boston Consulting Group, Boston, MA.

Boulding, K.E. (1942) The theory of the firm in the last ten years. *American Economic Review*, **32**, 791–802.

Boulding, K.E. (1950) *A Reconstruction of Economics*. Wiley, New York.

Boulding, K.E. (1952) Implications for general economics of more realistic theories of the firm. *American Economic Review*, **42**, Papers and Proceedings, 35–44.

Boulding, K.E. (1960) The present position of the theory of the firm. In Boulding, K.E., and Spivey, W.A. (eds) *Linear Programming and the Theory of the Firm*. Macmillan, New York.

Boulding, K.E. (1966) *Economic Analysis, Vol 1: Microeconomics*. Harper & Row, New York.

Bradburd, R.M. (1980) A model of the effect of conglomeration and risk aversion on pricing. *Journal of Industrial Economics*, **28**, 369–386.

Bradley, A. (1927) Financial control policies of General Motors Corporation and their relationship to cost accounting. *NACA Bulletin*, **8**, 412–433.

Brandt, K. (1953) Die Problemstellung in der gegenwaertingen Preistheorie. *Zeitschrift fuer die gesamte Staatswissenschaft*, **109** (2), 251–278.

Brovot, R. (1955) Betriebswirtschaftliche Grundlagen der Kapitalrentabilitaet und die Methoden ihrer Berechnung. PhD Dissertation, Universitaet Koeln, Koeln.

Brown, D. (1924a) Pricing policy in relation to financial control. *Management and Administration*, **7**, 195–198.

Brown, D. (1942b) Pricing policy in relation to financial control. *Management and Administration*, **7**, 283–286.

Brown, D. (1924c) Pricing policy in relation to financial control. *Management and Administration*, **7**, 417–422.

Brown, S.R. (1967) *Costs and Prices*. Law Book Company Ltd, Sydney, Australia.

Brown, W. and Jacques, E. (1964) *Product Analysis Pricing*. Heinemann, London.

Bruegelman, T.M., Haessly, G., Wolfangel, C.P., and Schiff, M. (1985) How variable costing is used in pricing decisions. *Management Accounting*, **67**, 58–65.

Buckner, H. (1967) *How British Industry Buys*. Industrial Market Research Ltd, London.

Burck, G. (1972) The myths and realities of corporate pricing. *Fortune*, April; reprinted in Vernon, I.R., and Lamb, C.W., eds (1976) *The Pricing Function*. Lexington Books, D.C. Heath & Co., Lexington, pp. 5–17.

Burnham, J. (1941) *The Managerial Revolution*. Day, New York.

Burns, L.S. (1959) Recent theories of the behaviour of business firms. *University of Washington Business Review*, October, 30–40.

Business Week (1963) Discounts that don't show. *Business Week*, March 2, p. 23.

Business Week (1974) Pricing strategy in an inflation economy. *Business Week*, 6 April, pp. 42–49.

Business Week (1977) Flexible pricing. *Business Week*, 12 December, pp. 78–88.

Cameron, S., and Shipley, D.D. (1985) A discretionary model of industrial buying. *Managerial and Decision Economics*, **6**, 102–111.

Campbell, P.A. (1988) An investigation into the pricing objectives of UK firms. MBA Dissertation, Department of Business Studies, University of Edinburgh.

Cannon, W.B. (1932) *The Wisdom of the Body*. Norton, New York.

Capon, N., Farley, J.U., and Hulbert, J. (1975) Pricing and forecasting in an oligopoly firm. *Journal of Management Studies*, **12**, 133–156.

Cassady, R. (1963) The role of economic models in microeconomic market studies. In Oxenfeldt, A.R. (ed.) *Models of Markets*. Columbia University Press, New York.

Chakravarti, D., Mitchell, A., and Staelin, R. (1979) Judgement based decision models: An experimental investigation of the decision calculus approach. *Management Science*, **25**, 251–263.

Chamberlain, N.W. (1955) *A General Theory of Economic Process*. Harper & Bros, New York.

Chamberlin, E.H. (1933) *Theory of Monopolistic Competition*. Harvard University Press, Cambridge, Massachusetts.

Chief Executive (1981) Finding the right price is no easy game to play. *Chief Executive*, September, pp. 16–18.

Chief Executive (1982) Alice-in-Wonderland pricing spells danger. *Chief Executive*, June, pp. 14–15, 19.

Churchill, W.L. (1932) *Pricing for Profit*. Macmillan, New York.

Clarke, R. (1985) *Industrial Economics*. Blackwell, Oxford.

Clelland, S. (1960) A short essay on a managerial theory of the firm. In Boulding, K.E., and Spivey, W.A. (eds) *Linear Programming and the Theoryy of the Firm*. Macmillan, New York.

Cocks, D.L., and Virts, J.R. (1974) Pricing behaviour of the ethical pharmaceutical industry. *Journal of Business*, **47**, 349–362.

Coe, B. (1983) Perceptions on the role of pricing in the 1980's among industrial marketers. *AMA Educators' Proceedings*. American Marketing Association, Chicago, Illinois.

Committee on Price Determination (1943) *Cost Behaviour and Price Policy*. National Bureau of Economic Research, New York.

Cook, A.C. and Jones, E.W. (1954) Full cost pricing in Western Australian manufacturing firms. Paper presented to Section G of 30th ANZAAS Congress, Canberra.

Cooper, R.G. (1979) The dimensions of new product failure. *Journal of Marketing*, **43**, 93–103.

Cooper, W.W. (1949) Theory of the firm: Some suggestions for revision. *American Economic Review*, **39**, 1204–1222.

Couch, D.D. (1958) Establishing pricing policies for different products and product lines. In *Competitive Pricing*. Report No. 17. American Management Association, New York.

Cournot, A.A. (1838) *Recherches sur les Principes Mathematiques de la Theorie des Richesses*. English translation by Bacon, N.T. (1897). Macmillan, London.

Cox, R. (1946) Non-price competition and the measurement of prices. *Journal of Marketing*, **10**, 370–383.

Cyert, R.M., and Hedrick, C.L. (1972) Theory of the firm: Past, present, and future. *Journal of Economic Literature*, **10**, 398–412.

Cyert, R.M., and March, J.G. (1963) *A Behavioral Theory of the Firm*. Prentice-Hall, Englewood Cliffs, NJ.

Cyert, R.M., Simon, H.A., and Trow, D.B. (1956) Observation of a business decision. *Journal of Business*, **29**, 237–248.

Dartnell Corporation (1957) *Pricing Policies*. Special Investigation Report No. 572. Dartnell Corporation, Chicago.

Davidson, J.H. (1976) Why most new consumer brands fail. *Harvard Business Review*, **54**, 117–122.

Davies, J., and Hughes, S. (1975) *Pricing in Practice*. Heinemann, London.

Day, G.S., and Montgomery, D.B. (1983) Diagnosing the experience curve. *Journal of Marketing*, **47**, 44–58.

Dean, J. (1947) Research approach to pricing. In *Planning the Price Structure*. Marketing Series No. 67. American Management Association, New York.

Dean, J. (1949) *Pricing from the Seller's Standpoint*. Columbia University Press, New York.

Dean, J. (1950) Problems of product line pricing. *Journal of Marketing*, **14**, 518–528.

Dean, J. (1951) *Managerial Economics*. Prentice-Hall, Englewood Cliffs, NJ.

Dean, J. (1961) The role of price in the American business system. In *Pricing: The Critical Decision*. Report No. 66. American Management Association, New York.

Dempsey, W.A. (1978) Vendor selection and the buying process. *Industrial Marketing Management*, **7**, 257–267.

Devine, P.J., Jones, R.M., Lee, N., and Tyson, W.J. (1974) *An Introduction to Industrial Economics*. Allen & Unwin, London.

Deyhle, A. (1967) *Gewinnmanagement: Gewinerzielung durch richtige Artikelstrategie, Verkaufspolitik und Kostensenkung mit Hilfe der Plankostenrehnung*. Verlag Moderner Industrie, Muenchen.

Dolan, R. (1980) The extent of suboptimality of myopic pricing rules. In Bagozzi, R.P. (ed.) *Marketing in the 1980's: Changes and Challenges*, American Marketing Association, Chicago.

Dolan, R., and Jeuland, A. (1981) Experience curves and dynamic demand models: Implications for optimal pricing strategies. *Journal of Marketing*, **45**, 52–62.

Dorward, N. (1987) *The Pricing Decision: Economic Theory and Business Practice*. Harper & Row, London.

Drucker, P.F. (1954) *The Practice of Management*. Harper, New York.

Earl, P.E. (1980) A behavioural view of economists' behaviour and the lack of success of behavioural economics. University of Stirling Discussion Papers in Economics, Finance and Investment, No. 84, August.

Earley, J. (1956) Marginal policies of excellently managed companies. *American Economic Review*, **46**, 44–70.

Edgeworth, F.Y. (1925) *The Pure Theory of Monopoly*. Macmillan, London.

Edwards, R.S. (1952) The pricing of manufactured products. *Economica*, **19**, 298–307.

Eiteman, W.J. (1960) *Price Determination in Oligopolistic and Monopolistic Situations*. Michigan Business Report No. 33. University of Michigan, Ann Arbor, Michigan.

Enke, S. (1951) On maximizing profits: A distinction between Chamberlin and Robinson. *American Economic Review*, **41**, 566–578.

Farley, J.U., Hulbert, J.M., and Weinstein, D. (1980) Price setting and volume planning by two European industrial companies: A study and comparison of decision processes. *Journal of Marketing*, **44**, 46–54.

Farmer, D.H. and Farrington, B. (1979) The buyer's influence on pricing decisions. *Journal of Purchasing and Materials Management*, Summer, 8–13.

Fellner, W. (1949) *Competition Among the Few: Oligopoly and Similar Market Structures*. Alfred A. Knopf, New York.

Fitzpatrick, A.A. (1964) *Pricing Methods of Industry*. Pruett Press, Boulder, Colorado.

Fleming Associates (1984) *1984 Key Pressure Points for Top Marketing Executives*. Fleming Associates, Sarasota, Florida.

Fleming Associates (1986) *1986 Key Pressure Points for Top Marketing Executives*. Fleming Associates, Sarasota, Florida.

Florence, S.P. (1961) *Ownership, Control and Success of Large Companies*. Sweet & Maxwell, London.

Flueck, J. (1961) Staff Paper No. 9 in *Price Statistics of the Federal Government*. Joint Economic Committee, US Government Printing Office, Washington, DC.

Fog, B. (1948) Price theory and reality. *Nordisk Tidsskrift for Teknisk Okonomi*, **12**, 89–94.

Fog, B. (1960) *Industrial Pricing Policies*. North Holland, Amsterdam.

Forbis, J.L., and Mehta, N.T. (1979) Economic value to the customer. McKinsey Staff Paper, February.

Foxall, G.R. (1972) A descriptive theory of pricing for marketing. *European Journal of Marketing*, **6** (3), 190–194.

Fremgen, J.M., and Liao, S.S. (1981) *The Allocation of Corporate Indirect Costs*. National Association of Accountants, New York.

Friday, F.A. (1955) Some thoughts on the pricing of television receivers. *Journal of Industrial Economics*, **3**, 111–121.

Gabor, A., and Granger, C.W.J. (1973) A systematic approach to effective pricing. In Rodger, L.W. (ed.) *Marketing Concepts and Strategies in the Next Decade*. Wiley, New York.

Galbraith, J.K. (1967) *The New Industrial State*. Hamish Hamilton, London.

Garda, R.A. (1984) Strategy vs tactics in industrial pricing. *The McKinsey Quarterly*, Winter, 49–64.

George, K.D., and Joll, C. (1981) *Industrial Organisation*. Allen & Unwin, London.

Gilbert, M. (1972) Introduction. In Gilbert, M. (ed.) *The Modern Business Enterprise*. Penguin, Harmondsworth, Middlesex.

Gordon, L.A., Cooper, R., Falk, H., and Miller, D. (1980) *The Pricing Decision*. Society of Management Accountants of Canada, Hamilton, Ontario and National Association of Accountants, New York.

Gordon, R.A. (1945) *Business Leadership in the Large Corporation*. Brookings Institution, Washington, DC.

Gordon, R.A. (1948) Short-period price determination in theory and practice. *American Economic Review*, **38**, 265–268.

Govindarajan, V., and Anthony, R. M. (1983) The use of cost data in pricing decisions. *Management Accounting*, **65**, 30–36.

Guiltinan, J.P. (1987) The price bundling of services: A normative framework. *Journal of Marketing*, **51**, 74–85.

Guiltinan, J.P., and Paul, G.W. (1985) *Marketing Management: Strategies and Programs*, 2nd edn. McGraw-Hill, New York.

Gutenberg, E. (1958) *Einfuehrung in die Betriebswirtschaftslehre*. Gabler, Wiesbaden.

Gutenberg, E. (1984) *Grundlagen der Betriebswirtschaftslehre*, 17th edn. Springer Verlag, Berlin.

Haas, R., and Wotruba, T. (1976) Marketing strategy in a make-or-buy situation. *Industrial Marketing Management*, **5**, 65–76.

Hague, D.C. (1949) Economic theory and business behaviour. *Review of Economic Studies*, **16** (3), 144–157.

Hague, D.C. (1971) *Pricing in Business*. Allen & Unwin, London.

Haldi, J. (1958) Pricing behaviour: Economic theory and business practice. *Current Economic Comment*, **20**, 55–66.

Hall, R.L., and Hitch, C.J. (1939) Price theory and business behaviour. *Oxford Economic Papers*, No. 2, May, 12–45.

Hamouda, O.F., and Smithin, J.N. (1988) Some remarks on uncertainty and economic analysis. *Economic Journal*, **98**, 159–164.

Hankinson, A. (1985) Pricing decisions in small engineering firms. *Management Accounting (UK)*, **63**, 36–37.

Hansen, H.L. and Nilland, P. (1952) Esso Standard: A case in pricing. *Harvard Business Review*, **30** (3), 114–132.

Hapgood, R. (1965) A new approach to profitable pricing. *Financial Executive*, **33**, 14–21.

Harper, D. (1966) *Price Policy and Procedure*. Harcourt Brace & World, New York.

Harris, C.E. (1978) Stability or change in marketing methods? *Business Horizons*, **21**, 32–40.

Harrison, R., and Wilkes, F.M. (1973) A note on Jaguar's pricing policy. *European Journal of Marketing*, **7**, 242–246.

Harrod, R.F. (1934) Doctrines of imperfect competition. *Quarterly Journal of Economics*, **48**, 442–470.

Hart, H., and Prusmann, D.F. (1963) A Report of A Survey of Management Accounting Techniques in the S.E. Hants Coastal Region. Department of Commerce and Accountancy, University of Southampton, December.

Hatten, M.L. (1982) Don't get caught with your prices down: Pricing in inflationary times. *Business Horizons*, **25**, 23–28.

Hatzold, O., and Helmschrott, H. (1961) *Analyse unternehmerischer Verhaltensweisen*. Schriftenreihe des Ifo-Instituts fuer Wirtschaftsforschung, No. 44, Berlin.

Hawkins, C.J. (1973) *The Theory of the Firm*. Macmillan, London.

Hay, D.A., and Morris, D.J. (1979) *Industrial Economics: Theory and Evidence*. Oxford University Press, Oxford.

Haynes, W.W. (1962) *Pricing Decisions in Small Business*. University of Kentucky Press, Lexington, Kentucky.

Haynes, W.W. (1964) Pricing practices in small firms. *Southern Economic Journal*, **30**, 315–324.

Heflebower, R.B. (1952) Comment. In Haley, B.F. (ed.) *A Survey of Contemporary Economics*, Vol. II. Irwin, Homewood, Illinois.

Heflebower, R.B. (1954) Towards a theory of industrial markets and prices. *American Economic Press*, **44**, 121–140.

Heflebower, R.B. (1955) Full costs, cost changes, and prices. In Stigler, G.J. (ed.) *Business Concentration and Price Policy*. Princeton University Press, Princeton, NJ.

Heidensohn, K., and Robinson, N. (1974) *Business Behaviour*. Philip Allan, Oxford.

Heinen, E. (1962) Die Zielfunktion der Unternehmung. In Koch, H. (ed.) *Zur Theorie der Unternehmung*. Gabler, Wiesbaden.

Heinen, E. (1966) *Das Zielsystem der Unternehmung: Grundlagen betriebswirtschafticher Entscheidungen*. Gabler, Wiesbaden.

Henderson, B.D. (1980) *The Experience Curve Revisited*. Boston Consulting Group, Boston, Massachussetts.

Hewitt, C.M. (1961) Pricing — an area of increasing importance. *Business Horizons*, **4**, 108–111.

Hicks, J.R. (1935) Annual survey of economic theory: The theory of monopoly. *Econometrica*, **3**, 1–20.

Hicks, J.R. (1939) *Value and Capital*. Oxford University Press, Oxford.

Higgins, B. (1939) Elements of indeterminacy in the theory of non-perfect competition. *American Economic Review*, **29**, 468–479.

Hirschleifer, J. (1980) *Price Theory and Applications*, 2nd edn. Prentice-Hall, Englewood Cliffs, NJ.

Hooley, G.J., West, C.J., and Lynch, J.E. (1984) *Marketing in the UK: A Survey of Current Practice and Performance*. Institute of Marketing, Maidenhead, Berkshire.

Horowitz, I. (1970) *Decision Making and the Theory of the Firm*. Holt Rinehart & Winston, New York.

Hotelling, H. (1929) Stability in competition. *The Economic Journal*, **39**, 41–57.

Howe, M. (1962) Marginal analysis in accounting. *Yorkshire Bulletin of Economics and Social Research*, **14**, 81–89.

Howe, W.S. (1978) *Industrial Economics — An Applied Approach*. Macmillan, London.

Hutt, M.D., and Speh, T.W. (1985) *Industrial Marketing Management*. Holt-Saunders, New York.

Jain, S.C. and Laric, M.V. (1979) A framework for strategic industrial pricing. *Industrial Marketing Management*, **8**, 75–81.

Jobber, D., and Hooley, G.J. (1987) Pricing behaviour in UK manufacturing and services industries. *Managerial and Decision Economics*, **8**, 167–171.

Joskow, P.L. (1975) Firm decision-making processes and oligopoly theory. *American Economic Review*, **65**, 270–279.

Kafoglis, M.Z. (1969) Output of the restrained firm. *American Economic Review*, **59**, 583–589.

Kahn, R.F. (1952) Oxford studies in the price mechanism. *Economic Journal*, **62**, 119–130.

Kaldor, N. (1934) The equilibrium of the firm. *Economic Journal*, **44**, 60–76.

Kaldor, N. (1935) Market imperfection and excess capacity. *Economica*, **2**, 33–50.

Kaplan, A.D.H., Dirlam, J.B., and Lanzillotti, R.F. (1958) *Pricing in Big Business.* The Brookings Institution, Washington, DC.

Karger, T., and Thompson, G.C. (1957) Pricing policies and practices. *Business Record,* National Industrial Conference Board, September, 434–442.

Kay, N.M., and Diamantopoulos, A. (1987) Uncertainty and synergy: Towards a formal model of corporate strategy. *Managerial and Decision Economics,* **8**, 121–130.

Kaysen, C., and Turner, D.F. (1959) *Antitrust Policy: An Economic and Legal Analysis.* Harvard University Press, Cambridge, Mass.

Kellogg, L.S. (1958) The administration of prices and price policy: A farm equipment manufacturer. In *Competitive Pricing.* Report No. 17. American Management Association, New York.

Kelly, P.S., and Coaker, J.W. (1976) The importance of price as a choice criterion for industrial purchasing decisions. *Industrial Marketing Management,* **5**, 218–293.

Knauth, O. (1956) *Business Practices, Trade Position and Competition.* Columbia University Press, New York.

Kniffin, F.W. (1974) Stagflation pricing — seven ways you might improve your decisions. *Marketing News,* 15 November, p. 10.

Knight, F.H. (1934) *Encyclopaedia of the Social Sciences,* Vol. 12. Macmillan, London.

Knox, R.L. (1966) Competitive oligopolistic pricing. *Journal of Marketing,* **30**, 47–51.

Koch, J.V. (1980) *Industrial Organization and Prices,* 2nd edn. Prentice-Hall, Englewood Cliffs, NJ.

Kotler, P. (1988) *Marketing Management: Analysis, Planning and Control,* 6th edn. Prentice-Hall, Englewood Cliffs, NJ.

Koutsoyiannis, A. (1979) *Modern Microeconomics,* 2nd edn. Macmillan, London.

Kraushar, P.M. (1970) *New Products and Diversification.* Business Books, London.

Krelle, W. (1961) *Preisthorie.* Mohr Siebeck Verlag, Tuebingen.

Krelle, W. (1976) *Preisthorie,* 2nd edn. Mohr Siebeck Verlag and Polygraphischer Verlag, Tuebingen and Zuerich.

Krupp, S.R. (1963) Theoretical explanation and the nature of the firm. *Western Economic Journal,* **1**, 191–204.

Kuhlo, K.C. (1955) Eine Analyse des Vollkostenprinzips. *Weltwirtschaftliches Archiv,* **75** (2), 137–195.

Ladd, D.R. (1965) *The Role of Costs in Pricing Decisions.* Society of Management Accountants of Canada, Hamilton, Ontario.

Ladd, G.W. (1969) Utility maximisation sufficient for competitive survival. *Journal of Political Economy,* **77**, 478–483.

Lambin, J.J. (1976) *Advertising Competition and Market Conduct in Oligopoly Over Time.* North Holland, Amsterdam.

Lambin, J.J., Naert, P.A. and Bultez, A. (1975) Optimal marketing behaviour in oligopoly. *European Economic Review,* **6**, 105–128.

Langholm, O. (1969) *Full Cost and Optimal Price.* Scandinavian University Press, Oslo.

Lanzillotti, R.F. (1958) Pricing objectives in large companies. *American Economic Review,* **48**, 921–940.

Lanzillotti, R.F., and Parrish, G.O. (1964) *Pricing, Production and Marketing Policies of Small Manufacturers.* Washington State University Press, Pullman.

Laric, M.V. (1980) Pricing strategies in industrial markets. *European Journal of Marketing*, **14** (5/6), 303–321.

Larner, R.J. (1970) *Management Control and the Large Corporation*. Dunellen, Cambridge, Massachussetts.

Lazer, W. (1957) Price determination in the Western Canadian garment industry. *Journal of Industrial Economics*, **5**, 124–136.

Learned, E.P. (1948) Pricing of gasoline: A case study. *Harvard Business Review*, **26**, 723–756.

Leland, H.E. (1972) The dynamics of a revenue maximising firm. *International Economic Review*, **13**, 376–385.

Lewellen, W.G. (1969) Management and ownership in the large firm. *Journal of Finance*, **24**, 299–322.

Lewellen, W.G. (1971) *The Ownership Income of Management*. Columbia University Press, New York.

Lewellen, W.G. and Huntsman, B. (1970) Managerial pay and corporate performance. *American Economic Review*, **60**, 710–720.

Lieberman, S. (1969) Has the marginalist–antimarginalist controversy regarding the theory of the firm been settled? *Schweizerische Zeitschrift fuer Volkswirtschaft*, **105** (4), 535–549.

Likierman, A. (1981) Pricing policy in the texturising industry 1958–71. *Journal of Industrial Economics*, **30**, 25.

Lintner, J. (1970) The impact of uncertainty on the 'traditional' theory of the firm: Price setting and tax shifting. In Markham, J.W., and Papanek, G.F. (eds) *Industrial Organization and Economic Development — in Honor of E.S. Mason*. Houghton Mifflin, Boston.

Little, J.D.C. (1970) Models and managers: The concept of a decision calculus. *Management Science*, **16**, 466–485.

Loasby, B.J. (1985) Herbert Simon's human rationality. University of Stirling Discussion Papers in Economics, Finance and Investment, No. 121, August.

Loasby, B.J. (1987) Baumol's 'managerial' theory of the firm. University of Stirling Discussion Papers in Economics, Finance and Investment, No. 131, March.

Long, B.G., and Varble, D.L. (1978) Purchasing's use of flexible price contracts. *Journal of Purchasing and Materials Management*, Autumn, 2–6.

Luce, R.D., and Raiffa, H. (1957) *Games and Decisions*. Wiley, New York.

Lund, D., Monroe, K., and Choudhury, P.K. (1982) *Pricing Policies and Strategies: An Annotated Bibliography*. American Marketing Association, Chicago.

Lydall, H.F. (1958) Aspects of competition in manufacturing industry. *Bulletin of the Oxford University Institute of Statistics*, **20**, 319–337.

Lynn, R.A. (1968) Unit volume as a goal for pricing. *Journal of Marketing*, **32**, 34–39.

Machlup, F. (1946) Marginal analysis and empirical research. *American Economic Review*, **36**, 519–554.

Machlup, F. (1952) *Economics of Sellers Competition*. John Hopkins Press, Baltimore.

Machlup, F. (1967) Theories of the firm: Marginalist, behavioural, managerial. *American Economic Review*, **57**, 1–33; reprinted in Needham, D. ed. (1970) *Readings in the Economics of Industrial Organization*. Holt, Rinehart and Winston, New York, pp. 3–31.

Mahajan, V., and Peterson, R.A. (1985) *Models for Innovation Diffusion*. Sage, London and Beverly Hills.

Margolis, J. (1958) The analysis of the firm: Rationalism, conventionalism, and behaviourism. *Journal of Business*, **31**, 187–197.

Marris, R.L. (1963) A model of the managerial enterprise. *Quarterly Journal of Economics*, 185–209; reprinted in Gilbert, M. ed. (1972) *The Modern Business Enterprise*. Penguin, Harmondsworth, Middlesex, pp. 211–237.

Marris, R.L. (1964) *The Economic Theory of Managerial Capitalism*. Macmillan, London.

Marris, R.L. (1971) The modern corporation and economic theory. In Marris, R.L. and Wood, A. (eds) *The Corporate Economy*. Macmillan, London.

Marshall, A. (1890) *Principles of Economics*. Macmillan, New York.

Marshall, A. (1979) *More Profitable Pricing*. McGraw-Hill, London.

Mason, E.S. (1939) Price and production policies of large-scale enterprise. *American Economic Review*, **29**, 61–74.

Mason, E.S. (1940) Price policies and full employment. In Friedrich, C.J., and Mason, E.S. (eds) *Public Policy*. Harvard University Press, Cambridge, Massachussetts.

Mason, E.S (1949) The current state of the monopoly problem in the United States. *Harvard Law Review*, **62**, 1265–1285.

Masson, R. (1971) Executive motivation, earnings and consequent equity performance. *Journal of Political Economy*, **79**, 1278–1292.

Maxcy, G. (1968) Profit maximisation for students and management. *Yorkshire Bulletin of Economic and Social Research*, **20**, 85–97.

McAllister, H.E. (1961) Staff Paper No. 8 in *Price Statistics of the Federal Government*. Joint Economic Committee, US Government Printing Office, Washington, DC.

McGoldrick, P.J., and Douglas, R.A. (1983) Factors influencing the choice of a supplier by grocery distributors. *European Journal of Marketing*, **17** (5), 13–27.

McGuire, J.W. (1964) *Theories of Business Behaviour*. Prentice-Hall, Englewood Cliffs, NJ.

McIntyre, S.H., and Currim, I.S. (1982) Evaluating judgement-based decision models: Multiple measures, comparisons and findings. In Zoltners, A.A. (ed.) *TIMS Studies in the Management Sciences*. Special Issue on Marketing Models. North-Holland, Amsterdam, pp. 185–207.

McKie, J.W. (1970) Market structure and function: Performance versus behaviour. In Markham, J.W., and Papanek, G.F. (eds) *Industrial Organization and Economic Development — in Honor of E.S. Mason*. Houghton Mifflin, Boston.

Miller, R.L. (1978) *Intermediate Microeconomics*. McGraw-Hill, New York.

Milliband, R. (1969) *The State in Capitalist Society*. Weidenfield & Nicolson, London.

Monroe, K.B. (1971) The information content of prices: A preliminary model for estimating buyer response. *Management Science*, **17**, 519–532.

Monroe, K.B. (1977) Objective and subjective contextual influences on price perception. In Woodside, A.G., Sheth, J.N., and Bennett, P.D. (eds) *Consumer and Industrial Buying Behaviour*. North-Holland, New York.

Monroe, K.B. (1979) *Pricing: Making Profitable Decisions*. McGraw-Hill, New York.

Monroe, K.B., and Zoltners, A.A. (1979) Pricing the product line during periods of scarcity. *Journal of Marketing*, **43**, 49–53.

Morris, M.H., and Joyce, M.L. (1988) How marketers evaluate price sensitivity. *Industrial Marketing Management*, **17**, 169–176.

Morton, J., and Rys, M.E. (1987) Price elasticity prediction: New research tool for the competitive '80s. *Marketing News*, January 2, p. 12.

Moskal, B.S. (1978) Pricing: New forces prompt new philosophies. *Industry Week*, 11 December, pp. 48–49, 52, 54, 56.

Nagle, T. (1983) Pricing as creative marketing. *Business Horizons*, **26**, 14–20.

Nagle, T. (1987) *The Strategy and Tactics of Pricing*. Prentice-Hall, Englewood Cliffs, NJ.

National Association of Cost Accountants (1953a) Direct costing. NACA Research Series No. 23. *NACA Bulletin*, **34**, 1079–1128.

National Association of Cost Accountants (1953b) Product costs for pricing purposes. NACA Research Series No. 24. *NACA Bulletin*, **34**, 1671–1729.

Needham, D. (1978) *The Economics of Industrial Structure Conduct and Performance*. Holt Rinehart & Winston, London, Sydney and Toronto.

Nelson, S., and Keim, W.G. (1941) *Price Behaviour and Business Policy*. TNEC Monograph No. 1, Washington, DC.

Ng, Y.K. (1969) A note of profit maximization. *Australian Economic Papers*, June, 106–110.

Ng, Y.K. (1974) Utility and profit maximization by an owner manager: Toward a general analysis. *Journal of Industrial Economics*, **23**, 97–108.

Nichols, T. (1969) *Ownership, Control and Ideology*. Allen & Unwin, London.

Niehans, J. (1948) Zur Preisbildung bei ungewissen Erwartungen. *Schweizerische Zeitschrift fuer Volkswirtschaft und Statistik*, **84**, 433–456.

Nimer, D.A. (1971) There's more to pricing than most companies think. *Innovation*, August; reprinted in Vernon, I.R. and Lamb, C.W. eds (1976) *The Pricing Function*. Lexington Books, D.C. Heath & Co, Lexington, pp. 19–33.

Nordquist, G.L. (1965) The breakup of the maximization principle. *Quarterly Review of Economics and Business*, **3**, 33–46; reprinted in Breit, W., and Hochman, H., eds (1968) *Readings in Microeconomics*. Holt Rinehart and Winston, Hinsdale, Illinois, pp. 287–295.

Nourse, E.G. (1944) *Price Making in a Democracy*. Brookings Institution, Washington, DC.

Nourse, E.G., and Drury, H.B. (1938) *Industrial Price Policies and Economic Progress*. Brookings Institution, Washington, DC.

Nowotny, E., and Walther, H. (1978) The kinked demand curve — some empirical observations. *Kyklos*, **31**, 53–67.

Olsen, D.E. (1973) Utility and profit maximization by an owner-manager. *Southern Economic Journal*, **39**, 389–395.

Ott, A.E. (1962) Preistheorie. *Jahrbuch fuer Sozialwissenschaft*, **13**, 1–60.

Oxenfeldt, A.R. (1951) *Industrial Pricing and Marketing Practices*. Prentice-Hall, New York.

Oxenfeldt, A.R. (1961) *Pricing for Marketing Executives*. Wadsworth, Belmont, California.

Oxenfeldt, A.R. (1966) Product line pricing. *Harvard Business Review*, **44**, 137–144.

Oxenfeldt, A.R. (1968) The role of price and pricing reconsidered. In Marting, E. (ed.) *Creative Pricing*. American Management Association, New York.

Oxenfeldt, A.R. (1973) A decision making structure for price decisions. *Journal of Marketing*, **37**, 48–53.

Oxenfeldt, A.R.; Miller, D., Shukman, A., and Winick, C. (1965) *Insights into Pricing from Operations Research and Behavioural Science*. Wadsworth, Belmont, California.

Pack, L. (1962) Maximierung der Rentabilitaet als preispolitisches Ziel. In Koch, H. (ed.) *Zur Theorie der Unternehmung*. Gabler, Wiesbaden.

Palda, K.S. (1969) *Economic Analysis for Marketing Decisions*. Prentice-Hall, Englewood Cliffs, NJ.

Palda, K.S. (1971) *Pricing Decisions and Marketing Policy*. Prentice-Hall, Englewood Cliffs, NJ.

Papandreou, A.G. (1952) Some basic problems in the theory of the firm. In Haley, B.F. (ed.) *A Survey of Contemporary Economics*, Vol. II. Irwin, Homewood, Illinois.

Pass, C. (1971) Pricing policies and market strategy: An empirical note. *European Journal of Marketing*, **5** (3), 94–98.

Patton, W.E., and Puto, C. (1979) Tactical aspects of variable price strategy in the pricing of new automobiles at the retail level. *Proceedings Southern Marketing Association*, 351–354.

Pearce, I.F. (1956) A study in price policy. *Economica*, **23**, 114–127.

Pearce, I.F., and Amey, L.R. (1956/57) Price policy with a branded product. *Review of Economic Studies*, **24** (1), 49–60.

Penrose, E.T. (1952) Biological analogies in the theory of the firm. *American Economic Review*, **42**, 804–819.

PEP Report (1965) The determination of prices. In *Thrusters and Sleepers*. Allen & Unwin, London.

Petrone, D.V. (1961) Price policy in selling through distributors, wholesalers, and jobbers. In *Pricing: The Critical Decision*. AMA Report No. 66. American Management Association, New York.

Phillips, A. (1967) An attempt to synthesize some theories of the firm. In Phillips, A., and Williamson, O.E. (eds) *Prices: Issues in Theory, Practice and Public Policy*. University of Pennsylvania Press, Philadelphia.

Phillips, A. (1970) Structure, conduct and performance — and performance, conduct, and structure? In Markham, J.W., and Papanek, G.F. (eds) *Industrial Organization and Economic Development — in Honor of E.S. Mason*. Houghton Mifflin, Boston.

Pickering, J.F. (1974) *Industrial Structure and Market Conduct*. Martin Robertson, Oxford.

Plinke, W. (1985) Cost-based pricing: Behavioural aspects of price decisions for capital goods. *Journal of Business Research*, **13**, 447–460.

Plunkett, J. (1964) The strategy of price leadership. *Sales Management*, June 5, pp. 25–29, 66, 67.

Preiser, E. (1934) *Gestalt und Gestaltung der Wirtschaft*. Mohr Siebeck Verlag, Tuebingen.

Raia, A.P. (1965) Goal-setting and self-control. *Journal of Management Studies*, **2**, 34–53.

Ranlett, J.G., and Curry, R.L. (1968) Economic principles: The monopoly, oligopoly and competition models. *Antitrust Law and Economics Review*, Spring, 107–145.

Rao, V.R. (1984) Pricing research in marketing: The state of the art. *Journal of Business*, **57**, 39–60.

Rao, A.G., and Shakun, M.F. (1972) A quasi-game theoretic approach to pricing. *Management Science*, **18** (5), 110–123.

Reder, M. (1947) A reconsideration of marginal productivity theory. *Journal of Political Economy*, **55**, 450–458.

Reekie, W.D. (1981) Innovation and pricing in the Dutch drug industry. *Managerial and Decision Economics*, **2** (1), 49–56.

Reekie, W.D., and Crook, J.N. (1987) *Managerial Economics*, 3rd edn. Philip Allan, Oxford.

Reibstein, D.J., and Gatignon, H. (1984) Optimal product line pricing: The influence of elasticities and cross-elasticities. *Journal of Marketing Research*, **21**, 259–267.

Ricardo, D. (1817) *Principles of Political Economy and Taxation*, edited by Sraffa, P. (1953) Cambridge University Press, Cambridge.

Richardson, G.B., and Leyland, N.H. (1964) The growth of firms. *Oxford Economic Papers*, **16**, 9–23.

Robicheaux, R.A. (1975) How important is pricing in competitive strategy? In Nash, H.W., and Robin, D.P. (eds) *Proceedings Southern Marketing Association*, January.

Robinson, J. (1933) *The Economics of Imperfect Competition*. Macmillan, London.

Robinson, B., and Lakhani, C.G. (1975) Dynamic price models for new product planning. *Management Science*, **21**, 1113–1122.

Rosendale, P.B. (1973) The short-run pricing policies of some British engineering exporters. *NIER*, No. 65, 44–51.

Rothschild, K.W. (1947) Price theory and oligopoly. *Economic Journal*, **57**, 229–320.

Sabel, H. (1973) Zur Preispolitik bei neuen Produkten. In Koch, H. (ed.) *Zur Theorie des Absatzes*. Gabler, Wiesbaden.

Said, H.A. (1981) The relevance of price theory to pricing practice: An investigation of pricing policies and practices in UK industry. PhD Dissertation, Department of Marketing, University of Strathclyde, Glasgow.

Samiee, S. (1987) Pricing in marketing strategies of US and foreign-based companies. *Journal of Business Research*, **15**, 17–30.

Samuelson, P.A. (1976) *Economics*, 10th edn. McGraw-Hill, New York.

Savage, L.J. (1951) The theory of statistical decision. *Journal of the American Statistical Association*, **46**, 55–67.

Sawyer, M.C. (1979) *Theories of the Firm*. Weidenfield & Nicolson, London.

Sawyer, M.C. (1981) *The Economics of Industries and Firms*. Croom Helm, London.

Saxton, C.C. (1942) *The Economics of Price Determination*. Oxford University Press, London.

Scapens, R.W., Cameil, M.Y., and Cooper, D.J. (1983) Accounting information for pricing decisions: An empirical study. In Cooper, D., Scapens, R.W., and Arnold, J. (eds) *Management Accounting Research and Practice*. Institute of Cost and Management Accountants, London.

Schackle, G.L.S. (1955) Businessmen on business decisions. *The Scottish Journal of Political Economy*, **2**, 32–46.

Scherer, F.M. (1970) *Industrial Pricing*. Rand McNally, Chicago.

Scherer, F.M. (1980) *Industrial Market Structure and Economic Performance*. Rand McNally, Chicago.

Scitovsky, T. (1943) A note on profit maximisation and its implications. *Review of Economic Studies*, **11**, 57–60.

Scotese, P.G. (1961) Return on investment as a pricing factor. In *Pricing: The Critical Decision*. Report No. 66. American Management Association, New York.

Sewall, M.A. (1976) A decision calculus model for contract bidding. *Journal of Marketing*, **39**, 92–98.

Shipley, D.D. (1981) Pricing objectives in British manufacturing industry. *Journal of Industrial Economics*, **29**, 429–443.

Shipley, D.D. (1983) Pricing flexibility in British manufacturing industry. *Managerial and Decision Economics*, **4** (4), 224–233.

Shipley, D.D. (1984a) Determinants of adjustment in price and non-price marketing intensities. *Mid-South Business Journal*, **3** (3), 3–9.

Shipley, D.D. (1984b) Followership of adjustments in price and non-price marketing intensities. *Review of Regional Economics and Business*, April, 7–15.

Shipley, D.D. (1985) Resellers' supplier selection criteria for different consumer products. *European Journal of Marketing*, **19** (7), 26–36.

Shipley, D.D. (1986) Dimension of flexible price management. *Quarterly Review of Marketing*, **11**, 1–7.

Shubik, M. (1959) *Strategy and Market Structure*. Wiley, New York.

Shubik, M. (1970) A curmudgeon's guide to microeconomics. *Journal of Economic Literature*, **8**, 405–434.

Silberston, A. (1970) Surveys of applied economics: price behaviour of firms. *Economic Journal*, **80**, 511–582.

Simon, H.A. (1955) A behavioural model of rational choice. *Quarterly Journal of Economics*, **69**, 99–118.

Simon, H.A. (1956) Rational choice and the structure of the environment. *Psychological Review*, **63**, 129–138.

Simon, H.A. (1957a) *Models of Man*. Wiley, New York.

Simon, H.A. (1957b) *Administrative Behaviour* (revised edition). Macmillan, New York.

Simon, H.A. (1958) The role of expectations in an adaptive or behaviouristic model. In Bowman, M.J. (ed.) *Expectations, Uncertainty and Business Behaviour*. Wiley, New York.

Simon, H.A. (1959) Theories of decision-making in economics and behavioural science. *American Economic Review*, **49**, 253–283.

Simon, H.A. (1962) New developments in the theory of the firm. *American Economic Review*, **52**, 1–15.

Simon, H. (1977) Preispolitik bei erwarteten Konkurrenzeintritt: ein dynamisches Oligopolmodell. *Zeitschrift fuer Betriebswirtschaft*, **47**, 745–766.

Simon, H. (1980) *Dynamisches Produktlinienmarketing*. Habilitationsschrift, Universitaet Bonn.

Simon, H. (1982) *Preismanagement*. Gabler, Wiesbaden.

Simons, L. (1967) Product analysis pricing. In Taylor, B. and Wills, G. (eds) (1969) *Pricing Strategy*. Staples Press, London.

Sizer, J. (1966) The accountant's contribution to the pricing decision. *Journal of Management Studies*, **3**, 129–149.

Skinner, R. (1970) The determination of selling prices. *Journal of Industrial Economics*, **18**, 201–217.

Smith, A. (1776) *An Inquiry into the Nature and Causes of the Wealth of Nations*, edited by E. Conman (1961). Methuen, London.

Sonkondi, H. (1969) *Business and Prices*. Routledge & Kegan Paul, London.

Sraffa, P. (1926) The laws of returns under competition conditions. *Economic Journal*, **31**, 535–550.

Staudt, T.A., and Taylor, D.A. (1965) *A Managerial Introduction to Marketing*. Prentice-Hall, Englewood Cliffs, NJ.

Stephenson, P.R., Cron, W.L., and Frazier, G.L. (1979) Delegating pricing authority to the sales force: The effects on sales and profits performance. *Journal of Marketing*, **43**, 21–29.

Stigler, G.J. (1962) Administered prices and oligopolistic inflation. *Journal of Business*, **35**, 1–13.

Stigler, G.J., and Kindahl, J.K. (1970) *The Behaviour of Industrial Prices*. National Bureau for Economic Research, Columbia University Press, New York.

Sturmey, S.G. (1964) Cost curves and pricing in aircraft production. *Economic Journal*, **74**, 954–982.

Sultan, R. (1974) *Pricing in the Electrical Oligopoly*. Harvard University Press, Cambridge, Massachussetts.

Tatham, R.L., and Allen, B. (1976) Industrial pricing systems and the changing roles of buyers and sellers. In Vernon, I.R., and Lamb, G.W. (eds) *The Pricing Function*. Lexington Books, D.C. Heath, Lexington.

Tellis, G.J. (1986) Beyond the many faces of price: An integration of pricing strategies. *Journal of Marketing*, **50**, 146–160.

Temporary National Economic Committee (1940) *Industrial Wage Rates, Labor Costs and Price Policies*, Parts I, II. TNEC Monograph No. 5, Washington, DC.

Thompson, G.C. (1947) How industry prices its products. *Business Record*, National Industrial Conference Board, NY, June, pp. 180–182.

Thompson, G.C., and MacDonald, M.B. (1964) Pricing new products. *Conference Board Record*, January, pp. 7–14.

Till, I. (1937) The fiction of the quoted price. *Law and Contemporary Problems*. Duke University School of Law, June, pp. 363–374.

Triffin, R. (1940) *Monopolistic Competition and General Equilibrium Theory*. Harvard University Press, Cambridge, Massachussetts.

Tull, D.S., Kohler, R. and Silver, M.S. (1986) Nachfrageerwartungen und Preisverhalten deutscher Unternehmen: Eine Empirische Studie. *Marketing*, **7**, 225–232.

Udell, J. (1964) How important is pricing in competitive strategy. *Journal of Marketing*, **28**, 45–78.

Udell, J.G. (1968) The perceived importance of the elements of strategy. *Journal of Marketing*, **32**, 34–40.

Udell, J. (1972) *Successful Marketing Strategies in American Industries*. Mimir Publishers, Madison, Wisconsin.

Udell, J.G. (1973) The pricing strategies of United States industry. In Greer, T.C. (ed.) *Increasing Marketing Productivity and Conceptual and Methodological Foundations of Marketing*. Combined Proceedings, American Marketing Association, Chicago.

Vanderblue, H. (1939) Pricing policies in the automobile industry. *Harvard Business Review*, **17**, 385–401.

Von Mering, O. (1954) Marginal Preistheorie und tatsaechliche Preisbildung. *Zeitschrift fuer die gesamte Staatswissenschaft*, **110** (1), 80–87.

Von Neumann, J., and Morgernstern. O. (1944) *Theory of Games and Economic Behaviour*. Princeton University Press, Princeton, NJ.

Vormbaum, H. (1959) Die Zielsetzung der beschaeftigungsbezogenen Absatzpolitik erwerbwirtschaftlich orientierter Bertriebe. *Zeitschrift fuer handelswissenschaftliche Forschung*, **11**, 624–632.

Wagner, W.B. (1981) Changing industrial buyer-seller pricing concerns. *Industrial Marketing Management*, **19**, 109–117.

Wald, A. (1945) Statistical decision functions which minimise the maximum risk. *Annals of Mathematics*, **46**, 265–270.

Walker, A.W. (1967) How to price industrial products. *Harvard Business Review*, **45**, 38–45.

Wasson, C.R. (1974) *Dynamic Competitive Strategy and Product Life Cycles*. Challenge Books, St Charles, Illinois.

Waterson, M. (1984) *Economic Theory of the Industry*. Cambridge University Press, Cambridge.

Watson, I.R. (1978) *Pricing and Scale in Australian Industry*. AIDA Research Centre, Melbourne.

Wentz, T. (1966) Realism in pricing analyses. *Journal of Marketing*, **30**, 19–26.

Weston, J.F. (1970) Pricing behaviour of large firms. *Western Economic Journal*, **10**, 1–18.

White, C.M. (1960) Multiple goals in the theory of the firm. In Boulding, K.E., and Spivey, W.A. (eds) *Linear Programming and the Theory of the Firm*. Macmillan, New York.

Wicksell, K. (1934) *Lectures on Political Economy*, Vol. 1. Macmillan, New York.

Wied-Nebbeling, S. (1975) *Industrielle Preissetzung*. Mohr Siebeck Verlag, Tuebingen.

Wied-Nebbeling, S. (1985) *Das Preisverhalten in der Industrie*. Mohr Siebeck Verlag, Tuebingen.

Wildsmith, J.R. (1973) *Managerial Theories of the Firm*. Martin Robertson, London.

Williamson, O.E. (1963a) A model of rational managerial behaviour. In Cyert, R.M., and March, G.J. *A Behavioural Theory of the Firm*. Prentice-Hall, Englewood Cliffs, NJ.

Williamson, O.E. (1963b) Managerial discretion and business behaviour. *American Economic Review*, **53**, 1032–1057; reprinted in Gilbert, M. (ed.) (1972) *The Modern Business Enterprise*. Penguin, Harmondsworth, Middlesex, pp. 238–266.

Williamson, O.E. (1964) *The Economics of Discretionary Behaviour: Managerial Objectives in the Theory of the Firm*. Prentice-Hall, Englewood Cliffs, NJ.

Wilson, J.R. (1952) Maximization and business behaviour. *Economic Record*, **28**, 29–39.

Wind, Y., Green, P.E., and Robinson, P.J. (1968) The determinants of vendor selection: The evaluation function approach. *Journal of Purchasing*, August, 29–41.

Winter, S.G. (1964) Economic 'Natural Selection' and the theory of the firm. *Yale Economic Essays*, **4**, 225–272.

Woodside, A.G., and Davenport, J.W. Jr (1976) Effect of price and salesman expertise on customer purchasing behaviour. *Journal of Business*, **49**, 51–59.

Wray, M. (1956) Uncertainty, prices and entrepreneurial expectations — an applied study. *Journal of Industrial Economics*, **5**, 107–128.

Yelle, L.E. (1979) The learning curve: Historical review and comprehensive survey. *Decision Sciences*, **10**, 302–328.

Zarth, H.R. (1981) Effizienter Verkaufen durch die richtige Strategie fuer das Preisgespraech. *Markenartikel*, **43**, 111–113.

Zeuthen, F. (1932) *Problems of Monopoly and Economic Warfare*. Routledge and Kegan Paul, London.

Zimmermann, D. (1971) *Marktforschung und Absatzplannung in schweizerische Unternehmungen*. Institut fuer Wirtschaftsforschung ETH, Zuerich.

APPENDIX 1. OVERVIEW OF EMPIRICAL STUDIES ON PRICE DETERMINATION

Author(s)/ topic(s)	Research design	No. of firms studied	Type of sample	Data collection method(s)	Statistical analysis
Brown (1924a,b,c); Bradley (1927) (PO, PM, PE)	Case study (USA, F)	1	—	Executive's self-report	No
Churchill (1932) (PO, PM)	Survey (USA, M)	N/A	N/A	N/A	Yes (D)
Vanderblue (1939) (PO, PM, PE)	Case study (USA, M)	1	—	Document analysis	Yes (D)
Hall and Hitch (1939) (PM, PE)	Survey (UK, E)	38	Convenience	Self-admin. questionnaire/ personal interviews	Yes (D)
TNEC (1940) (PO, PM, PE)	Case study (USA, E)	1	—	Document analysis/ personal interviews	Yes (D)
Saxton (1942) (PM, PE)	Survey plus unknown number of case studies (UK, E)	50	N/A	Mail questionnaire*/ personal interviews/ document analysis	Yes (D)
Thompson (1947) (PO, PM, PE)	Survey (USA, M)	N/A	N/A	N/A	No
Learned (1948) (PO, PM, PE)	Case study (USA, M)	1	—	Document analysis	Yes (D)
Fog (1948) (PO, PM, PE)	Case study (Denmark, E)	N/A	Convenience	Personal interviews	No
Hague (1949) (PO, PM, PE)	Survey (UK, E)	20	N/A	Personal interviews	Yes (D)
Hansen and Nilland (1952) (PO, PM)	Case study (USA, M)	1	—	Document analysis	No
Edwards (1952) (PM, PE)	Case study (UK, E)	2	—	Document analysis	No
NACA (1953a) (PM)	Case study (USA, F)	18	Purposive	Personal interviews	No

Author(s)/ topic(s)	Research design	No. of firms studied	Type of sample	Data collection method(s)	Statistical analysis
NACA (1953b)** (PM, PE)	N/A (USA, F)	N/A	N/A	N/A	N/A
Cook and Jones (1954)** (PM)	N/A (Australia, E)	N/A	N/A	N/A	N/A
Friday (1955) (PM, PE)	Case study (UK, E)	N/A	N/A	N/A	No
Schackle (1955) (PO, PM)	Field experiment (UK, E)	15	Convenience	Self-admin. questionnaire*	Yes (D)
Balkin (1956) (PM, PE)	Case study (UK, E)	1	—	Executive's self-report	No
Wray (1956) (PM, PE)	Case study (UK, E)	N/A	N/A	N/A	No
Pearce (1956) (PM, PE)	Case study (UK, E)	1	—	Personal interviews/ document analysis	Yes (D)
Pearce and Amey (1956/57) (PO, PM, PE)	Case study (UK, E)	1	—	Personal interviews/ document analysis	Yes (D)
Earley (1956) (PM, PE)	Survey (USA, E)	110	Population	Mail questionnaire* (48.2%)	Yes (D, H)
Lazer (1957) (PO, PM, PE)	Case study (Canada, E)	26	Purposive	Personal interviews	No
Dartnell Corporation (1957) (PM, PE)	Survey (USA, M)	N/A	N/A	N/A	Yes (D)
Karger and Thompson (1957) (PO, PM, PE)	Survey (USA, M)	155	N/A	N/A	No
Lydall (1958) (PM, PE)	Survey (UK, E)	876	Systematic random	Personal interviews	Yes (D)
Kellogg (1958) (PE)	Case study (USA, M)	1	—	Executive's self-report	No
Couch (1958) (PE)	Case study (USA, M)	1	—	Executive's self-report	No

Author(s)/ topic(s)	Research design	No. of firms studied	Type of sample	Data collection method(s)	Statistical analysis
Kaplan, Dirlam and Lanzillotti (1958); Lanzillotti (1958) (PO, PM, PE)	Case study (USA, E)	20	Purposive	Personal interviews*/ document analysis	No
Fog (1960) (PO, PM, PE)	Case study (Denmark, E)	185	Convenience	Personal interviews*	No
Eiteman (1960) (PO, PM)	Case study (USA, E)	N/A	N/A	Personal interviews	No
Scotese (1961) (PO, PM)	Case study (USA, M)	1	—	Executive's self-report	No
Petrone (1961) (PO, PM, PE)	Case study (USA, M)	1	—	Executive's self-report	No
Hatzold and Helmschrott (1961)** (PE)	N/A (Germany, E)	N/A	N/A	N/A	N/A
Howe (1962) (PM)	Case study (UK, E)	28	N/A	N/A	No
Hart and Prusmann (1963) (PO, PM, PE)	Survey (UK, F)	132	Simple random	Mail questionnaire* (33.0%)	Yes (D)
Haynes (1962, 1964) (PO, PM, PE)	Case study (USA, E)	88	Purposive	Personal interviews	No
Sturmey (1964) (PM, PE)	Case study (UK, E)	N/A	N/A	N/A	Yes (D)
Richardson and Leyland (1964) (PO, PE)	Case study (UK, E)	16	Purposive	Personal interviews	No
Thompson and MacDonald (1964) (PO, PE)	Survey (USA, M)	146	N/A	N/A	Yes (D)
Fitzpatrick (1964) (PO, PM, PE)	Survey (USA, E)	83 20	Stratified random Purposive	Mail questionnaire* (45.1%)/ personal interviews	Yes (D)

Author(s)/ topic(s)	Research design	No. of firms studied	Type of sample	Data collection method(s)	Statistical analysis
Barback (1964) (PO, PM, PE)	Case study (UK, E)	7	Convenience	Personal interviews*/ document analysis	Yes (D)
Lanzillotti and Parrish (1964) (PO, PM, PE)	Survey (USA, E)	165 91	Stratified random Purposive	Mail questionnaire* (35.3%)/ personal interviews	Yes (D, H)
Brown and Jacques (1964); Simons (1967) (PM, PE)	Case study (UK, M)	1	—	Executive's self-report/personal interviews/ document analysis	No
PEP Report (1965) (PE)	Case study (UK, M)	47	Purposive	Document analysis/ personal interviews	No
Hapgood (1965) (PM)	Case study (USA, F)	1	—	Executive's self-report	No
Raia (1965) (PO)	Case study (UK, M)	1	—	Document analysis/ personal interviews	Yes (D)
Ladd (1965) (PM)	Case study (Canada, F)	1	—	Document analysis	No
Heinen (1966) (PO)	Survey (Germany, M)	25	N/A	Personal interviews	Yes (D)
Sizer (1966) (PM, PE)	Survey (UK, M)	21	Purposive	Mail questionnaire (36.2%)	Yes (D)
Wentz (1966) (PM)	Case study (USA, Mk)	2	Purposive	Document analysis	No
Knox (1966) (PM, PE)	Case study (USA, Mk)	N/A	N/A	Personal interviews	No
Nimer (1971)*** (PM, PE)	Survey (USA, F)	121	N/A	Mail questionnaire*	Yes (D)
DIB (1967)*** (PM, PE)	Survey (Germany, F)	74	N/A	Mail questionnaire* (1.2%)	Yes (D)

Author(s)/ topic(s)	Research design	No. of firms studied	Type of sample	Data collection method(s)	Statistical analysis
SIB (1967)*** (PM, PE)	Survey (Switzer., F)	22	N/A	Mail questionnaire* (0.4%)	Yes (D)
Skinner (1970) (PO, PE)	Survey (UK, E)	179	Population	Mail questionnaire*/ personal interviews (26 respondents)	Yes (D, H)
Weston (1970) (PO, PE)	Case study (USA, E)	50	N/A	Personal interviews	No
Zimmerman (1971)** (PO)	N/A (Switzer., Mk)	N/A	N/A	N/A	N/A
Hague (1971) (PO, PM, PE)	Case study (UK, E)	13	Convenience	Personal interviews	No
Nimer (1971) (PO, PM, PE)	Survey (USA, M)	100+	N/A	Mail questionnaire*	Yes (D)
Pass (1971) (PO)	Survey (UK, Mk)	85	N/A	Mail questionnaire/ personal interviews (with 'representative sample of respondents')	Yes (D)
Foxall (1972) (PM, PE)	Case study (UK, Mk)	17	N/A	Personal interviews	No
Udell (1972, 1973) (PM)	Survey (USA, Mk)	485	Purposive	Mail questionnaire* (50.0%)	Yes (D, H)
Rosendale (1973) (PM, PE)	Survey (UK, E)	29	N/A	Personal interviews*	Yes (D)
Wied-Nebbeling (1975) (PO, PM, PE)	Survey (Germany, E)	401 20	Stratified random N/A	Mail questionnaire* (40.1%)/ personal interviews	Yes (D, H)
Atkin and Skinner (1975) (PM, PE)	Survey (UK, Mk)	220	Systematic random	Mail questionnaire* (21.9%)	Yes (D)

Author(s)/ topic(s)	Research design	No. of firms studied	Type of sample	Data collection method(s)	Statistical analysis
Capon, Farley and Hulbert (1975) (PE)	Case study (UK, M)	1	—	Personal interviews	No
Nowotny and Walther (1978) (PE)	Survey (Austria, E)	187	N/A	Mail questionnaire/ personal interviews	Yes (D, H)
Watson (1978) (PO, PM, PE)	Survey (Australia, E)	28	N/A	Mail questionnaire	Yes (D)
Farley, Hulbert and Weinstein (1980) (PE)	Case study (USA, Mk)	2	Purposive	Personal interviews	Yes (D)
Gordon *et al.* (1980) (PO, PM, PE)	Survey (USA/Can., F)	44	Purposive	Personal interviews	Yes (D, H)
Said (1981) (PO, PM, PE)	Survey (UK, Mk)	356	Stratified random	Mail questionnaire* (17.5%)	Yes (D, H)
Likierman (1981) (PO, PM, PE)	Case study (UK, E)	1	—	Executive's self-report	No
Fremgen and Liao (1981) (PM, PE)	Survey (USA, F)	123 9	Purposive Convenience	Mail questionnaire* (16.1%)/ personal interviews	Yes (D, H)
Shipley (1981, 1983, 1984a,b, 1986) (PO, PM, PE)	Survey (UK, E/M/Mk)	728	Stratified random	Mail questionnaire (12.1%)/ personal interviews (111 respondents)/ telephone interviews (148 respondents)	Yes (D)
Govindarajan and Anthony (1983) (PM)	Survey (USA, F)	501	Population	Mail questionnaire* (50.1%)	Yes (D, H)
Scapens, Cameil and Cooper (1983) (PE)	Survey (UK, F)	99	Stratified random	Mail questionnaire (28.3%)	Yes (D, H)

Author(s)/ topic(s)	Research design	No. of firms studied	Type of sample	Data collection method(s)	Statistical analysis
Hooley, West and Lynch (1984); Jobber and Hooley (1987) (PO, PM, PE)	Survey (UK, Mk/E)	1775	Population	Mail questionnaire* (13.9%)/ personal interviews (100 respondents and non-respondents)	Yes (D, H)
Hankinson (1985) (PO, PM, PE)	Survey (UK, F)	50+	N/A	N/A	No
Bruegelman *et al.* (1985) (PM, PE)	Case study (USA, F)	11	N/A	Personal interviews	No
Abratt and Pitt (1985) (PO, PE)	Survey (S. Africa, Mk)	21	Purposive	Personal interviews	Yes (D)
Wied-Nebbeling (1985) (PO, PM, PE)	Survey (Germany, E)	286 10	Stratified random N/A	Mail questionnaire* (40.1%)/ personal interviews	Yes (D, H)
Tull, Kohler and Silver (1986) (PO, PE)	Survey (German, Mk)	80	Purposive	Mail questionnaire/ telephone interviews (with 'a series of' respondents)	Yes (D)
Samiee (1987) (PO, PE)	Survey (USA, Mk)	192	Stratified random	Mail questionnaire (22.7%)	Yes (D, H)
Bartholomew (1987); Campbell (1988) (PO, PE)	Survey (UK, E)	77	Simple random	Mail questionnaire* (43,5%)	Yes (D, H)
Morris and Joyce (1988) (PE)	Survey (USA, Mk)	83	Simple random	Mail questionnaire (37.7%)	Yes (D)

PO, pricing objectives; PM, pricing methods; PE, pricing environment. F, finance; M, management; E, economics; Mk, marketing. D, descriptive analysis; H, hypothesis testing. N/A, information not disclosed.
* Research instrument disclosed. ** Original study could not be located. *** Study's results disclosed in Deyhle (1967).
Note: Mail response rates shown in parentheses where disclosed.

APPENDIX 2. COMPOSITION OF THE PRICING ENVIRONMENT

ORGANIZATIONAL ENVIRONMENT

Firm demographics

Company size
Company age
Corporate image
Divorce of ownership from control
Company experience/market familiarity
Profitability and market position
Marketing mix advantages

Structural characteristics

Decentralization/divisionalization
Responsibility for pricing decisions
Functional involvement in pricing
Hierarchical involvement in pricing
Formalization of price-setting
Bottom up *vs* top-down planning

Supply characteristics

Ability to increase supply
Cost structure
Cost advantages over competition
Inventory situation
Production method
Size/complexity of product range
Fullness of order book/back orders
Product advantages
Relative product importance (80/20 rule)

Information systems

Knowledge about competitors' offerings and prices
Knowledge about customers' reactions to price
Accounting system(s)
Forecasting activities
Availability of information on past prices
Demand estimation procedures
Computer utilization in price calculation

Sociopsychological characteristics

Background/experience of price-setter(s)
Personal objectives of price-setter(s)
Conflict between decision-makers on price
Market perceptions/expectations of price-setter(s)

MARKET ENVIRONMENT

Industry demographics

Vertical integration
Distribution arrangements
Manufacturer–distributor agreements
Technological developments
Patent protection
Industry maturity
Industry profitability

Demand conditions

Price elasticity of demand
Demand growth/decline
Cyclical/seasonal fluctuations
Derived demand
Market size/potential
Value of typical purchase
Market saturation

Product shortages
Excess capacity
Economies of scale/experience effects

Customer characteristics

Price sensitivity
Type of buyer
Buying motives
Product awareness/knowledge
Buyer effort
In-house production capability
Ordering patterns
Bargaining power
Reputation and past record
Negotiation tactics
Price expectations
Psychological factors
Knowledge about product/price variations among suppliers
Value/importance of product to customer
Importance of price as a supplier/product choice criterion
Presence/absence of purchasing power
Repeat sales possibilities
Proportion of total expenditures spent on product
Special requirements

Price traditions

Existence of conventional prices/price classes and margins
Loss leader practices
Preference for price stability
Promotional (temporary) price-cutting
Trade association pricing guidelines
Frequency/timing of price revisions
Historical price patterns/trends
Payment terms/credit facilities
Price rumours
Public interest in price changes
Use of escalation clauses/open contracts
Discount practices
Relation of list to transaction prices
Incidence of price leadership
Government price control/scrutiny
Use of price in advertising/promotional claims
Cost of implementing price changes
Formal/informal price consultation among competitors

Future demand expectations
Regional demand variations

Product characteristics

Product life cycle
Existence of second-hand market
Product complexity
Product type
Product perishability
Product differentiation/branding
Product utility
Product add-ons

Competitive conditions

Number/size of competitors
Product/price variations of competitive offerings
Threat of potential entry
Collusion potential
Prices of competing products in other industries

General economic climate

Inflation
Recession/boom
Taxation

Extraordinary events

Weather
Raw material shortages
Disasters

CHAPTER 4

Product Policy: Perspectives on Success

Patricia Snelson[1] and Susan Hart[2]

[1] *Grant Thornton, Glasgow;*
[2] *Department of Marketing, Strathclyde University*

INTRODUCTION

Marketing, both in concept and practice, espouses the notion that, given the dynamic nature of demand, technology and competition in today's markets, the delivery of satisfaction has to be managed actively. This entails the constant adaptation of product ranges to enhance long-term growth and profitability. In practical terms, however, this means more than adding products to or deleting products from a company's portfolio. Simply carrying out these tasks is no guarantee of success. They have to be carried out *well.* A point of pedantry? We think not. Much of the textbook material on product policy does not, in fact, concentrate on the portrayal of best practice, but focuses instead on describing the decision variables in normative decision processes. In contrast, this chapter attempts to look at product policy from the perspective of decision *outcomes*.

Marketing literature dealing with product policy suffers from two crucial shortcomings. First, as is pointed out above, adapting the product mix entails both adding products to and deleting products from the company's portfolio. Yet a majority of marketing textbooks seem implicitly to equate product policy with new product development *only* (Baker, 1985; Cannon, 1986; Kotler, 1988; Pride and Ferrell, 1989). While this reflects the relative neglect of product deletion by researchers, equating product mix *change* with product *proliferation* leads to an incomplete understanding of product policy which eclipses the crucial task of identifying and withdrawing products no longer achieving company objectives.

Secondly, while studies of new product development, and in particular success and failure in new product development, make interesting

Perspectives on Marketing Management, Volume 1
Edited by M.J. Baker

reading, their impact on managerial and research practice is unclear. From the findings of major research studies there is a growing consensus that success is dependent upon dynamic and flexible processes with inputs from all key functions throughout. How can we reconcile the traditional task-stage models of the new product development process with these newer findings?

This chapter addresses these important issues in two sections. First, the issues of new product development (NPD) are dealt with by summarizing and analysing 'the success literature' and feeding back salient success factors into our conception of the NPD process. In other words, an attempt is made to suggest how success factors can be integrated into NPD practice and into academic research frameworks. Secondly, marketing literature and thought in the field of product deletion are summarized in such a way as to focus on how the procedures of product deletion might generate successful outcomes.

NEW PRODUCT DEVELOPMENT

How does a company get from an idea for a new product to the eventual successful launch? How does an idea become converted into a product, with a recognizable form, function and features? And why, sometimes, does the process go wrong?

When recalling successful 'industrial' products like facsimile machines, autopilot controls, microchips or computer-controlled machine tools, it is tempting to think that the way they developed was obvious from the outset, because they were good ideas. Initially researchers and managers felt that all that was necessary for successful product development was a good idea, but since then major research projects have consistently shown that the execution of the development process — the conversion activities between the idea and the product launch — is at least as important as the idea itself.

An example might illustrate a good idea that was not transformed into a successful new product.

The launch of ZX and Spectrum computers by the UK company Sinclair Research singlehandedly created the market for home computers. Following on from this success, the company developed and launched a powerful desk-top computer capable of handling small business operations yet priced well below the computer systems available at the time. The 'Quantum Leap' did not live up to expectations. Manufacturing and distribution problems were compounded by design faults. While the company struggled to rectify these problems, other computer manufacturers recognized the enormous market potential and rapidly developed comparable products. The Quantum Leap was eventually withdrawn and the company was ultimately taken over by the UK electronics firm Amstrad.

From this, it is apparent that good ideas can easily 'go wrong' on their way through the development process. It follows, therefore, that conversion activities have to be managed properly in order for companies to capitalize on the opportunities afforded by a good idea. Looking more closely at academic research into success and failure in new product development allows us to see what activities in the new product development process are critical.

SUCCESS AND FAILURE IN NEW PRODUCT DEVELOPMENT

There has been a lot of research into why some new products have failed, why some have been successful, and why some have been more successful than others. Of course, there is no single explanation of success. Not only are there many different factors, but they operate at different levels within an organization. By distilling and analysing the results of this research we can see that these factors operate at either the management or project level.

Management-level factors relate to the way in which a firm 'approaches' a programme of product development: how top managers encourage product development and who in the firm are brought together to carry through developments.

Project-level factors relate to a specific product and the way it has been developed.

Although there has been a plethora of writing on the subject of NPD, this chapter concentrates on some 'milestone' studies, together with some key findings from two recent projects carried out by the authors of this chapter (Rothwell, 1977; Cooper, 1979, 1984; Booz, Allen and Hamilton, 1982; Johne and Snelson, 1988; Hart and Service, 1988).

Failure in New Product Development

Table 4.1 summarizes the key recurrent reasons for failure in new product development. As it shows, at the management level three issues are important. First, where the organization does not encourage entrepreneurial or risk-taking activity, research shows this has a negative impact on product development. Clearly, NPD is a risky undertaking, and therefore some endeavours *will* fail. Cooper's (1979) project NewProd revealed that 22% of new product developments are 'killed' prior to launch. This in itself shows that not all development

Table 4.1 Sources of failure in product development

Management level
Entrepreneurial activity and risk-taking not encouraged
Lack of communication and cooperation between functions, and appropriate structures to encourage this
Lack of top management support
Project level
Marketing inputs
Failure to meet customer needs
Relative advantage weak:
– product not differentiated
– pricing inappropriate
Poor launch execution
Technical input
Technology does not work
Increased technological performance has no relevance to customer needs

Source: Hart and Snelson (1989).

programmes will come to fruition. If the company will not recognize the inherent risk involved in product development to tolerate this type of 'failure', then it will actively discourage innovators from coming forward with and pursuing new product ideas.

Secondly, where there is a lack of interfunctional communication — particularly between technical and commercial functions — there is more likelihood of failure. Again, the logic is simple. A new product should have some added benefit to the customer. While the added benefit may be conceived by people with technical or design expertise, ensuring that the benefit is *relevant* and *communicated* to the customer is largely in the hands of people with commercial or marketing expertise. Yet the functional divisions inside companies, with marketing expertise locked inside the marketing departments and technical expertise confined to the laboratory, actually work against the effective communication that is so necessary for successful NPD. There is clearly a need for an integrating mechanism that encourages the cross-fertilization of development activities during the course of the NPD process.

These two issues are closely connected to the third: top management support. If the company's senior management is not openly supportive of product development efforts, those below are unlikely to shoulder the risks involved or be encouraged to cooperate with other functions in the development work.

Table 4.1 also highlights the project-level reasons for failure and, as is shown, these reasons can be further divided into two sets of problems: marketing and technical.

Marketing problems such as a new product failing to meet user needs were highlighted by Cooper's project NewProd (1979, 1984). Another marketing problem has been shown to be a lack of customer acceptance due to a new product's imperceptible relative advantage over other products on the market. One of Baker's (1985) maxims for success is that you either make a better product for the same price as others on the market or you make a similar product at a lower price. This essentially means that customers need to see some relative advantage in buying your new product. If it is too similar to a product already on the market (and not cheaper) or if the differences are not *perceptible* to the buyer, the chances of success are reduced. These issues clearly relate to the ability of a company to assess the market properly, to pinpoint needs that are not satisfied, to evaluate the benefit to the customer of satisfying those needs and to appraise their willingness to pay for such satisfaction. Unfortunately, while its importance has been highlighted, very little research has been done on the critical task of market assessment for product development. Academics are still in the unhappy state of knowing *what* is necessary without being able to say *how* it should be done. Even in cases where a new product does meet customer needs and offers relative advantage, research shows that it can still fail in the marketplace because of the company's failure to launch it effectively. The product's benefits need to be successfully communicated to the marketplace and distribution channels need to be properly organized and managed.

Technical problems with the product might occur during development, or worse, after launch. Technical problems during development can either be put right or delay project completion, but those manifesting themselves after launch can cause serious problems for the entire reputation of a company. They are particularly difficult to handle in the industrial market, where the technical testing of a product may be difficult to manage. For example, a company (which remains nameless for confidentiality) studied by one of the authors developed a new lorry-loaded concrete mixing machine from a basic design of its sister company in France. The machine was tested over a four-week period in this country and its perfect functioning was recorded and substantiated by several hundred reports from the French users of the similar basic design. However, within four months of the UK launch, users began to make irate complaints about the machine's tendency to get thoroughly clogged within a matter of weeks. After some basic technical research, the company found that the way in which the machines were cleaned by British workers differed from that used by the French workers. This was a matter of in-use behaviour that could not have been identified through technical assessment only. The company rectified the problem by incorporating some minor design changes in the light of this evidence, but diversifying into this type of product cost it dearly in terms of profit and general reputation.

Another 'technical' problem is actually related to marketing, in that a technical solution to a problem does not *automatically* sell. There is a tendency, particularly with products of a high technological content, for manufacturers to assume that customers will automatically view new technical capabilities as an added advantage. As we have already seen, unless the technology gives customers perceptible in-use benefits (particularly if the product is more costly), market demand will not be realized.

Success in New Product Development

Table 4.2 summarizes the key reasons for success and categorizes them in a similar fashion to the reasons for failure. It comes as no surprise that the reasons for success are, in essence, the reverse of those for failure.

Table 4.2 Sources of success in product development

Management level
Team structures to manage product development
Top management enthusiasm and support
Appropriate authority given to staff
Appropriate long-term financing
Project level
Marketing inputs
Product meets customer needs
Launched efficiently
Technical inputs
Product technologically sound
Product has technological advantage that meet customer needs
NPD process efficiently carried out with no delays

Source: Hart and Snelson (1989).

At the management level, enthusiasm and support for what is a risky endeavour are apparent in successful projects, and team structures are developed *across* functional divisions to encourage collaboration and communication during the development process. Such organizational support is also manifested in the way those individuals responsible for NPD are given the authority appropriate for the effective discharge of their responsibilities. The correct level of financial support is also found to be forthcoming in companies with successful product development track records.

At the project level, successful programmes are characterized by two factors. First, the balance between technical advancement and customer need is correct. In other words, the firm's marketing and technical skill bases have been successfully integrated. Secondly, the development process is surprisingly speedy and efficient, culminating in a successfully executed product launch.

Recent Research: Johne and Snelson (1988)

The recent work by one of the authors was developed out of some of the milestone research described above and sharpened the focus of what distinguishes NPD success from failure. Further, the work recognizes that there will be differences in the managerial approach needed for *new* product development (i.e. entirely new products) and *old* product development (i.e. improving and developing current products). In contrasting the policies of 20 experienced product developers and 20 inexperienced and less successful product developers, Johne and Snelson (1988) used the McKinsey 7-S framework for the analysis. This framework was originally developed by Peters and Waterman (1982) to diagnose the managerial practices of top-performing firms at the corporate level. Because product development is a strategically important activity and involves a wide spread of the firm's functional skills, this framework is capable of being operationalized in order to investigate the management of product development programmes.

Table 4.3 indicates how experienced product developers approach the tasks of old and new product development. The results both support previous research in the area and elaborate upon it.

For example, in pursuing old product development, experienced firms institute multifunctional teams of low-level line managers (*s*tructure, *s*taff), sponsored by top management (*s*tyle) and guided by detailed procedural control (*s*ystems). These same firms recognize the need for a different managerial approach to the inherently more risky and uncertain task of new product development. For instance, different skills are required and a different type of top management support. The authors maintain that each of the 7-Ss needs to be managed in a mutually supportive way, and in a way that is compatible with the intricacies and characteristics of each type of development task.

Recent Research: Hart and Service (1988)

Based on the logic of much of the findings described thus far, the work of the second author concentrated more specifically on the 'management' level of new product development. The research, based on the

Table 4.3 Successful product development: Managing the 7-Ss

	Old product development	New product development
Management level		
Strategy	Explicit and incorporated into corporate plans	Broad growth objectives: market/ technology targets
Top management style	Sponsorship	Leadership
Shared values	Shared commitment to development work	'Vision of future'
Structure	Multifunctional part- or full-time teams of line managers	Skeletal business units outside mainstream organization
Project level		
Staff	Low level with enhanced authority	Senior-level managers
Skills	Market analysis, segmentation; technical analysis	'Intrapreneurial': interpret macrochanges in environment
Systems	Close procedural control	'Free-wheeling' development

Source: Johne and Snelson (1988). Reproduced by permission.

opinions of top management in 369 firms, found seven different managerial orientations regarding NPD. These are summarized in Table 4.4, and again back up the results of previous studies.

The most successful management orientation when compared to company performance (measured in terms of absolute and relative growth in sales turnover) is the balanced orientation. This orientation rejects the notion of developing products only to suit existing manufacturing capability and the notion that current product designs are the only way to do things. Rather, this stance acknowledges that the role of marketing involves more than 'selling': the balanced orientation encourages a more synergistic relationship between marketing and engineering, with marketing having an input into design and development activities. The positive association between this orientation and overall company performances reflects the advantage that companies can gain when they combine a commitment to lead the field technically with a sound marketing input.

Table 4.4 Managerial orientations to new product development

Name of orientation	Attitudes that count in orientation
Incremental orientation	We have a continuous programme of R&D to back up our new efforts We review product design and development expenditure regularly We always spend a set percentage of our sales revenue on product development We actively commission market research to identify new product opportunities
Long-term/ radical orientation	We support product development only when we recognize a specific need for it* We mostly redesign to lower the cost and price of our products* The design and development budget is set according to how much money there is to spend* Long-term R&D projects have got to fit in with our current technological knowhow* Unconventional ideas are not actively encouraged*
Balanced orientation	Our engineers solve the technical problems only; it's marketing's job to go out and sell* Unconventional ideas are not actively encouraged* We only develop products to suit existing plant* If there was a different way to design the type of products we make, it would have been done by now*
Added-value orientation	The way the product looks is an important selling point for us We redesign products to introduce them to more expensive market segments We try to influence the market through design
Fashion orientation	In our new product developments speed is of the essence The way a product looks is an important selling point for us Our engineers solve the technical problems; it's marketing's job to go out and sell
Independence orientation	Our customers tell us when we need to redesign products* We review product design and development expenditure regularly
Design orientation	It is our objective to develop our own internal design expertise We actively commission market research to identify new product opportunities*

* Respondents strongly disagreed with these statements.
Source: Hart and Service (1988). Reproduced by permission

LINKING SUCCESS AND FAILURE TO THE NPD PROCESS

From the foregoing discussion of success and failure in new product development it should be clear that getting from an idea to a successfully launched product is a complex matter, one that needs to be managed carefully. Specifically, from the review of success and failure, three factors dictate the need for the careful management of the NPD process:

1. The need for interdisciplinary inputs. In order to combine technical and marketing expertise, a number of company functions have to be involved: R&D, manufacturing, engineering, marketing and sales. As the development of a new product might be the only occasion when these people meet, it is important that the NPD process adopted ensures that they work well and effectively together.
2. The need for quality inputs. Both technical and marketing information, which are the building blocks of NPD, have to be accurate and timely, and must be continually reworked in the light of changing circumstances during the course of the development.
3. The need for speed. The NPD process has to be managed in such a way as to be quick enough to capitalize on the new product opportunity before competitors do so. The value of being first with a new product in a marketplace is often significant, and the window of opportunity for a particular development may be fleetingly open. The speedy undertaking of the complex and intricate product development task requires sophisticated management.

Given the points which characterize success and failure in product development, along with the factors listed above which identify the need for good management, how well do accepted models of the new product development process encapsulate these issues? As a basis for discussion, we will use Booz, Allen and Hamilton's (BAH) portrayal of the product development process. It is this model which is accepted and used widely in marketing education. As will be seen, although the BAH model identifies the key core activities of the process, it does not portray all the factors that have an impact on the successful management of product development.

The Booz, Allen and Hamilton Model

The BAH model is incoporated into Table 4.5. To help link the model with what we now know from research into success and failure in product development, it is characterized in terms of information needed, its source and expected output at each stage of the NPD process. Booz, Allen and Hamilton's empirical research found that:

- Those companies that were successful at NPD were more likely to have a *formal* system for managing NPD, which identified key stages and key participants at each stage. The system in successful companies was typically in place for a long time.
- Successful companies spent more time on *up-front* activities, in particular on the first three stages. This means that more information seeking and analysis are carried out *before* major costs are incurred in the later stages of the process.

Distilling the lessons from our review of research into new product success and failure, we cannot say that the BAH model is endorsed *per se*. We can say, however, that the model, at least implicitly, highlights some of the key activities which have been shown by the research to be necessary for effective product development. Specifically, the *tasks* (outputs) identified throughout the BAH model have to be addressed, and these are, as can be seen in Table 4.5, dependent upon the information *inputs*. Apart from these elements, the precise unfolding of the process as described by BAH has been criticized on two counts:

1. In reality, the NPD process is idiosyncratic to the firm and to the project. It depends on the type of new product being developed and its relationship with the firm's current activities (Cooper, 1988; Johne and Snelson, 1988).
2. There is no linear beginning, middle and end to the NPD process. For example, from one idea, several product concept variants may be developed each of which might be pursued. Also, as an idea crystallizes, the developers can assess the nature of market need more easily, and the technical and production costs also become more readily evaluated. The issues, problems and solutions become clearer as the process unfolds: it is easier to decide on which variants to pursue and how worthwhile the whole endeavour may be in the later stages of the process. While, because of the costs involved, process models stress that such evaluations should be made up front, their credibility and accuracy are at their weakest during the early phases of development.

The iterative nature of the NPD process results from the fact that each stage or phase of development is capable of producing numerous outputs which implicate both previous development work and future

Table 4.5 An analysis of the NPD process based on Booz, Allen and Hamilton (1982)

Stage of development	Information needed for stage; nature of information	Sources of information	Likely output of stage in light of information
1. Explicit statement of new product strategy, budget allocation	Preliminary market and technical analysis; company objectives	Generated as part of continuous MIS and corporate planning	Identification of *market* (NB not product) opportunities to be exploited by new products
2. Idea generation (or gathering)	Customer needs and technical developments in *previously* identified markets	Inside company: salesmen, technical functions Outside company: customers, competitors, inventors, etc.	Body of initially acceptable ideas
3. Screening ideas: finding those with most potential	Assessment of whether there is a *market* for this type of product, and whether the company can make it. Assessment of financial implications: market potential and costs. Knowledge of company goals and assessment of fit	Main internal functions: — R&D — Sales — Marketing — Finance — Production	Ideas which are acceptable for further development
4. Concept development: turning an idea into a recognizable product concept, with attributes and market position identified	*Explicit* assessment of customer needs to appraise market potential. *Explicit* assessment of technical requirements	Initial research with customer(s). Input from marketing and technical functions	Identification of: key attributes that need to be incorporated in the product, major technical costs, target markets and potential
5. Business analysis: full analysis of the proposal in terms of its business potential	Fullest information thus far: — Detailed market analysis — Explicit technical feasibility and costs — Production implications — Corporate objectives	Main internal functions Customers	Major go/no go decision: company needs to be sure the venture is worthwhile as expenditure dramatically increases after this stage Initial marketing plan Development plan and budget

Table 4.5 (contd.)

Stage of development	Information needed for stage; nature of information	Sources of information	Likely output of stage in light of information
6. Product development: crystallizing the product into semi-finalized shape	Customer research with product. Production information to check 'makeability'	Customers Production	Finalize product specification Explicit marketing plan
7. Test marketing: small-scale tests with customers	Profile of new product performance in light of competition, promotion and marketing mix variables	Market research; production, sales, marketing, technical people	Final go/no go for launch
8. Commercialization	Test market results and report	As for test market	Incremental changes to test launch Full-scale launch

Source: Hart and Snelson (1989)

development progress. For example, suppose an idea has reached the concept testing stage. The logic of the BAH model is that, if a new product concept fails the concept test, then the development itself is terminated. But a number of outcomes may result from a 'failed' concept test:

- Maybe the original concept is faulty but a better one is found; it would then 're-enter' the development process at the screening stage.
- Maybe a new customer need is identified through the process of concept testing: after all, the company is out in the market listening to customer needs when concept testing; this new opportunity would thus need to be subject to idea generation processes and formed into a concept that could itself be tested.

The possibilities at this stage of the process are shown in Figure 4.1, and this illustrates how, viewed as linear or sequential, the BAH model is unrealistic, particularly regarding up-front activities.

A further point in relation to the sequencing of product development tasks is the existence of related strands of development. These complicate the picture further because they mean that product development activity is not only iterative *between* stages but also *within* stages.

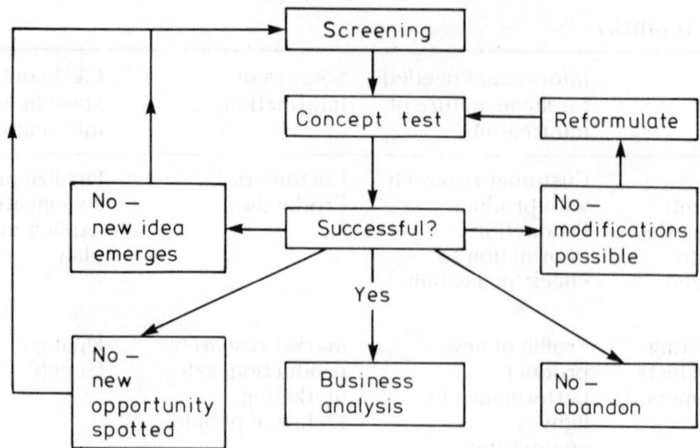

Figure 4.1 An example of iteration in the NPD process. *Source*: Hart and Snelson (1989)

These related strands of development refer to the marketing, technical (or design) and production tasks and decisions that occur as the process unwinds. Each strand of development gives rise to problems and opportunities within the other two. For example, if, at the product development stage, production people have problems which push the costs up, this could well affect market potential. The marketing and technical assumptions need to be reworked in the light of this new information. A new design may be considered, or a new approach to the marketplace. Whatever the nature of the final solution, that solution has to be based on the interplay of technical, marketing and manufacturing development issues.

Using an example of the development of a new car-steering system, the way these different strands of development operate is shown in Figure 4.2. The crux of the matter is that the horizontal dimension of development is not adequately communicated by the BAH model. However, recognition of this flaw has led to the idea of parallel processing, which acknowledges the iterations *between* and *within* stages and categorizes them along functional configurations.

This idea of parallel processing is highly prescriptive: it advises that the major functions should be involved from the early stages of the NPD process to its conclusion. This, it is claimed, allows problems to be detected and solved much earlier than in the classic task-by-task, function-to-function models. In turn, the entire process is much speedier, which has the advantages described earlier. In addition it encourages a multidisciplinary approach, which we know is also crucial to successful product development.

Because of the importance of parallel processing, and the

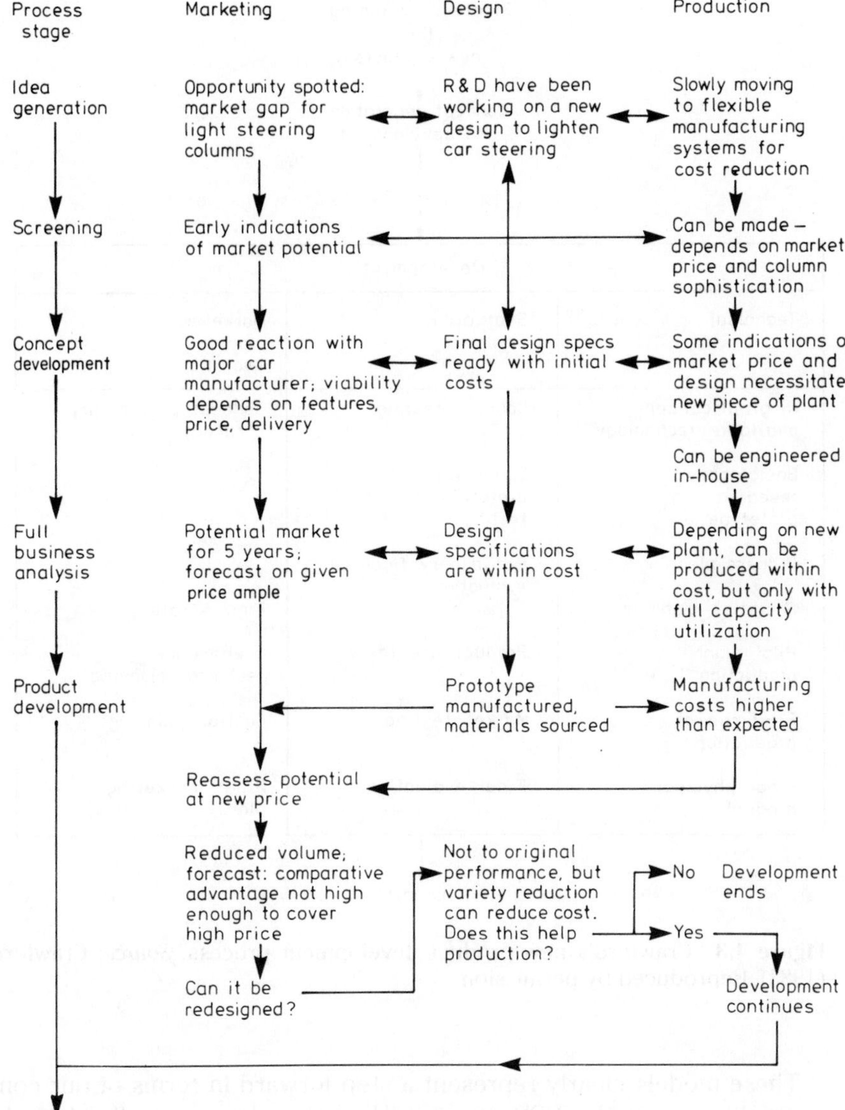

Figure 4.2 An example of the impact of individual interrelated strands of development. *Source*: Hart and Snelson (1989)

inadequacies of the BAH model in respect of it, revised models of the NPD process have been put forward by Crawford (1983) and Cooper (1988). These take cognizance of the key tasks explicit in the BAH approach, and cater for the multidisciplinary parallel approach (see Figures 4.3 and 4.4).

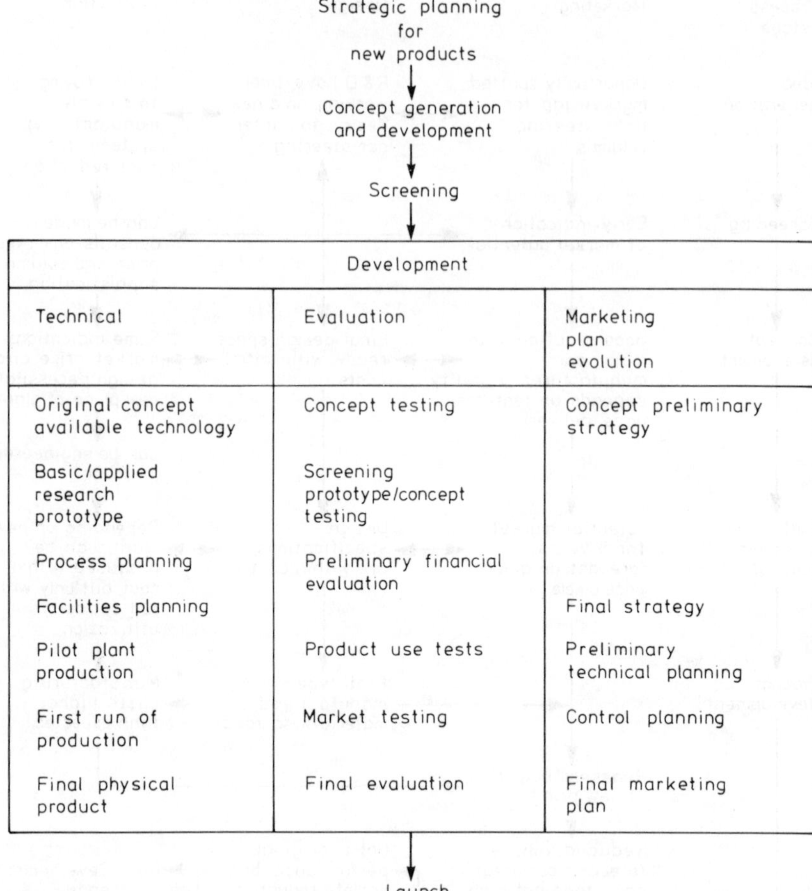

Figure 4.3 Crawford's new product development process. *Source*: Crawford (1983). Reproduced by permission

These models clearly represent a step forward in terms of our conceptualization of the NPD process. However, they are still relatively simplistic portrayals of what is a complex, intricate and interactive process. Despite the plethora of research in the area, our conceptual understanding of product development remains highly stylized. It may be that the search for an accurate representation of the process of product development is misjudged, and that a more fruitful endeavour would be to focus on the necessary outputs of development work, the activities and actions required to generate such outputs being highly project- and firm-specific.

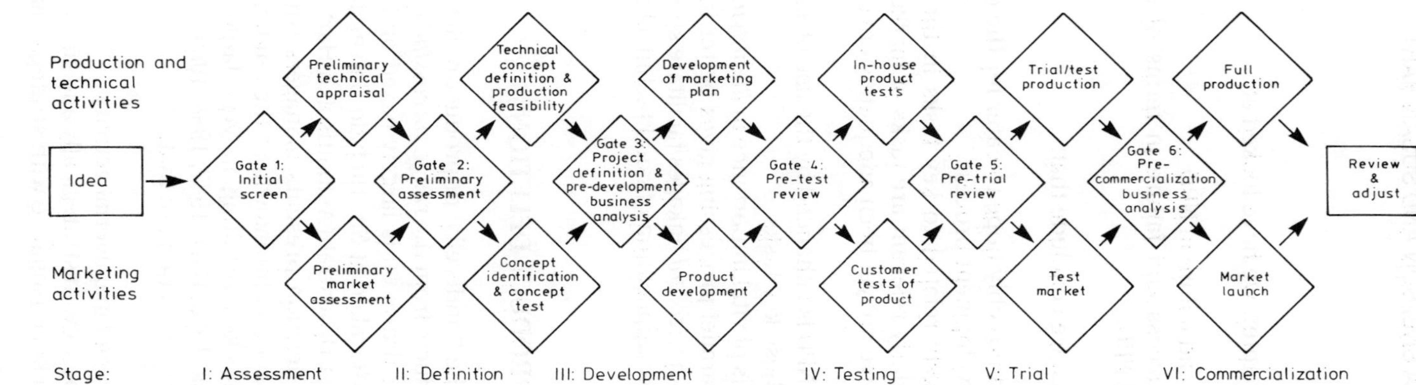

Figure 4.4 Cooper's stage-gate new product process. *Source*: Cooper (1988). Reproduced by permission

SUMMARY

In this first part of the chapter, we have looked at:

- the causes of success and failure in NPD
- the implications of success and failure in terms of managing and guiding the process of NPD.

From these discussions, we conclude that:

1. No single model could possibly hope to cater for the circumstances of every individual development process.
2. Failure in NPD is largely related to key tasks in the NPD process being left out. Particularly relevant are tasks of market assessment, the details of which have not yet been adequately covered by empirical study.
3. Success and speed in NPD is enhanced by the use of a multidisciplinary team to address these key tasks.
4. While the BAH model is of vital importance in *identifying* the key NPD tasks, the notion of parallel processing gives better insight into the NPD process in which *horizontal* linkages facilitate speed in development, together with the application of good technical and marketing input at each stage.

PRODUCT DELETION

In this second section, the 'Cinderella' of product policy, namely, how to go about deleting products from the range *successfully*, is considered. The material the chapter draws on is largely based on insights from a research programme undertaken at Strathclyde University's Marketing Department called Project Dropstrat (Avlonitis and Hart, 1985).

The issue of product deletion presents managers with many problems, particularly in market conditions where the tendency is for products to proliferate unchecked resulting in very large and unwieldy product ranges (Avlonitis, 1983; Hart, 1987, 1988, 1989).

The main messages of this section are that:

- product deletion is a *useful* managerial activity
- product deletion can be viewed strategically and successful deletions tend to be those taken in consonance with strategic plans.

DELETION — A NATURAL CONSEQUENCE OF THE PRODUCT REVIEW SYSTEM?

Once a product has been introduced onto the market, normative theory holds that it will be assessed constantly in terms of its financial performance, its compatibility with market requirements and its fulfilment of the objectives set for it. Should there be shortfall on any criteria, the prescriptive approach advocates that remedial action be taken, or, where this is deemed impossible or undesirable, that the product be removed from the company's range (Alexander, 1964; McSurely and Wilemon, 1973; Hise and McGinnis, 1975; Kotler, 1988). However, empirical study of this process suggests that this chain of events is not easily followed in practice (Salerno, 1982; Avlonitis, 1983; Hise, Parasuraman and Viswanathan, 1984; Hart, 1987). The process instead appears to be plagued by indecision and delay, particularly when making a choice between dropping a product and keeping it. Indeed, the delete option seems to be one that is commonly avoided, for a number of reasons that will now be examined.

THE REASONS FOR NEGLECT OF PRODUCT DELETION

The reasons why the deletion decision is often avoided or delayed can be grouped into two: rational reasons and not-so-rational reasons. Both are summarized in Table 4.6.

Table 4.6 Reasons for neglect

Rational reasons for neglecting product deletion
Revitalization
Product line scope
Defrayal of overheads
Not-so-rational reasons for neglecting product deletion
Lack of appropriate financial data
'Ostrich attitudes'

One rational reason for avoiding a deletion decision is that a situation may be 'savable': a product could be revitalized in some way. This can be explained if we view the deletion process as a multistage decision-making process, as depicted in Figure 4.5 (Avlonitis, 1985; Hart, 1989).

Some occurrence or set of circumstances turns management's attention to a problem (or opportunity) which might be solved (or exploited)

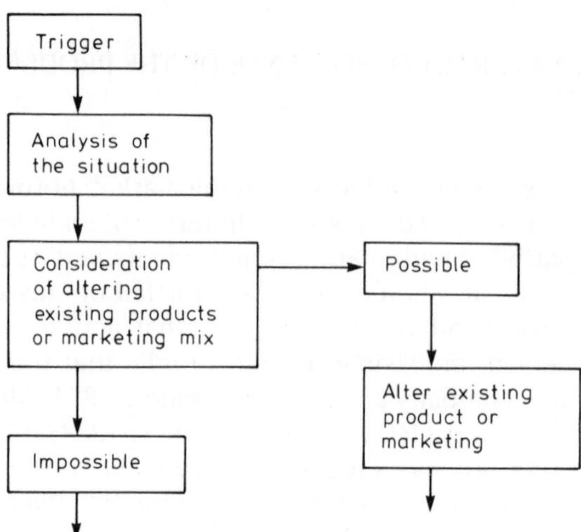

Figure 4.5 The initial steps in the product deletion process

by the deletion of a product. This occurrence is called a trigger. The situation is then analysed, and depending on what emerges, there might be a way of remedying the problem *without* deleting a product. For example, if the price of the product is too high to generate the required volume of sales, then the company might be able to lower its production costs (and hence the price), it might be in a position simply to decrease the price, or it might be able to add value to the product to bring it to a level that is consistent with its price.

To take another example, one of the managers participating in Project Dropstrat considered dropping a product because, unlike the competitors, only one version was marketed. Most other companies offered a *range* of products, which made it easier to be stocked by wholesalers. In the end, the way the product was assembled (the production line) was reorganized so that a variety of the products could be made, thus making them more competitive. These types of reasons are perfectly valid for not deleting a product. However, even when a remedy is either not possible or deemed by management to be not worth pursuing, a product might be retained for valid reasons which might have to do with evaluating the effect the deletion would have on the rest of the company's operation (see Figure 4.6). For instance, the effect of deletion on the scope of the product line may be judged too severe where management values the concept of a full range. In these circumstances, management considers that the losses incurred by offering the product are less than those incurred by having a hole in the product line. Typically, market leaders carry a full range and to cut down is felt somehow to belittle their status.

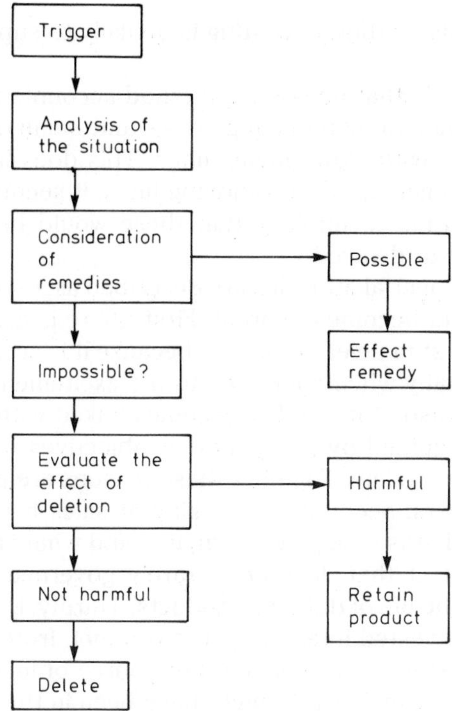

Figure 4.6 The product deletion process

Customer patronage may also encourage the retention of dubious products, particularly in the industrial market where customers often like to purchase materials from a single source. Another reason a product may be retained is to assist the defrayal of overheads. Many of the costs of the average industrial multiproduct company are joint. Raw materials, product lines and labour may be interchangeable and shared between products. If one product is removed then the share of the burden is increased for the remaining products.

All of the above are plausible managerial reasons for not deleting a product, but there are also less rational reasons. Quite simply, there are often inadequate financial data available to judge whether or not a product should be continued in the portfolio. This leads to inactivity. This is because all of the standard measures of profitability, the bottom line for making deletion decisions, are based on arbitrary methods of costing. For example, total absorption costing may yield a different profit figure from other costing methods. This can cause decision-makers to be unsure about whether to drop a product.

Further, deletion does little to affect the fixed costs of an organization, so this method of costing is unlikely to support the argument for deletion.

Another problem is that no costing method accounts for the intangible costs like production-line changeovers and small-order handling that are associated with slow-moving lines. This does little to strengthen the resolve to get rid of slow-moving lines. It seems ridiculous in the age of information technology that these would be reasons why deletion is avoided or delayed.

A number of managerial attitudes are described as 'ostrich attitudes', for reasons that will become apparent. First, there is a general lack of management interest in deletion. This is because it is seen as a dull and boring task, especially when compared to the excitement of new product development. Also, it inevitably becomes linked with the notion of failure, and is not guided by any policy or objectives which could be used to gauge the outcome. Together these reasons are powerful disincentives to managers. Secondly, in looking at sales figures, it can be difficult to know what is a 'blip' in the figures and what is a trend. This, coupled with the fact that deletion is rarely governed by deadlines, serves to prolong the life of dubious products. Thirdly, there are often a whole collection of vested interests in the product, from product managers to salesmen (for whom it is another source of income, however small) to the MD, whose 'baby' it might have been in the first place.

In view of these reasons for not deleting products, it is necessary to examine whether proliferation of the product line really harms the company at all, and to review the benefits of pruning back the product line.

THE IMPORTANCE OF PRODUCT DELETION

Product deletion is important for a variety of reasons. First, a weak product places a burden on the company's resources, such as funds, facilities and management attention, which is disproportionate to its contribution. It may require excessive managerial effort with respect to pricing, sales, distribution and communication, and it may also require warehouse space, which is usually a premium resource for companies selling from stock.

Given the finite resources of the company, those devoted to the weak product are less profitably invested than they might be if they were available to produce, promote and distribute either a new product or other existing products. The opportunity cost is therefore potentially enormous.

A weak product is also damaging with respect to the future. Not only can it tarnish the company's image and promote dissatisfaction in the marketing channel but the company may incur additional opportunity costs. By camouflaging the need for new product development and draining necessary resources, a weak product may delay the process of developing new products.

The expense of carrying a product which is weak, that is, one which is deteriorating in terms of profitability, sales volume or contribution to the objectives of the company, goes beyond production costs. No method of financial accounting can adequately report all indirect costs incurred by a weak product, which disappear in general 'overhead' classes in the accounts. Such costs include: (a) the costs of changeovers in the production lines for short runs; (b) handling costs for small orders; (c) inventory-carrying costs for slow-moving items. Having too many products increases the company's costs of doing business and having too few permits market opportunities to slip away and results in excess capacity. Both extremes are costly and affect profit adversely.

Product overpopulation spreads a company's productive, financial and marketing resources too thinly. This in turn leads to further problems. Forecasting becomes more difficult and even the mechanics of product-pricing become complex and time-consuming. Also, the use of informative advertising as a means of persuasion, particularly by companies manufacturing shopping goods and industrial goods, may be difficult where an extensive product range is being promoted. Moreover, an excess of products in the line not only creates internal competition among the company's own products but also creates confusion in the minds of customers, since perceived differences among individual products usually diminish as more products are added to a given range.

Planning and controlling a large number of products present serious problems. For instance, management must contend with coordinating shared parts and ingredients when planning production schedules, allocating production costs to products and purchasing additional production equipment. Also, as management attempts to spread its efforts over a wide and varied product mix, its ability to coordinate and control the portfolio is weakened. When a company has only a few products, its management can scrutinize and control each product's problems as they arise.

The implications of proliferated product lines such as those detailed above suggest that deletion needs to be considered for reasons other than simply stopping a cash drain from a company. By extension, the reasons for (or aims of) deletion are likely to be diverse. For example, a product could be removed from the product range with the aim of freeing resources to exploit new opportunities, or to simplify a company's product positioning or marketing communication strategy.

Potentially, each of the implications of carrying extensive product lines gives rise to a different aim for deleting a product. These are shown in Table 4.7.

Table 4.7 Derivation of deletion aims

Implications of carrying excess products	Aims of deletion
Excessive burden on company resources:	
Physical	Create warehousing space for quick delivery of key lines
Financial	Transfer promotional funds from several slow-moving lines to fewer, buoyant lines
Managerial	Simplify product positioning
'Immeasurable' costs	Streamline selling procedures Cut the costs of distributing small orders
Opportunity costs	Create physical, financial and managerial resources to exploit a new product opportunity
Resources are spread too thinly	Simplify production planning
Old products are damaging to market image	Initiate the development of new products

What may be inferred from Table 4.7 is that it is not *purely* because of poor sales and profits that products are withdrawn. Of course, highly successful products are unlikely to be removed, but deletion candidates need not be outright loss-makers either. A couple of examples might help to explain what we mean here. During the research study Project Dropstrat, the interviewed managers described the reasons why they had deleted products in the past.

A large manufacturer of electronic testing equipment which fosters a pioneering image started moves to remove from the range a product that it perceived to be somewhat outmoded in terms of technological developments. The product manager had been trying to bring the outmoded product to top management's attention for some time. The latter were moved to act when the competition announced a new product launch. In this case the driving force was to remove a product that compared badly in image terms with the company's competitive aspirations.

Another example is a manufacturer of automotive components which had developed a variety reduction policy to reduce the number of different products it actively manufactured and stocked. The decision was motivated by:

- uncontrollable number of products to manage;
- inventory control problems;
- the desire to simplify selling.

What is important about this decision is that it breaks out from the traditional manner in which business in this industry is done — making parts for every vehicle — but was nevertheless successful in terms of the standards set by the initial reasons for undertaking the rationalization. The deletions were thus tackled strategically, as part of overall company policy. The issue at stake here is that, because products can be deleted for reasons other than poor sales and profits, then from these reasons we can derive *objectives* for product deletion. Such objectives are very important for guiding the process of managing product deletion. So, by way of a summary to this discussion, it is important to understand:

- as an under-rated activity associated with failure, deletion will never get full managerial attention;
- the benefits of deletion are rarely articulated in such a way as to help managers *achieve* something from deleting products;
- the benefits of addressing product deletion are more than 'stopping problems';
- these benefits could be used as blueprints for setting objectives.

The logical conclusion from these summary points is that *objectives* have to be developed to guide and manage product deletion.

VIEWING DELETION IN TERMS OF SUCCESS

Defining deletion as a success may be seen to be rather a contradiction in terms. However, before management can set objectives for the task, there has to be some definition of a good deletion and a not-so-good deletion. One of the aims of Project Dropstrat was to define what constituted a successful deletion. The research aimed to investigate respondents' opinions on successful and less successful outcomes by examining specific products which had been deleted.

Project Dropstrat comprised two stages: a personal interview and survey and a mail survey. The interviews with 31 managing or marketing directors provided the ideal setting for eliciting and probing ideas about the outcomes of specific product deletion decisions. From these interviews, a list of consequences deriving from product deletion was compiled. This list is given in Table 4.8.

Table 4.8 Consequences of product deletions

After deleting the product, stocks (raw and/or finished) had to be written off
There was adverse customer reaction to the deletion
The deletion led to enhanced company profits
After the product was dropped, no further orders or enquiries were received for it
The deletion led to a loss of confidence in the salesforce
The deletion adversely affected sales volume and market share
The deletion led to enhanced sales and profits of other products
The gap left in the market by dropping the product was filled by competition

Source: Avlonitis and Hart (1985).

As can be seen by scanning the table, some statements are positive — for example, 'the deletion led to enhanced company profits' — while some are more negative — 'after deleting the product, stocks had to be written off'.

Perhaps more interesting than the direction of the outcome statements are the dimensions they are seen to represent. Specifically, writing off stocks, increasing overall profits or increasing sales and profits of other products share an obvious financial tone. On the other hand, the salesforce's confidence, enquiries after deletion, customer reaction and competitors filling any gap relate more directly to marketing issues.

With these possible dimensions in mind, the mail survey stage was used to analyse these outcome statements more thoroughly, using factor analysis. This analysis of 156 specific deletions described by the mail survey respondents yielded four dimensions or outcome profiles that explained 70% of the variance. Table 4.9 presents these findings.

The four outcome profiles are now described briefly in turn:

Maintaining Competitive Position

Where a deletion results in the maintenance of the company's competitive position, the company has managed to drop a product without leaving the field open to development by competitors. Furthermore, no overall loss in market share has resulted, and there has been no loss in the confidence of the salesforce — which can be a major consideration in deletion.

Table 4.9 Success profiles for deletion: a factor analytic solution ($N = 156$)

Factor name (% variance explained)	Variables on factor	Variable loading
Maintaining competitive position (24.3%)	The decision led to a loss of confidence in the salesforce*	0.53
	The decision adversely affected sales volume and market share*	0.81
	The gap left by dropping the product was filled by the competition*	0.81
Retaining customer goodwill (17.7%)	There was adverse customer reaction*	0.84
	The decision led to a loss of confidence in the salesforce*	0.45
	After the product was dropped, there were no further enquiries or orders for it	0.73
Improving profitability (14%)	Dropping this product led to enhanced company profits	0.73
	This decision led to enhanced sales and profits of other products	0.81
Improving financial structure (14%)	No stocks have been written off	0.90
	Dropping this product led to enhanced company profits	0.39

* These items were reverse scored. High totals (disagreement with statements) were interpreted as a successful outcome and low totals (agreement with statements) were interpreted as an unsuccessful outcome.
Source: Avlonitis, G.J. (1987). Project Dropstrat: What types of product elimination decisions are likely to be successful? *International Journal of Research in Marketing*, **4**(1), 43–57. Reproduced by permission.

Retaining Customer Goodwill

Where the customer's goodwill is retained, there is usually no residual demand for the deleted product nor any expression of dissatisfaction on the customer's part.

Improving Profitability

Where profitability improves, this refers to the profits of other products (which run the risk of becoming less profitable as they absorb more overheads) as well as to that of the company as a whole.

Improving Financial Structure

Where there is an improved financial structure, this means that the deletion was well managed and did not entail any writing off of finished or raw material stocks.

In describing these 'outcome profiles', Avlonitis (1987) stressed that no deletion decisions would be successful on all four counts. That this is so should not come as any surprise. As outlined earlier, products are often deleted for a variety of different reasons, which would result in different foci and outcomes. For example, if a product were to be removed from the range in order to divert resources into ventures with greater long-term potential, then there might well be some negative repercussions such as adverse customer reaction or the resulting gap in the market being filled by competitors. In such an instance, it would be the responsibility of the managers involved to assess these repercussions in the light of the overall objective of the deletion decision. With these issues in mind, Avlonitis (1987) sought to investigate whether there was any relationship between the outcome policies described above and the type of deletion. The type of deletion was defined as comprising:

- the original circumstances triggering the decision to delete the product
- whether the deleted product was replaced
- the product's position on the product life-cycle curve
- whether the deletion was considered to be part of overall product-market strategy.
- the importance of the product (measured in terms of the percentage of sales volume it accounted for at the time of deletion and whether any fixed capital was *solely* invested in it)

Avlonitis' analysis of these features produced eight types of deletion (for a full discussion of these see Avlonitis (1987)):

1. Product elimination due to coercion by external forces
2. Replacement of a 'major' product facing competitive pressures and declining demand
3. Replacement of a poorly designed and unprofitable product hurting the company's image

4. Product elimination for the purpose of diverting the resources released onto new strategic ventures
5. Product elimination due to decline in market potential
6. Product elimination due to the development of an active variety reduction policy
7. Product elimination due to poor financial performance and declining demand
8. Elimination of an 'unsuccessful' new product experiencing problems at the early stages of its life

In order to see what outcomes were associated with which type of product deletion decision, canonical analysis was used to interpret the data. Of the eight types of deletion decision identified by Avlonitis, four were significantly associated with particular outcomes (Table 4.10).

Table 4.10 Associations between types of deletion and outcome profile

Outcome profile	Deletion type			
	Replacement of a major product	Development of an active variety reduction programme	Product deletion to release resources	Deletion of an unsuccessful new product
Positive	Maintenance of competitive position	Improvements in overall profitability; improvements in financial structure	Retention of customer goodwill; improvements in overall profitability; improvements in financial structure	
Negative		Poor prospects for maintaining customer goodwill	Poor prospects for maintaining competitive position	Poor prospects for overall profitability and financial structure

Note: for a summary of the statistics see Appendix 1.

As can be seen from Table 4.10, where associations are found between the type of deletion and outcome, no deletion type is successful on all four dimensions identified in Table 4.9. However, those deletions that are taken as strategic decisions (for instance developing a variety reduction programme, replacing a major line with a new improved product or deleting a product to make way for alternative developments) are more strongly associated with more of the successful outcomes than those which are taken as an *ad hoc* or crisis decision. The failure of a new product and its subsequent deletion is negatively associated with the features of successful deletion outcomes, while those deletions brought about by external forces or poor product performance, be it technical or commercial, are not associated with any of the successful outcomes (see Appendix 1).

This research demonstrates that the outcomes of deletion decisions can be both positive and negative, and that managerial trade-offs are required. However, Project Dropstrat concluded that those decisions that were initiated for strategic reasons were more likely to be successful on more counts than those taken in a reactive, crisis-type manner.

PRODUCT DELETION OBJECTIVES

From the above discussion on the nature of success in product deletion, it is apparent that time is needed to plan it properly. This in itself is a good enough reason for reviewing the product line regularly with an explicit view to considering products which may, in the future, have to be deleted or replaced. However, whatever the window or lead-time on the final decision, we can derive the following theoretical list of objectives for deletion from the description of successful outcomes presented above.

1. No gap must be left for competitors to fill
2. Overall company market share should not drop significantly
3. No customers should express dissatisfaction as a result of the deletion
4. No raw or finished stocks should be written off
5. The salesforce should not lose confidence in the range
6. The sales of other products should not be affected
7. The profits of other products should not be affected
8. Overall profitability should not drop

However, in viewing these suggested objectives, two factors must be borne in mind. First, not all objectives can be achieved. A trade-off among them will have to be made. Secondly, they are expressed in absolute terms. For example, objective 1 is *No* gap must be left for competitors'. In reality, this might be impossible and managers would then set the objective at the maximum gap tolerable.

SUMMARY

In this second part of the chapter, we have looked at:

- the importance of product deletion as a managerial activity;
- the reasons for neglect of product deletion;
- how to view product deletion as a successful activity;
- how to construct objectives for product deletion.

From the discussion it is clear that, while there are sound and legitimate reasons for neglecting deletion, it can be ignored to the point that the only option open to management is the 'crisis' solution. Since the most successful deletions tend to be those that have been managed *strategically*, it is important for managers to plan product deletion in such a way as to set objectives that can be realistically achieved.

CONCLUSIONS

This chapter has attempted to shed fresh light on product policy by adopting a number of perspectives which are not apparent in textbook coverage of this important and complex subject. It has dealt with product development and deletion, both of which are vital for the effective management of the firm's product portfolio and, in the last analysis, impact on each other. In each of these subject areas, recent empirical research has been applied to develop our understanding of the procedures and decision processes involved. In the case of new product development, the research serves to demonstrate the inadequacies of normative representations of the development process, and how success in this task involves the management of parallel strands of development and the generation and handling of sophisticated marketing and technical information. In the case of product deletion, recent empirical research has sought to lay the groundwork for understanding this activity in a conceptual sense, thereby allowing for the proactive management of the deletion process to achieve positive outcomes. In both areas, research tends to raise more questions than answers, but nevertheless demonstrates the importance of understanding what constitute successful outcomes in order to devise and manage appropriate inputs.

REFERENCES

Alexander, R.S. (1964) The death and burial of 'sick' products, *Journal of Marketing*, **28**, April, 1–7.

Avlonitis, G. (1983) Product elimination decisions and strategies. *Industrial Marketing Management*, **12**, February, 31–43.

Avlonitis, G. (1985) Revitalising weak industrial products. *Industrial Marketing Management*, **14**, May, 93–105.

Avlonitis, G. (1987) Linking different types of product elimination to their performance outcome. *International Journal of Research in Marketing*, **4**(1), 43–57.

Avlonitis, G., and Hart, S.J. (1985) Product elimination decision-making in British manufacturing industry: 4 conceptual frameworks and preliminary results. Presented at Research In Management Conference, Ashridge Management College, January 1985.

Baker, M.J. (1985) *Marketing: An Introductory Text*, 4th edn. Macmillan, London.

Booz, Allen, and Hamilton (1982) *New Products Management for the 1980s*. Booz, Allen and Hamilton, New York.

Cannon, T. (1986) *Basic Marketing: Principles and practice*, 2nd edn. Holt, Rinehart and Winston, London.

Cooper, R.G. (1979) The dimensions of industrial new product success and failure. *Journal of Marketing*, **43**, 93–103.

Cooper, R.G. (1984) New product strategies: What distinguishes top performers? *Journal of Product Innovation Management*, **1**(2), 151–64.

Cooper, R.G. (1988) The new product process: A decision guide for managers. *Journal of Marketing Management*, **3**(3), 238–255.

Crawford, C.M. (1983) *New Products Management*. Irwin, Homewood, Illinois.

Hart, S.J. (1987) An empirical investigation of the product elimination decision-making process in British manufacturing industry. Unpublished PhD thesis, University of Strathclyde.

Hart, S.J. (1988) The causes of product deletion in British manufacturing companies. *Journal of Marketing Management*, **3**(3), 328–343.

Hart, S.J. (1989) The analysis and revitalisation of problem products. Presented at the XVIII Annual Conference of the European Marketing Academy, Athens, April 1989, 1125–1150.

Hart, S.J., and Service, L. (1988) The effects of managerial attitudes to design on company performance. *Journal of Marketing Management*, **4**(2), 217–229.

Hart, S.J., and Snelson, P.A. (1989) The new product development process: Areas for research. Department of Marketing Working Paper, WP89/4. University of Strathclyde.

Hise, R.T., and McGinnis, M.A. (1975) Product elimination: Practices, policies and ethics. *Business Horizons*, June, 25–32.

Hise, R.T., Parasuraman, A., and Viswanathan, R. (1984) Product elimination: A neglected management responsibility. *Journal of Business Strategy*, Spring, 56–63.

Johne, F.A., and Snelson, P.A. (1988) Auditing product innovation activities in manufacturing firms. *R&D Management*, **18**(3), 227–233.

Kotler, P. (1988) *Marketing: Analysis, Planning and Control*, 6th edn. Prentice-Hall, Englewood Cliffs, New Jersey.

McSurely, H.B., and Wilemon, D.L. (1973) A product evaluation, improvement and removal model. *Industrial Marketing Management*, **2**, 319–331.

Peters, T.J., and Waterman, R.H. (1982) *In Search of Excellence: Lessons from America's Best-Run Companies*. Harper & Row, New York.

Pride, W.M., and Ferrell, O.C. (1989) *Marketing*, 6th edn. Houghton Mifflin, Boston, Mass.

Rothwell, R. (1977) The characteristics of successful innovators and technical progressive firms (with some comments on innovation research). *R&D Management*, **7**(3), 191–206.

Salerno, F. (1982) Processes et Comportements d'Abandon de Produits: Analyse et Implications. Thèse de Doctorat d'Etat et Science de Gestion, Université de Lille.

APPENDIX 1

Canonical summary statistics

Variates	Canonical	R, F	D.F.	Prob.	Criterion set redundancy	% total redundancy
1	0.61	3.38	32	< 0.0001	0.0919	60
2	0.41	1.79	21	< 0.05	0.0432	29
3	0.23	0.85	12	NS	0.0124	8
4	0.15	0.59	5	NS	0.0051	3
					0.1517	100

Relationships between variables and significant canonical functions

Variables	Canonical loadings 1	2
	Criterion set	
Maintaining competitive position	–0.92	–0.17
Retaining customer goodwill	0.32	–0.10
Improving profitability	–0.20	0.84
		0.52
	Predictor set	
Elimination due to coercion by external forces	0.09	0.09
Replacement of a 'major' product	–0.31	0.50
Replacement of a poorly designed product	–0.26	0.24
Product elimination to release resources	0.74	0.61
Elimination due to decline in market potential	–0.01	0.11
Development of an active variety reduction policy	–0.48	0.42
Elimination due to poor product performance	–0.12	–0.12
Elimination of an 'unsuccessful' new product	0.16	–0.30

Note: The results of this canonical analysis were verified using cluster analysis and one-way ANOVAs. For details, refer to Avlonitis (1987).

CHAPTER 5
Managing the Mix in Europe

Paul Fifield

The Winchester Consulting Group, Winchester

PREAMBLE

This work is derived from the author's research, which was carried out between 1980 and 1984 and submitted in 1985 for the degree of PhD at Cranfield School of Management.

During the period of the research the magic phrase 'Single European Marketplace by 1992' had still not been formulated. Now at the turn of the decade the relevance of the work has been accentuated by the shift in political direction in the EC.

This abridged version of the final thesis omits much of the basic literature review and theoretical arguments contained in the original and concentrates more on the practical applications of the findings. It is important also that the reader should understand the original intention behind the work. Unlike many pieces of academic research which concentrate on the depth analysis of minutiae, the main interest here was always to take a 'macro' approach to the vast problem of European market segmentation. This, of course, means that practical application of the findings will be dependent upon additional, more directed, research being carried out either within academia or preferably by commercial organizations.

The primary objective of this research was to open the way for the more detailed work which is so desperately needed in the area of European marketing.

Looking now towards the 1990s, the pressures on business of all kinds to embrace the Single European Market are intense. Of course, much of this pressure is politically inspired and commercial organizations should, as always, temper the political encouragements with economic reality. The core question when considering a wider activity in Europe must be 'is there a sufficient demand for our products and services in the other European countries?'

Perspectives on Marketing Management, Volume 1
Edited by M.J. Baker
Published 1991 by John Wiley & Sons Ltd

Before embarking on any expensive growth plans in Europe, the organization must find out who the potential customers are and what they want. The drive to political and economic union of 'the twelve' may well have significant short- and long-term effects on the business infrastructure. What is much less certain is the effects it will have on consumer buying habits.

The term 'Single European Market' is in itself a huge assumption. It will be clear to those organizations that take the time to think about it that the wider markets and economies of scale promised by the SEM do not depend upon the harmonization of VAT rates or the dismantling of trade barriers alone; they will depend finally upon the homogeneity of buying motives among the European population of some 320 million consumers. In other words, we are to expect that, say, the German mother, the British mother, the Italian mother and the Dutch mother will all start to buy the same products and services for their families after 1992. Not only is this patently unreasonable, but an equally good case can be made for the increasing fragmentation of Europe after 1992, as the various national and cultural groups strive to assert their individuality within an imposed European 'norm'.

Back in 1980 when this research was started, the issues and the level of uncertainty were much the same. The problems facing the existing or would-be pan-European organization have not changed in the interim. The need to make some sense of the confusion of the European market is still critical to market success. This book has provided a golden opportunity to raise these important issues among a wider audience at a time when Europe is coming to the front of all of our minds.

PART 1. A REVIEW OF CURRENT PRACTICE

INTRODUCTION

THE STIMULUS FOR THE RESEARCH

It is important to put the research project into context at this early stage by identifying how the idea for the work was born. The first spur to the research originated from the author's own experience over a number of years marketing consumer products in Belgium. During this period a number of products were maintained in the product range and an average of five new products a year was launched, all marketed and supported on a national basis. It soon became evident that a number of products marketed by the company experienced differing degrees of sales success in the two principal regions of the country (Dutch-speaking Flanders and French-speaking Wallony). On closer observation it was also evident that these differences could not be attributed directly to differences in pricing policy, promotional policy or anomalies in the distribution system.

Since the physical product was identical in both regions and the product platform was supposedly common for the entire national market, the answer was presumed to lie in a variance in the marketplace itself. Further investigation showed that the classic segmentation process was sound.

At this stage the only reasonable explanation for the difference appeared to be located in the consumer personality/character profiles of the two regional groupings, i.e. differences in the 'regional character' somehow affected the way in which the product benefits were perceived. It is significant that in Belgium the two principal regions have their own distinctive languages rather than simply different dialects of a common tongue. They also have very different cultural backgrounds and origins.

This supposedly cultural effect was also present (it later transpired) in the sales of some of those products which appeared to maintain equal sales levels in both regions. On closer examination it was apparent that original text supplied to the advertising agency (in French) had been *transposed* rather than simply translated, and that in the process the 'product promises' had been subtly altered. This often happened when a copywriter of Dutch language mother tongue had handled the work; he presumably brought his cultural perceptions as well as his translation abilities to bear on the product.

At this point the question arose, national prejudices and infrastructures apart, of whether it might be more functional if the two regions of Belgium were reassigned to the neighbouring countries of France and the Netherlands; France to market products to French-speaking Wallony and the Netherlands to market products to Dutch-speaking Flanders. However, although a rapid review of the current marketing literature categorically vetoed the idea of dispensing with the 'nation' as the prime marketing unit, no empirical evidence to back this point of view could be found nor any evidence of this approach having been used in the past and failing.

Such 'acceptance' of the *status quo* is unusual in domestic marketing but perhaps more common in the area of international marketing. The current research has not taken the Belgian case in isolation although much emphasis is placed on the Belgian data in the analysis because of its unique 'dual-culture' situation. The interaction between culture and product positioning has, however, remained the primary target for the investigation.

THE AIM OF THE RESEARCH

The central aim of the research is to investigate the role of culture as an international marketing variable, to better understand how cultural groupings could provide an alternative segmentation base.

This research will test the hypothesis that cultural groupings exist in Western Europe. These cultural groupings are larger than individual nation-states and should offer considerable potential for cost savings if employed as a base for international segmentation.

Owing to the wide nature of international segmentation and the all-pervasive nature of the culture, the work will approach the problem from a 'macro' standpoint. In this way the findings will be as generally relevant as possible to multinational and international organizations. The use of this 'macro' approach, however, means that it will be unlikely that the findings will be directly applicable to a given organization in their raw state.

The principal aim of this work is, then, to provide the justification for interested organizations to undertake the extensive and expensive research required to apply the findings in their own markets. The justification will be provided by showing that a relationship exists between personal values and culture.

THE SCOPE OF THE RESEARCH

The wide-ranging nature of the work makes it important to define clearly the exact scope and limits of the study. The objective is to test the validity of cultural groupings as a segmentation base. A 'macro' approach will be taken by considering consumers in general rather than as specific to any one company or product range.

Objectives

The research is considered as 'pioneering' in nature. It is thought unlikely that the results obtained will be of *immediate* practical value to the international organization. In any research project, the decision must be made to tackle either a very restricted area of the problem but in sufficient depth to allow relatively rapid implementation of the results or to approach the problem 'in total', thereby sacrificing a degree of direct applicability. Owing to the scale of the international operations involved it was decided to adopt the latter approach. This means that the precise objective of the research must be to provide enough evidence to justify further more detailed research into the commercial exploitation of culture as an international segmentation base.

Products

The research concentrates primarily on consumer products. Future studies may well extend the work into areas of industrial products but in the meantime we will concentrate on directing the efforts towards those industries in which brand image and correct product positioning are crucial to marketing success. Fast-moving consumer goods (FMCG) are typically highly competitive and involve a high degree of product differentiation. The manufacturers/marketers of FMCG products will probably be the first to recognize the benefits of a quantifiable culture–purchase behaviour relationship.

Geographical

The area of Western Europe has been selected for the analysis. As well as being known to the author and accessible, it is unique in that it comprises a large number of independent nation-states within a concise geographical area. The separate nations are all densely populated and have good internal and external communications and commercial infrastructures. It is also hypothesized that Europe maintains only a small number of distinct cultural groups, fewer than the number of nation-states, and so will allow a good comparative analysis to be made between the validities of cultural and national segmentation bases. The European nations eventually included in the data analysis are:

1. United Kingdom.
2. France.
3. Belgium.
4. Denmark.

Marketing Mix

The marketing function in any organization, domestic or international, is a detailed and complicated task. It involves the constant setting and 'fine-tuning' of the marketing mix to match the opportunities offered by a continually changing market. Although product policy is only one component of McCarthy's marketing mix (product, price, place and promotion), it is the point at which all subsequent mixes start. Only when the product mix has been determined (product attributes, position and concept) can the pricing, promotional and distribution plans be prepared. It is because of this central importance that the research concentrates on product policy decisions and, more specifically, on the product–market match.

Management Decision-making

Every organization maintains a number of separate management levels each with its own responsibilities and decision-making problems. With the geographical area and objectives of the exercise clearly set, the hypothesized cultural groupings are considerably larger than nation-states. This implies a process of market segmentation being carried out before reducing Europe to a collection of national markets; such a process of 'macro-segmentation' is of prime importance to the head office or other centralized control function which has responsibility for decision-making above the level of local (normally national) unit chief executives. The research is directed at improving control at this 'super-national' level. Often the bulk of the work carried out at a local level consists of ensuring the execution of plans within the context of local conditions. Due to the pioneering nature of the research and the practical constraints upon the researcher, the problems of application will be considered at some length but more detailed analysis will be left to future researchers.

THE PRACTICAL BENEFITS ACCRUING FROM THE RESEARCH

The research has been conducted with the intention of being useful to multinational corporations and international companies marketing consumer products to Western European markets. The work has been directed with the specific problems of these organizations in mind, although any organization responsible for its own marketing activities in foreign markets must benefit from a better understading of how its customers behave.

Europe is special in that it represents a collection of densely populated independent national states all within a concise geographical area with good communications. Although comparisons between Europe and the United States of America are often made, marketing practice differs widely between the two areas; any European move towards the level of integration existing in the USA would result in spectacular savings in marketing costs for Europe-based organizations.

Assuming that there are fewer cultural groupings in Western Europe than nation-states, the international organization which employs cultural rather than national segmentation can expect to reap considerable benefits from a reduced number of different product platforms, according to Terpstra (1983):

1. Economies of scale in production through longer production runs
2. Economics of scale in research and development as fewer products are required on a world basis
3. Economies in marketing such as packaging design, communications design, etc.
4. Increased management control over more similar products and marketing

THE INTERNATIONAL MARKETING TASK

The trend over recent years has been for an increased number of companies to move into international markets. According to Majaro (1982):

> Two major developments have imperceptibly become the vital forces that have determined the strategic route that modern firms have taken. They are:
> The marketing concept
> Internationalisation.

This move away from the 'secure' home market has not always been the logical, well-planned strategic action foreseen by some marketing theorists. Frequently the company is forced into international markets, unprepared, as a defensive ploy against increasing international competition in its hitherto 'safe' home market. In fact Piercy (1980), from a survey of 231 companies, showed that the decision to 'go international' is not necessarily a rational seeking after business opportunity but rather the result of a series of chance decisions. Piercy suggests six stages:

1. No interest, would not even fill unsolicited foreign orders
2. Fills unsolicited orders but does not seek to export actively
3. Active exporting considered
4. Experimental activity in some 'psychologically close' country
5. Company becomes established in that market
6. Possibilities of other 'psychologically more distant' countries considered

Nationally successful companies have not always reaped the benefits they expected from their forays into foreign markets. There are a number of important factors in the successful marketing of a company's products internationally. The classic approach of the 4Ps as suggested by McCarthy (product, price, place, promotion) demonstrates that the task of marketing management is not an easy one, especially in a dynamic environment embodying constant market change. The international marketing task, involving as it does multimarkets, adds extra dimensions of complexity.

It is well accepted that marketing success is depedent upon *all* of the principal components of the marketing mix being correctly manipulated; a flaw in any one area of the mix can negate all the good work done in the other areas. The first area of interest for the marketer (domestic or international) is always the product–market match. This operation is central to the marketing concept of producing benefits or solutions (products) for customers' needs or problems (markets), and the product–market match is the starting point for subsequent mixes and marketing decisions. According to Kotler (1972):

> These [products] are the foundation of the marketing program. The choice of products affects the choice of trade channels, promotional media and messages, physical distribution arrangements and other significant dimensions of the marketing program. (p. 423)

And from Gordon Oliver (1980):

> The essential vehicle for the provision of customer satisfaction is the product or service that the company offers in the market place. The array of decisions associated with that offer becomes the base ingredients in the development of the total marketing plan. All other marketing mix decisions need to be integrated with those of product planning, since they are about how to promote, price and distribute the product. (p. 145)

Because of the central importance of the product mix in the overall marketing strategy and the enormous amount of work still to be done in the area of international marketing research, this project will concentrate on the area of international product policy. While any realistic implementation of the research results cannot be made without consideration of the other areas of the mix, it is more practical at this stage to limit the scope of the research to a clearly defined area. A more detailed discussion of the research scope and terms of reference will be found later.

As was explained in the introductory section, we will be concentrating on the problem of product positioning as it confronts the international marketer. To explain briefly the concept of product positioning and its importance to the marketing function, we can turn again to Kotler (1972), who describes it thus:

> A product is always part of a field of competing products. . . . It is from the *competitive field* that the buyer makes his choice. . . . Distinctive products are those that have some differentiated product attributes or appeals. They occupy a distinct position in the market, offering certain things and not others. An indistinct product is not likely to survive in a field of distinct products, unless buyers attach little value to the distinctive qualities . . . Good marketing practice calls for trying to endow the company's product (or brand) with real or psychological differences. *A differentiated product* is one that is seen as desirably different from others by some of the buyers. (p. 425)

The essence of both national and international product management is that success and failure are both created at the planning stage prior to actual market entry. The question of which product to market in fact conceals three distinct questions which must be addressed by the company.

1. What are the main product attributes which are differentially responded to by the buyer? (Product attributes)
2. What are the positions of the various competing products in the product space? (Product positions)
3. What is the best position for this product in the product space? (Product concept) (Kotler, 1972)

Minor realignments of the product position as it travels through the stages of the product life cycle are relatively easy to accommodate, but major repositioning of a product after launch can be extremely expensive, as Campbell's Soups found out in the 1950s when launching condensed soups into the UK market; only after two years and $30 million did the company succeed in satisfactorily explaining the benefits of the product to the British customer (Ricks, Arpan and Fu, 1974).

The central question for the international marketer is which product to market in each country. Should a standardized approach be attempted, the success stories are as enticing as the disaster stories are discouraging. If he approaches the problem on a market-by-market basis, can he be sure that the increased marketing investment will be justified by increased sales levels? Are apparent market differences real or the effect of local patriotic sentiment?

We will first consider how multinational and international organizations actually handle these problems and then look at the marketing theory available to guide them.

INTERNATIONAL PRODUCT POLICY — COMPANY EXPERIENCE

The first point which we note from the literature relating to company experience in international markets is the very wide range of approaches that have been attempted by different organizations. It is not possible here to catalogue the entire range of material which recounts company experience in international markets, but it is important to try to draw the main conclusions from our collective past experience.

The great 'success' stories in international marketing tend to recount the success of a standardized product policy, and examples cited are of Coca-Cola, Levi-Strauss (Terpstra, 1983), and IBM (Cateora, 1983), among others. The advantages of a standardized product range in international markets are considerable and are explained in more depth below. What is not clear in these cases is whether the move was a calculated strategy to satisfy identified universal wants or the naive export of a domestic product which luckily happened to appeal to similar segments in foreign markets.

More recent examples of success through standardization can be cited, McDonald's, Kentucky Fried Chicken, Sony Walkman, etc., and much effort has been dedicated to discovering the reasons for this success, as will be discussed below.

The 'disasters' are even better documented than the successes and constantly show the dire results of exporting a domestically successful 'marketing package' to foreign markets where needs and wants are different. In the late 1960s Campbell's Soups, General Foods and General Mills all tried to repeat their domestic (US) successes in European markets by following the same product and marketing procedures which had worked so well at home (Ricks, 1983). General Foods later reapproached the European markets with one of its products, coffee, and by adapting the product to a range of different regional tastes succeeded in building a respectable brand share in most markets.

Another point revealed by a study of the various case histories is the apparent lack of knowledge transfer among companies. Despite the well-documented failures, Radio Shack followed exactly the same procedure of exporting domestic products and marketing from the US into Europe during the late 1970s (Terpstra, 1983). Radio Shack's results were not good. The company was so insensitive to local environmental factors that it timed the big Christmas promotion to peak towards December 25, so missing the St Nicholas (December 6) present-exchanging date dominant in many European countries. Also, the product and company image which was so successful in the home market appeared to be less attractive to many European markets.

Another apparent example of standardization is typified by the Jeep experience. By 1980 American Motors Corporation was exporting the Jeep to most world markets and manufacturing, assembling or licensing in over 20 countries. The basic Jeep product may be standardized but the particular role of the product varies from country to country. For example, in developing countries they are multipurpose vehicles for transportation, in developed countries they are primarily recreational. They also serve as taxis in the Philippines, coffee transport in Colombia and as ambulances in Norway (Terpstra, 1983). Such a product range is an example of adaptation to local requirements.

At the opposite end of the scale are the large multinational and international companies with a history of localized growth. Beechams, the UK toiletries company, for example, operates throughout Europe and maintains separate product ranges on a country basis, with Italian products being, for the most part, specific to the Italian market and marketed nowhere else in Europe. Other companies (e.g. Unilever, Van den Berghs) operate this policy of different brands on a national or grouped national basis; such companies are typified by their relatively high expenditure on market research needed to ensure optimal product–market matches in different environments. It is significant that the companies operating this multibrand policy tend to be in the FMCG market, where unit sales are high and relatively long production runs can be achieved in even the smaller markets.

What then can be concluded from observation of company practice? Clearly the benefits of a standardized international product range are tempting to every company management. The case for standardization has been recently reinforced by Levitt (1983), who has forecast the imminent demise of the multinational corporation and the rise of the 'global corporation'. The latter corporation, it is suggested, is typified by its

> . . . need to be competitive on a world-wide basis as well as nationally and seeks constantly to drive down prices by standardizing what it sells and how it operates. It treats the world as composed of few standardized markets rather than many customised markets. It actively seeks and vigorously works toward global convergence. (p. 96)

According to Levitt, there remain certain cultural and environmental differences among markets but these are diminishing with the growth in technology and communications; he also suggests that a company successful in a domestic segment should look for similar segments which almost certainly exist in other markets.

This approach obviously worked for McDonald's; it evidently did not work for Radio Shack.

The principal question then remains: how is the company to plan its international marketing? Standardized or adapted products? What is the cost/benefit of either approach? Aside from experiential learning and its associated high costs, we must consider the available theory which might serve to indicate the company's best approach.

INTERNATIONAL PRODUCT POLICY — THE SUPPORTING THEORY

A discussion of the supporting theory in the area of international product policy should begin with an examination of exactly what is meant by 'product'. The classic marketing-oriented definition is based on the task which the product performs, the benefit it offers or the role it plays in the customer's consumption system. A product can also be defined in terms of its physical or chemical characteristics. A detailed analysis of the term 'product' can be taken from Kotler (1972):

> . . . we can distinguish three distinct concepts of a product: the tangible product, extended product and generic product . . . The tangible product is the physical entity or service which is offered to the buyer. It is what is immediately recognised as the things sold. . . . The extended product is the tangible product along with the whole cluster of services that accompany it. . . . The generic product is the essential benefit that the buyer expects to get from the product . . . The important contribution of the generic-product idea is that benefits rather than features should guide the marketer's strategy. He must find ways to 'benefitize' his product. (p. 424)

And from Cateora (1983):

> The benefits or bundle of satisfactions received . . . includes three major components. At the centre is the core, the physical product and all its functional features. This part of the product along with the other two components, provides the bundle of utilities that the market derives from use of the product. Surrounding the core component is the packaging component that includes the physical package in which the product is presented as well as the brand name, trademark, styling and design features, price, and quality levels. The support services component completes the product buyers receive and from which the bundle of satisfactions are derived. This support services component includes repair and maintenance services, installation, delivery, warranty, spare parts, training and instructions, credit, and any other services related to the use and purchase of the product. (p. 411)

Progressing from the concept of the product in its domestic context to its international context, we can learn from Terpstra (1983) that:

> . . . But when the adjective 'foreign' or 'international' is added to a product, any of the definitions will change in some significant way.

Often the international products which a company markets are different either physically or chemically from the domestic production. The foreign customer's definition of the product is often different in terms of either the benefits it offers or the role it performs. At a more basic level, the packaging, labelling, branding and warranty aspects of the product are likely to be different in response to different languages, government restrictions and local customs.

The most basic contribution of marketing thought in the area of product policy has been to shift emphasis from the physical product itself to the needs and desires of the consumer. (This concept is at the heart of *Marketing Myopia* published by Theodore Levitt (1960) over 20 years ago.) It follows logically that product management should be primarily concerned with decisions which affect the consumer's perception of the firm's product offering.

When we move on to what is probably the key question in international marketing, 'what product(s) should the company be selling in its foreign markets?', an examination of the literature presents the operating company with a dilemma. Stress is placed upon the advantages of product and marketing standardization while at the same time it is explained at length how the differences in international markets act as traps for the unwary. Until the recent appearance of Levitt's article on market globalization (1983), it was difficult for the international business to reconcile these two approaches.

If we approach the problem from the viewpoint of standardization, the potential advantages open to the company have been summed up by Buzzell (1968) as follows:

Cost savings
- Economies of mass production
- Economies of product design
- Economies of packaging costs
- Economies of advertising and promotion costs

Consistency with customers
- The increase in customer mobility and international communications means that standardized brands can both promote purchase abroad and reinforce loyalty back home. The standardized product/brand can exploit international communications convergence. The international producer is coming under increasing pressure from international customers to standardize ranges (e.g. IBM's standardized range matches the requirements of its international (multibranch) banking clients).

Improved planning and control
- Marketing standardization may help to avoid wasteful competition between subsidiaries working on different models or cost/pricing strategies.

Exploiting good ideas
- Since good marketing ideas and people are hard to find, they should be used as widely as possible. Buzzell is also of the opinion that good ideas tend to have a universal appeal, especially with regard to the 'creative' areas of advertising and promotion.

Buzzell continues by describing those differences among countries which might act as a barrier to effective standardization; these are listed as:

Market characteristics
- Physical environment
- Stage of economic/industrial development
- Cultural factors

Industry conditions
- Stage of product life cycle by market
- Competition

Marketing institutions
- Distributive systems
- Advertising media and agencies

Legal restrictions

Buzzell concludes:

> Despite the potential benefits of standardization, the great majority of companies still operate on the premise that each national market is different and must be provided with its own, distinctive marketing program. Why is diversity still the rule of the day in multinational marketing? In many cases differences simply reflect the *customary* ways of doing business which have evolved in an earlier period when national boundaries were more formidable barriers than they are today. But even if tradition did not play a role, it must be recogised that there are and will continue to be some important obstacles to standardization. (p. 109)

Buzzell, however, does not give the practising businessman any indication of how he might discover which barriers to standardization are 'real' and which are 'customary'.

Majaro (1977) builds upon the work of Buzzell and gives some guidance as to the types of product/market which would encourage standardization. He makes the following points:

1. Corporative objectives. A firm which strives for profit maximization rather than international market penetration will be more attracted to standardization.
2. The markets and their needs. The international marketer must ask whether the needs of individual markets are really so different from each other that the adoption of standardization would limit the use of the product to uneconomic levels. Systematic and detailed data collection for each market must be made. (Majaro gives a detailed table of the types of data required.)
3. Company resources. Differentiation is an expensive exercise.
4. Nature of the product. Different products have different potentials for standardization. Majaro suggests the following areas for consideration:

   The product life cycle
   The universality of the product's appeal
   Level of service required
   Branding
   Ease of production
   Legal constraints

So we can see that the question of standardization or product adaptation is based on extensive research of the target international markets in order to determine the potential in both the market and the product for a standardized marketing approach. This reliance upon market research obviously raises questions of accuracy, confidentiality and dependability of international sources and methods.

More importantly, we find that the various authors stress a change in the way in which international companies should approach marketing. Traditional marketing orientation stresses the importance of using market wants to determine marketing and product strategy. In international marketing this may not be the most efficient way to proceed. Levitt (1983) states:

> The successful global corporation does not abjure customization or differentiation for the requirements of markets that differ in product preferences, spending patterns, shopping preferences, and institutional or legal arrangements. But the global corporation accepts and adjusts to these differences only reluctantly, only after relentlessly testing their immutability, after trying in various ways to circumvent and reshape them. There is only one significant respect in which a company's activities around the world are important, and that is in what it produces and how it sells. Everything else derives from, and is subsidiary to these activities. (p. 101).
>
> Companies that do not adapt to the new global realities will become victims of those that do.

And more precisely from Majaro (1977):

> International marketing is a vastly more complex process than marketing in one national marketplace. At the same time it must be recognised that nobody becomes an international marketing expert without having first won his spurs in a few micro-markets. The transition is difficult and often full of pitfalls. The essential pre-requisite is to develop the ability to rise above the immediate environment to a vantage point from which the global marketplace can be analysed and international strategies evaluated. How far a product can be standardised is a vital question and it can be answered only by those who have relinquished their micro-market orientations.

The question still remains, what are the practical alternatives open to the international company and how can it translate theory into practice?

WHAT IS A COMPANY TO DO?

So far we have considered the significant benefits inherent in a standardized approach to international markets while at the same time illustrating the many differences among markets and the considerable barriers to standardization which exist. The conclusion was that the degree to which the benefits of standardization are achievable depends upon the type of market(s), products, corporate objectives, resources, etc. In short, every company's position is different and only detailed research will reveal any potential.

In this section we will consider the approach outlined above in addition to two other alternative strategic approaches to international product management and product positioning. The aim of this analysis is to determine the *practical* advantages/disadvantages of the various approaches from the viewpoint of the international company. This section will also evaluate the alternative methods and will isolate the principal areas of wastage and inefficient operation.

The three methods together cover the range of alternatives open to the international company. The first method considered is the traditional market-oriented approach to world markets which places emphasis upon thorough research of individual market requirements and the production and marketing of the most appropriate products. The second method involves the grouping of markets into relatively homogeneous sets; the sets are then used as the marketing unit and larger-scale operation may be achieved. The third method is direct transposition of a domestic success into foreign markets without any adaptation.

METHOD 1: TRADITIONAL MARKET-ORIENTED APPROACH

The first method we consider is the traditional marketing approach of analysing each target market in order to determine the optimum product positioning for that market. The optimum product position as described here must be properly understood. This terminology is taken from domestic marketing and refers to the satisfaction of customer wants with an appropriate product. Customer satisfaction leads to sales maximization which in turn is a recognized route towards profit maximization. We have already seen that this relationship may not hold good in the international area.

Traditional market orientation calls for a researched understanding of customer wants as a basis for product development. Internationally, the implication for the company is often slightly different; the company already may have a product or range of products which it markets domestically and in which it has a degree of experience. If the company is to adhere faithfully to the marketing concept it must research *each* individual target market to determine customer needs and wants and then carry out the necessary product and marketing adaptations in order to match local requirements as closely as possible.

This market-by-market company practice may be a logical consequence of organization into localized profit-centre operations.

International companies are usually organized on a national basis for obvious reasons. Marketing is usually based on the national scale while manufacture, research and distribution may be national or 'shared' depending on the company's market requirements and scale of operations. National differences in legal systems, taxation, communications and distribution infrastructure have always encouraged international companies to see their operations as a collection of *national* subsidiaries. The implication for a company structured in this way and contemplating a pan-European launch consists of initial exploratory research in up to 15 national markets.

Although it might be argued that this market-by-market approach must in the long run be the most efficient in terms of the product–market match, the practical marketing man cannot ignore the very high investment costs of the approach in terms of time and money, especially if the industry has a tradition of new product failure.

To consider the time problem first, it is well accepted that depth research and commercial confidentiality rarely exist side by side. The time needed to properly research each national market may give an agile competitor ample time to react, lay contingency plans or even arrange a pre-emptive launch. Wastage in terms of executive time will be particularly high if the company is organized on a profit-centre basis and local management has to be convinced of the need for research; more centralized operations will be better placed to impose a common research structure and centralize an amount of the initial research work (barring local fieldwork).

Apart from the obvious costs of multicountry research the major 'wastage' often occurs after research results are produced. When the data are returned, the proposed product positions in each market are unlikely to be identical. There are a number of reasons for this divergency; the separate markets may in fact require different product positions to optimize company sales in response to consumer predispositions or market conditions. Unfortunately, there are other explanations of these differences such as the following.

Nationalism

Nationalism of the company's local operation or the research organization. It is not the purpose of this work to deal in stereotypes, but the expression 'Ah yes, but you must understand that in France it is different' has become something of a monument in European marketing. Behind this rather glib statement we meet for the first time (but not for the last) the conscious or subconscious desire of local operations to search for differences rather than similarities in markets.

Politics

In any large-scale organization, internal politics is a force which is accepted, underestimated and rarely discussed. Its power to affect local research results is all too real. Protestations of professional integrity from respected research organizations notwithstanding, it is a commercial reality that a local operating subsidiary which directly commissions (and pays for) current and future research projects will not be ignored. The consequences should the local unit have preconceived ideas on what the product position should be, or indeed does not wish to launch the product in its market (for whatever reason), are obvious.

The 'Not-Invented-Here' Syndrome

This is a real problem in research bias, especially in those markets that have a strong sense of national pride and chauvinism. The problem is aggravated where the research facilities are also decentralized and professional pride becomes involved.

Research Problems

Research problems such as differing methodologies and linguistic/translation problems are well documented in the literature and common in multicountry projects. Although the research agencies are well aware of these problems, the degree to which each agency is able, or indeed willing, to compensate for these effects becomes an unknown variable and must reduce the trustworthiness of the results.

Company's Choice

The ultimate problem facing the company is whether to follow the directives of the research or ignore them. Not surprisingly, there is strong pressure to implement research results once they have been presented (and paid for) although not enough companies appreciate the problems involved in a diversified product programme. Besides foregoing all the benefits of economies of scale that can be achieved by a standardized product position, the company incurs substantially higher marketing investment costs when launching what is in fact a number of *different* products. In the long term any benefits of transnational promotion will be forfeited and, more importantly, it will not be possible to properly compare sales results among different countries. This lack of long-term control is probably the highest cost of a diversified launch since head office will not be able to pinpoint areas of inefficient management in their organizations. This is a problem not only for the product in question but for the company's entire product range and future international business.

In conclusion, we must pose the question: even if we accept the traditional argument that each market must be independently researched and *sales* will be maximized by an adapted market-by-market launch, will the extra sales generated by an optimal product–market match exceed the extra costs involved in managing such a launch? In short, the company may be achieving sales maximization but not *profit* maximization.

Critically, can the company place enough trust in the research results to justify a course of action which will not only commit it to significant expenditure (in the short term to satisfy local needs and in the long term to maintain different product platforms in various markets) but also deprives the management of good control mechanisms?

METHOD 2: MARKETING-ORIENTED APPROACH PLUS GROUPING

The second approach considered by many companies involves following current marketing theory and attempting to determine the optimum product position for each national market then, in order to achieve a degree of standardization, attempting to rationalize the number of product positions used in the total international market.

Majaro (1982) offers a detailed account of this grouping or 'clustering' process. He suggests:

> with adequate information one should be able to 'pair' markets that manifest similarities in their vital characteristics. Whilst one recognises that complete pairing is not likely to occur where foreign markets are concerned, one is prepared to accept minor differences. Thus, for instance, Norway and Denmark are different countries; in marketing terms there is a strong case for unifying the approach to both these markets. Finland has a language and a culture which differ from the other Scandinavian countries, nonetheless it has enough in common with others to justify a clustering approach when applying a concentrated marketing strategy. (p. 58)

Majaro suggests a method of clustering which involves the company selecting a 'benchmark' territory which represents either the company's strongest marketing centre or the intended focal point for international marketing. The aim of clustering is, then, to identify in some qualitative way how far other markets come close to the benchmark.

This approach would appear to offer the best opportunity of making an efficient compromise between traditional marketing theory and cost savings. Cost savings, however, are only made after all the initial market-by-market research has been carried out. Also, once the market research results are assembled, the company still has no solid theoretical guidelines as to the number of different product positions it should eventually support in, say, the European market. From the discussion above, we have already seen that the potential for standardization tends to be specific to a given product or market.

What happens in practice is that the company relies heavily upon qualitative data, perhaps including exploratory market research, and groups those countries whose (data) profiles are most similar. This method should indeed help to reduce marketing investment costs. The attendant problems are, however, quite serious. The major danger is that grouped platforms may be made based on erroneous research data or on conscious or unconscious subjective bias. Moreover, by depending heavily upon this qualitative data, the company is not guaranteed any long-term stability within the groups or clusters.

The company using the grouping approach may, in fact, be storing up very serious long-term problems for itself in return for relatively insignificant short-term cost savings. For the grouped approach to be worthwhile, the market groups must not only be stable over the life cycle of the product but they should also be relevant to other products in the company's range.

More importantly, the groupings must be relevant for new products. If the company is to invest heavily in its marketing, the international groupings should be consistent over the longer term (payback period) and offer the company a reasonably homogeneous market for its new products. Such market groups cannot be determined on the basis of normal initial market research, which is, by definition, limited to the acceptance of *one* given product in *one* given market at *one* given time. Nor can such groups be defined by an analysis of existing product sales. Predictability is dependent upon an understanding of *why* people buy, not just *what* people buy.

The only reliable method of grouping national markets that may produce groups which are stable in the longer term involves a shift of marketing emphasis as described by Levitt and Majaro (see above). For the company that wishes to benefit from a more standardized approach, management appears to have little alternative but to reject current domestic marketing theory which is based on *differences* between markets and concentrate its research effort upon identifying the *similarities* among markets. In addition, the information needed must shift from observation and description to understanding and motivations. Such a shift of emphasis could be expected to produce research that is more internationally comparable.

The question of grouping or clustering international markets, either prior to market entry or of existing markets, is in fact a problem of international market segmentation on a macro-scale. Although much has been written on the topic of market segmentation in a domestic market context, international market segmentation is a relatively under-researched area. It is sufficient to say at this point that the absence of good guiding theory does not make it easy for the company to determine the best base(s) for the segmentation of its international markets.

In conclusion, it must appear from the company point of view that market grouping, while 'probably worth a try', has few guarantees of success. Grouping on the basis of market-by-market research or sales results may offer cost savings and standardized product positions but still entails considerable investment in terms of research as well as dubious market groups. For the company which markets or plans to market a range of products over the long term, tackling the problem of market grouping involves 'going it alone' without constructive theoretical guidance on what might constitute a good marketing base for international segmentation.

METHOD 3: DIRECT EXPORT FROM DOMESTIC SUCCESS

The third alternative strategy we will consider implies that the company makes no allowances for international differences of environment or customer tastes, etc., but simply produces more domestic product and markets a completely standardized product to all markets. Some allowance will naturally have to be made for language, voltage differences, etc., but these modifications are considered production, not marketing modifications.

This third method of international product positioning deserves mention if only because it is still employed by some companies, often typifying their first foray into international markets. Despite the denigrating remarks which this approach receives in almost all of the marketing literature, it is not difficult to understand the temptation of a completely standardized and uniform approach to all world and European markets. If we think back to the work presented by Piercy, most UK companies who start in international business do so after they have been notified of an international demand by unsolicited export orders for their *domestic* product; product adaptation is a second-level consideration for the newly international organization. Also the one or two examples of companies who have managed to succeed with the 'one-product-to-all-markets' approach act as powerful magnets to the internationally inexperienced.

Coca-Cola, JCB, Sony, IBM and Burberry's are after all very visible success stories, while Campbell's Soups' $30 million mistake in attempting to launch condensed soups outside the US (Ricks, Arpan and Fu, 1974) is less well known. While Coca-Cola's uniform projected image has been successful with a segment in each target market, Campbell's refusal to adapt their product to local requirements meant that opposition was met in England, where the consumer was used to ready-to-eat soups not concentrates, and in Italy, where great emphasis is placed on home cooking.

Nevertheless, it is probably unreasonable that the direct approach should receive its 'bad press' in the marketing literature and perhaps short-sighted of most commentators to dismiss it as an invalid approach to international marketing. By merely dismissing the direct export approach, marketing tends to divorce itself from business reality, where the initial reason for a company 'going international' is normally to increase the potential market for its *existing* product range. The literature might do better to accept that standardization is a practical objective, but should stress that initial research must be conducted to determine the degree to which this standardization is possible and adaptation is essential for success. This shift in emphasis might, at the same time, prevent major disasters as experienced by Campbell's Soups and General Foods, ensure maximum cost savings in terms of product adaptation and maintaining different product platforms, and ensure maximum benefits from standardization.

Looked at from this angle, it could be argued that the direct approach is preferable to the traditional marketing-oriented method described above. However, the company embarking on this course still has the problem of how to manage a total European market where most national markets appear at first glance to require differing degrees of product adaptation. Unfortunately, as we have seen, no clear guidelines exist to help us in this area of international marketing.

CONCLUSION

From this first part of the chapter it can be concluded that generally the modern theories of diversified markets determining the optimum product positioning stance are accepted. Companies are also aware of the benefits of a standardized approach but are unsure of how to obtain these benefits. The company that follows domestic marketing concepts to the letter in its international markets may attain maximum sales in each market but may reduce profits, owing to high costs of both the set-up and the on-going control of a diversified product platform. The company that carries out research and then attempts to group countries into manageable product position segments without knowing the validity of the base it is choosing may be putting its long-term marketing strategy at risk. The company that, either through ignorance or a gambling spirit, chances all on a blanket approach to European markets is running a high risk of heavy losses.

It would almost seem that the international marketing company has problems however it tries to tackle the total market. Concentrating specifically on Europe at this point, the commonly held view at the moment is that Europe provides a potentially lucrative market of some 300 million-plus consumers but that it is inconveniently divided into a large number of small and not easily managed national units. There may, however, be a solution to this seemingly 'lose–lose' situation.

The first area of change involves the way in which the company regards its European market. As we have seen above, modern domestic marketing thought emphasizes differences among groups of consumers and then follows logically to the satisfaction of different needs with tailor-made product offers. The change of emphasis in this thinking as proposed by Buzzell and Majaro has yet to have a significant effect upon the literature in general, but the added weight of Levitt's article in 1983 may speed the process of adoption.

The same degree of product–market match could still be achieved working from the opposite end of the spectrum, so to speak, by determining the minimum degree of adaptation required to satisfy local needs. This approach by similarity may be 'new' in connection with marketing to Europe as a whole but has long been the *status quo* for companies marketing in the United States of America, which has only 20 million fewer potential consumers in its less than homogenous population. Although it is not proposed that a 'United States of Europe' will come into being in the foreseeable future, it *is* proposed that the 15 nations of Western Europe might be reduced to a smaller number of grouped markets.

The second area of change is probably the most important and involves a careful analysis and understanding of current marketing theory. We have already seen that the most pressing need of a 'grouping-oriented' company is for a guiding theoretical base which will permit the company to take a broader, more efficient view of the European market. For the moment, the company has no way of telling whether its groups are based on factors which will provide stable groups for its whole product line over the longer term.

It is the aim of this work to provide a piece of research work which will enable the company to discriminate between those European market groups based on 'unstable' variables (such as short-term distribution factors, availability, etc., or product-offer specific variables) which will produce groups valid for a given product at a given time, and those market groups based on 'stable' variables (such as consumer predispositions to whole product classes) which will produce groups valid for the company's product range over the long term. A piece of research that could point to the existence of such stable European groups would also give international marketers the incentive to rethink their approach to European markets and encourage more companies to employ similarity rather than difference as their benchmark.

PART 2. THE RESEARCH HYPOTHESIS AND RESULTS

INTRODUCTION

From the review of current practice considered in the preceding chapter, it would appear that international marketers are in a position of some uncertainty. The benefits from an increased degree of standardization are obvious and tempting to all companies. There is a desire on the part of international marketers to 'short-cut' the classical marketing concept when dealing with international markets in Europe, but they are unsure of the best way of achieving this. The question that begs an answer is: 'Looking beyond the political–national boundaries that divide Europe, is there a valid base for segmentation that would permit a more manageable division of the total market?' — more precisely, a base which is likely to be stable over the long term and hold valid for all companies.

The search for such a segmentation base must then concentrate its attention on the one area common to all companies, the consumers who comprise the separate markets for different consumer goods. The first step in this investigation will be to consider the question of segmentation and the accepted criteria for a 'good' segmentation base, after which the work will proceed to try to identify acceptable bases for Western Europe.

SUMMARY OF ARGUMENT PRODUCED FROM LITERATURE REVIEW

The original literature search and review of current thinking has been omitted from this overview. Nevertheless it is important to understand the progress which was made in this section and to review the main conclusions reached. It will be remembered that our initial objective was to critically appraise the actual practice of segmenting Western Europe on the basis of nationality and to investigate the likely existence of other, more efficient segmentation bases. A critical analysis of current literature and theoretical thought has produced a number of pointers for our search. The essentials of the discussion are reproduced below.

1. Market segmentation, to be a valid marketing approach in the longer term, must exploit segmentation bases which are securely founded on behavioural differences. Socioeconomic groupings and other descriptive variables are inappropriate, since they

describe a current segment without necessarily predicting future purchase behaviour.

2. The various models of consumer behaviour which might shed some light on potential segments are very diverse and use different theoretical bases. The most common model used in the area of marketing is the attitude model.
3. Attitude research, in isolation, forms an unreliable method of predicting consumer behaviour. After the steady stream of research produced in this area, there is no definitive agreement that behaviour is a consequence of attitude.
4. Personal value research, which has grown out of attitude and lifestyle research, does appear to offer a more reliable determinant of consumer behaviour. From the pioneering research already conducted, we have good reason to believe that personal values are a significant factor in consumer behaviour and as such will provide us with a reliable predictive tool. The early research in this area has produced exciting results and it may be only a matter of time before the relationship between personal values and behaviour is quantified in a scientific, operational manner.
5. Personal values can form the basis of a sound market segment in that they are instrumental in behaviour and as such can be used as predictors of future behaviour.
6. Groupings of people with like values are termed cultural groupings.
7. Culture is a self-perpetuating phenomenon in that the personal value systems relevant to that culture are learned from the individual's cultural institutions.
8. Culture imposes strict conformity to its value system.
9. A culture is concerned with maintaining its sense of identity and also differentiating itself from other cultures.
10. There are a number of ways in which a cultural group might be recognized; the point of emphasis depends largely upon the type of research being undertaken. The constraints of the current research require that one measure be taken, and spoken language and linguistic origins has been selected. It is expected that the use of just one differentiating factor will produce groupings which although imperfect are reliable enough to produce satisfactory relationships.
11. Western Europe is made up of two dominant language family groupings.
12. These dominant language groupings identify the two main cultural groups in Europe — Latin (Romance) languages and Germanic languages.

13. The international marketer will be able to approach Europe as two cultural segments, the Latin and Germanic cultures; these cultures will maintain their own value systems and these value systems will be different between the two cultural groups. The value systems will enable the marketer to predict with more certainty the reaction of the two groups to any given product and its promoted benefits. The use of two cultural groupings rather than over a dozen separate nationalities should also enable economies of larger-scale production and marketing.

THE HYPOTHESIS

So far this work has concentrated on the problems facing the international marketing company in its operation within its Western European market. The main dilemma facing the company was seen to be centred on the queston of segmentation in a marketplace made up of a large number of small autonomous national states. Having now reached the end of our review of current theory, we would seem to have arrived at a number of conclusions, the most important of which is that culture appears to play an important role in determining consumer behaviour. Marketing theorists have long accepted that culture is one of the underlying determinants of consumer behaviour, but the notion of such a causal relationship seems to be based more on intuitive assumptions than on any close theoretical argument or supporting empirical evidence. As long as there is no attempt to either prove or disprove the assumed role of culture in determining consumer behaviour, the discussion will remain in the area of theory and will not progress to implementation at company level.

The rest of this chapter will look at precisely what the theoretical reasoning means in practical terms and its implications for operating management. The hypothesis assumes a prime importance in any piece of marketing research since the 'acid test' of marketing research should be practical application and improved efficiency in achieving the company's objectives. Normally, more efficient marketing is achieved only through a better understanding of market forces.

What, then, are the basic theoretical conclusions that can be drawn from the discussion and what exactly are the propositions which remain to be tested empirically?

The basic model shown in Figure 5.1 summarizes the 'flow of influences' as uncovered in the literature and theoretical review. This model demonstrates the essence of the hypothesis contained within this research, that an understanding of cultural groupings will improve the international company's efficiency in European operations through a more robust segmentation policy towards its European markets. The literature and theory review, of course, worked back from the problem to the concept of cultural groupings, in a sense 'up' the model.

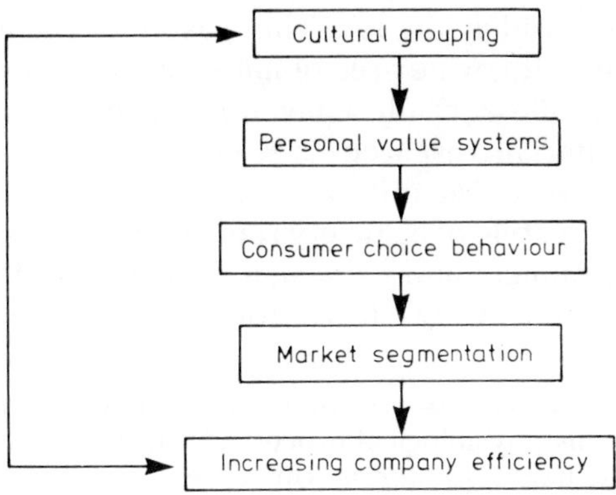

Figure 5.1

The remainder of Part 2 will consider each of these key relationships and will introduce the analysis undertaken to validate the key relationship.

THE RELATIONSHIPS

This section will examine each of the relationships included in Figure 5.1 with the express intention of now placing the theoretical processes into a practical context. In short, we will try to answer the traditional managerial question 'So what does that mean for me?'.

Relationship 1 — Cultural Groupings and Personal Values

In the literature review we considered the wealth of work, emanating chiefly from the realm of anthropology, which has been carried out in the area of culture and its effects on human behaviour. Without delving unnecessarily deeply into the decades of research that has been conducted among both primitive and advanced societies, it is clear that culture effectively 'conditions' human behaviour. Culture, or society's 'behavioural blueprint', is manifested at the level of the individual in the personal value system. By enforcing a common set of personal values, society ensures relative harmony among its members and a degree of security for all. The external observer simply sees a group of people holding roughly the same views, having the same priorities and making similar choices in life.

Culture has been defined in a number of different ways, although Kluckhohn's (1951) definition, being a consensus of anthropological definitions, is most widely quoted. The reason for the proliferation of definitions is due to the wide area of influence of culture. It affects so much of our daily life and all behaviour that definitions have been formulated by different researchers which clarify its effect on their special area of interest. Essentially, culture refers to social heritage. It is the distinctive lifestyle of a society representing its particular adaptation to its environment and its design for living. As to the immense scope of cultural influence, we learn from Ralph Linton (1973):

> Man appears to have very few unconditioned reflexes aside from those connected with his physiological processes. Although his behaviour is motivated by his needs, the forms which it assumes are normally conditioned by experience. Thus although eating is a response to the individual's need for nourishment, the way in which he eats depends upon how he has learned to eat. (p. 466)

We must remember also that beyond man's purely (Maslowian) physiological needs, what he considers to be his needs is also determined by his cultural background and what he has learned to need or value in life.

As we learn from Sturdivant (1973), the impact of culture on behaviour, including consumption behaviour, has not always been well recognized — probably because this impact has been so pervasive yet difficult to quantify empirically:

> Anthropologists have tended to ignore consumption as a distinguishing, researchable feature of society and have restricted their observations to other rituals such as marriage, religion, and childbearing.

When we stop to consider Sturdivant's terminology and recognize consumption behaviour as a 'ritual' like marriage and childbearing, it does tend to provoke a reevaluation of past thinking. As specialists in consumer behaviour, maybe we too have been guilty of examining only one specific area while ignoring the whole.

Nevertheless, to communicate the importance of culture to marketers it must be translated into marketing terms. Hofstede (1977) states:

> Culture is to human collectivity what personality is to an individual.

and Guildford (1959) has defined personality as:

> The interactive aggregate of personal characteristics that influences the individual's response to an environment.

In this light, culture defines the identity of the group in the same way that personality defines the identity of the individual. The concept of personality or personal identity has long been appreciated by marketers, especially its impact on the types of products which are purchased to enhance the individual's sense of personal identity. Culture moves this concept from the area of individual to group, the operating unit of marketing segmentation.

In concise form, then, this reasoning must lead us to the conclusion that the individual's personal value system determines his behaviour (in consumption as elsewhere). The personal value system is a product of the individual's culture (and society's value system). Convergence of the individual's and the society's values is enforced by society's reward–punishment action and the individual's need for identity. Consequently, the company which actively promotes a product which is perceived as not being congruent with the higher-ranking values of the individual and his society not only runs the risk of bad sales but also risks incurring penalties by attacking the identity of the group.

Relationship 2 — Personal Values and Consumer Behaviour

Historically, research in marketing has tended to be dominated by attitude research; more recently in the 'expectancy-value' analysis based on the models of Fishbein (1967) and others. Research has concentrated on attempting to predict consumer behaviour and brand choice behaviour and assessing the importance of various product attributes for choice behaviour. Attitude research has progressed and has been some help in predicting brand choice in a few instances. It has, however, always been plagued by two main problems. First, it does not satisfactorily explain the reasons why (or how) the consumer differerentially evaluates product attributes and thus prefers one brand over another (any generally applied predictive tool must be based on proved causality). Secondly, attitudes are always product- or situation-specific, which means that results have not been generally applicable across product ranges or markets.

Moving on from attitude research, we have seen that the individual is by nature 'an evaluating animal' and that he comes to the purchasing decision between competing brands in the same way that he approaches any other decision in his life. It was explained that the consumer has his set of personal values arranged into a hierarchical system which he uses as a framework for ordering his life. Further, it is implicit within the argument that from an understanding of the consumer's value system it will be possible to predict his reaction to different product attributes and consequently his purchase choice behaviour. Such prediction is possible thanks to the very strong pressures society puts upon the individual to act according to his values.

Although compared to attitude research value research is still in its infancy, the results so far obtained by the studies which have been carried out demonstrate a clear and positive causal relationship between personal values and behaviour. We have seen results obtained by a number of researchers, including the very conclusive work carried out by Hofstede (1980) on work-related values and in the area of consumer choice behaviour, the separate studies conducted by Vinson, Scott and Lamont (1977) and Walter Henry (1976) into motor car purchase in the USA, and the study by Alfred Boote (1981) into restaurant choice, etc. All the studies examined show that there is a clear link between personal values and consumer choice behaviour. Given the time and a wider appreciation of these techniques, it is inevitable that the process will be not only understood but quantified in a more scientific way to allow proper prediction and commercial application in domestic market situations. No work has yet been conducted into the international applications of value analysis, the extra problems created by international research being considerable.

For the marketing executive wishing to make practical use of this predictive tool there are three main elements he will require:

1. A knowledge of personal value systems
2. Salient values (consumption-related)
3. Beliefs relating to product attributes

since the basic model proposed by the current studies in value research is as follows:

> The consumer, when confronted with two competing brands, will use his personal value system to guide his choice. He will purchase the brand he perceives as offering benefits congruent with the highest-ranking salient values.

Relationship 3 — Consumer Behaviour and Market Segmentation

We have seen that the segmentation bases that have been used at one time or another in the past are legion. We have also seen the vast amount that has been written on the subject of what makes an ideal base for market segmentation. From the conclusions that we were able to draw in the review, it was evident that Wind (1978) has produced the most concise description of what makes a good base with his five 'rules' for validation:

1. Measurability
2. Accessibility
3. Substance
4. Mutual exclusivity
5. Homogeneity of response

and that for a segment to be valid in the longer term it should be based on differences in consumer *behaviour* rather than any other characteristics, since it is behaviour which holds the key to predictability and it is future buying behaviour that is of central interest to marketeers.

Also according to two prominent researchers in the area, Russell Haley (1968) and Daniel Yankelovich (1964), personal values hold the key to segmentation by behaviour.

Following logically along this path, we can see that on a broader 'macro' level we must be concerned with 'cultural segmentation', since behaviour is determined by personal values which in turn are determined by cultural background.

Subcultural segmentation has been used to a limited extent in some larger national markets where the applications tend to be fairly obvious, such as the negro cosmetics range in the USA. Also the case is often cited of international subcultural segmentation policy effected by certain products such as Coca-Cola and Blue Jeans, etc., although in the case of this latter section it is not clear whether the early companies involved actively promoted the international subcultures or simply exported their product to other countries where, by coincidence, these subcultures also existed.

In spite of these undoubted successes, the concept of cultural segmentation has not yet been extended to the European market in preference to a policy of national segmentation. The concept of market segmentation is one of the foundation stones of modern marketing and is actively employed by most marketing organizations on a national market basis. We have seen that there exists no theoretical rationale why one should not step back from national frontiers and consider the segmentation of the 'European market' to reap some of the benefits of standardization.

The test of what makes a good segmentation base has already been established. If we compare cultural grouping against these criteria, we can see:

1. Substantial. Assuming the eventual cultural groups are to be about the size that linguistic families would imply, and similar to the size discovered by Hofstede, then the major cultural groups will be larger than many European countries.
2. Accessible. Relatively easy; more difficult where cultural frontiers cross national boundaries such as can be expected in the case of Belgium and Switzerland, and possibly in France. Again, if the cultural grouping shows a relationship to families of spoken language, accessibility is increased due to a monolingual media structure.
3. Measurable. A more difficult problem due to the all-encompassing nature of culture. There are many aspects to culture and this research has opted to use spoken language in the full knowledge that one variable in isolation will be insufficient to fully delineate the various cultural groups in Europe. The measurement of culture is a key problem and is probably the root cause of the dearth of usable research in this area. In practical terms it is also true that cultural groupings will be measurable by the differences in their value systems (by definition, since culture is a grouping of people with common values). This route of measurement appears to be most fruitful for future use but is dependent upon the wider use and greater acceptance of value analysis as mentioned above.
4. Homogeneity of response. Since the initial search for bases was centred on the identification of groupings of like behaviour, it follows that homogeneity of response will be achieved. We have also seen that culture is the accepted code of behaviour of a given group and it is behavioural differences themselves which determine the differences between groups. It then must be true that behavioural response within a cultural group will be homogeneous since this is the *raison d'être* of that group. Also that two groups will produce different behavioural responses, since the difference is the *raison d'être* of the frontier.

Employing culture as a base for European segmentation could, of course, give extra problems to the marketer, especially where cultural and national frontiers do not coincide. The company will undoubtedly experience problems in implementing the marketing mix in a uniform manner where differences in marketing infrastructure exist. The marketing infrastructure, like the company, is normally centred on the nation with its political–legal and economic individuality. It will vary from company to company, but the benefits obtainable from increased standardization, increased management control and more accurate product positioning can be expected to outweigh the increased costs of the intermediate transfer period in a number of cases.

Relationship 4 — Cultural Segmentation and Company Efficiency

The significant potential for financial savings in a movement towards international standardization was explained in Part 1 and has been constantly referred to during the course of the discussion on marketing theory and practice.

Assuming for the moment that the argument outlined in Part 1 is valid and that proper testing can justify it to the satisfaction of operating management, we must consider the implications of cultural segmentation for the international company. For the sake of clarity and illustration we will consider here the problem confronting the company planning a new product launch on a European scale. So far we have concentrated heavily on the basic theoretical reasoning concerning the behaviour of the consumer market and we have questioned the automatic use of the national frontiers as market divisions. Although cultural factors may take priority over national factors in determining consumer reaction to a given product, the political–legal and commercial environment cannot be ignored by the company at the planning stage of its operations. Combining all aspects of the problem, practical and theoretical, a six-step process producing three successive segmentations would appear to be relevant.

Step 1 Head office (or central planning and coordination depending upon the type and structure of the organization) initially screens all European national markets to isolate those countries where the product cannot be marketed due to 'flaws' in the purchasing environment. Such flaws can be political–legal, constraints on the company, the product or the method of operation — lack of sufficient disposable income to produce a market for the product, insufficiency of marketing infrastructure that does not allow for any special marketing, for example after-sales service, that the product requires. This analysis will produce the following:

Step 2 — First Segmentation Head office now has results of initial screening and can isolate those countries allowing marketing and those where market launch is not possible, at least at this time. (Launch may be possible in *all* or *none* of the countries considered.) This produces two segments: go and no-go markets.

Step 3 Next, head office can shift its attention away from a country base to that of cultural group. Research should now be conducted within the two/three cultural groups to determine the optimum product positioning for that culture. The predominant value system for each grouping, once identified, will be a constant and used by the group as a frame of reference for considering all products. For the company the questions that must be answered are:

1. Which are the salient values that are 'activated' by the given product offer?
2. What are the product benefits as perceived by the consumer?

The process will probably also entail the matching of existing brands in the marketplace against their salient values. This must then be followed by strategic decisions such as whether to attack existing product positions against high-ranking values or to select lower-ranked salient values where no competition is positioned.

Step 4 — Second Semgentation Head office is now able to fix the optimum positions of its product in the Latin and Germanic cultures that will facilitate attainment of the company's objectives.

Step 5 Head office is now able to pass the product over to the local subsidiary units. The 'package' which the local unit receives at this point is the proposed product and the product benefit platform which will be used in the relevant culture. At this stage the local operating unit is best placed to handle local marketing arrangements and segmentation. It is important to note at this point that changes and adaptations will be required to cater for special circumstances in the local environment; these changes must not, however, impinge upon the basic product platform developed in step 4 — to do so would negate the benefits accruing from cultural segmentation.

Step 6 — Third Segmentation Within each cultural 'macro'-segment the local unit is able to segment along normal market lines. The research conducted at the level of cultural group gives a reading of the acceptability of any given product promise to the culture as a whole. At the local level it is still possible to 'fine-tune' the concept to take account of local variations of value systems which can be expected within the culture. Also classic demographic variables are important at this level to be able to describe the target market and allow communication contact.

This process of multiple segmentation shows how the company as a whole can maximize the effects of its international marketing effort. Control of the segmentation process is held for longer at head office level than is often the current practice. Involvement of head office central marketing is greater and local operating units are left less operational marketing freedom to alter the basic platforms of the product offer. They are still allowed the marketing 'fine-tuning' of the product to meet local requirements, so their contribution is still extremely valuable.

This process can be described diagramatically (see Figure 5.2).

It should not be concluded that this is a novel approach to international market segmentation; it would appear that most modern international companies are following these steps already — with one important difference. Most companies already operate segmentation procedures for steps 1 and 3. Cultural segmentation as proposed in step 2 is actually replaced by *national* segmentation, whereby the company has decided to segment its European market by nation-states and subsequently segment within these states.

As we have seen, in Europe cultural and political frontiers do not always coincide. Nation-states are, for the most part, the result of the different zones of influence of major powers (both past and present). Although orientation of the company and market on a national rather than a cultural basis may seem a contravention of basic marketing philosophy, it is understandable for two reasons.

First, there are significant differences in national legal systems, taxation, political orientation and general administration which make it more convenient and economic for the company to organize and account for its subsidiaries on a strictly national basis. It must also be remembered that although a convincing argument for the cultural segmentation of Europe can be made at a theoretical level, no research has yet shown that Europe can be segmented satisfactorily by culture. It is not surprising that in the present economic climate management has preferred certain administrative savings at the expense of only 'possible' profit improvements. However, the benefits to be obtained by moving to segments based on differences in consumption behaviour rather than politics should, in the longer term, far outweigh any increased costs — a lesson which is slowly being learned in domestic

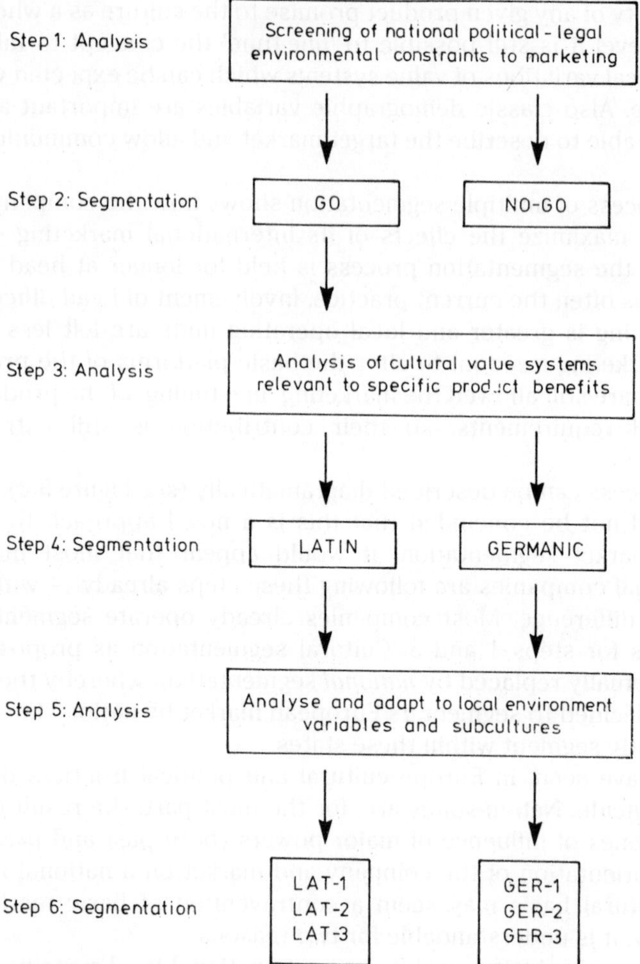

Figure 5.2

marketing. Understandably, companies will be unwilling to venture into the unproven if not the unknown and this research must be regarded as the first step along the road.

CONCLUSION

It is worthwhile at this point repeating the illustrative diagram produced at the beginning of Part 2.

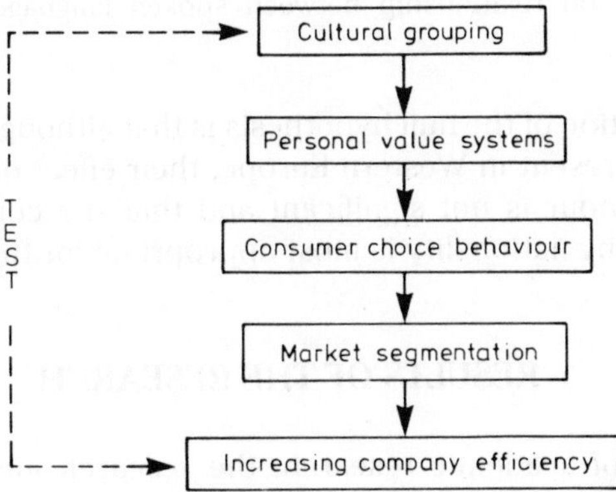

Figure 5.3

From this diagram (Figure 5.3) and the preceding discussion it is evident that the primary area of concern relates to the 'broken-line' relationship between the first and last boxes. When we consider the various research findings and evidence presented so far, it is apparent that there is significant potential in the exploitation of cultural segments. The one question which has not been answered by any of the quoted research is — 'Are there identifiable cultural segments in Western Europe for the international company to access?'.

The assumption has been made that Western Europe is made up of a number of distinct cultural groupings, that there exist a smaller number of cultural groups than nation-states. Clearly this assumption must be tested.

As has already been stated in the Preamble, it is not the aim of this study to encompass the whole problem of cultural segmentation up to practical implementation but to open up the way for future research in the area which will concentrate on more accurately quantifying the already exposed relationships. As a consequence, the emphasis of the hypothesis and the subsequent data analysis will be concerned with the *existence* of cultural groupings as distinct from national groupings in the Western European marketplace.

It is expected that the analysis of the data will show a significant relationship between spoken language and personal values held. This result would then lend substance to the assumption that cultural groupings exist within Western Europe and that these groupings, by transcending national frontiers, are significantly larger than the individual nations.

The null hypothesis, then, is:

> There exists no relationship between spoken language and personal values.

The implication of the null hypothesis is that although cultural groupings may be present in Western Europe, their effect on consumer purchasing behaviour is not significant and that the current practice of segmentation by nationality is most appropriate for this marketplace.

RESULTS OF THE RESEARCH

In any piece of academic research, the research methodology takes prime position and is key to the specialist understanding of results obtained. In this review, however, the detailed research approaches and statistical methodology have been omitted. Readers with a specialist interest are invited to consult the original research or to contact the author directly for more information.

Based primarily on a detailed reanalysis of secondary data generously provided by the RISC organization, the final research considered the cultural dimensions in four European countries, the United Kingdom, France, Denmark and Belgium. This was further broken down to 17 standard European regions which formed the central research base. From the RISC data it was possible to identify 18 separate personal values across a total respondent base of 8979 throughout the 17 geographic regions. To these value data a number of key demographic variables were added to be analysed simultaneously so that the effect of these variables could be measured upon value differences.

The core of the argument, it will be remembered, is that the current business practice of (effectively) segmenting the European market according to nationality is not the most efficient method. A better approach would be to segment the market according to culture since this has a greater effect upon human behaviour and purchase behaviour. Since culture is difficult to define and measure with certainty, we have decided to use language as a descriptor for culture. From the research, then, we were primarily concerned with two relationships: first the relationship between personal values and language, and secondly the relationship between personal values, language and nationality.

Looking first at the relationship between personal values and spoken language, of the 11 value items remaining in the analysis after cases of high intercorrelation were eliminated, seven were (statistically) significantly related to the spoken language of the region.

Taking then the relationship between personal values, spoken language and nationality, it was found that in only one case (the personal value of ‘patriotism’) did the relationship appear more significant than the relationship with language in each region. While at a basic statistical level the results here did not seem to be conclusive, however, when we translate the findings to the business world, we can say that a company which tailors its marketing effort to these four countries will not only be incurring higher marketing costs but will also be matching personal values less well than it would when segmenting by language group. Looking at the national scores together, it was evident that language offers the best *overall* measure in eight of 11 cases. In other words, 70% of the time the organization will be matching market needs more accurately if it segments its European market by language families rather than by national boundary. This is patently not what happens at the moment.

CONCLUSIONS

It will be remembered from Part 2 that the null hypothesis was:

> There exists no relationship between spoken language and personal values.

In view of the results obtained in the analysis of personal values on a European scale and the significant relationships exposed through a correlation process, we can safely reject the null hypothesis.

The rejection of the null hypothesis allows us to suggest a number of subsidiary conclusions from the analysis:

1. *Culture*. Through the research we have leaned heavily upon spoken language as a primary indicator of cultural grouping. This selection of indicator was made in the full knowledge that spoken language would be unable to *fully* describe cultural groupings and that other factors (historical, sociological, legal, etc.) all contribute to what Krejci and Velimsky (1981) call the sense of ethnic or cultural consciousness. The fact that spoken language is so consistently (eight of 11 values) and significantly related to personal values would imply that culture is not only a stronger factor in buyer behaviour than had previously been supposed, but that it may be more easily exploited than current theorists suggest, at least within the context of the Western European marketplace.

   There is a clear and urgent need for more detailed research into the precise measurement of culture as a prelude to its more widespread usage as an international segmentation base.

2. *Nationality*. Another point to arise from the analysis is the inconsistency of the relationship between personal values and nationality, especially bearing in mind the smallness of the sample and the bias produced in the figures by the weighting of the original data to nationally representative samples.

   In view of these results and the surprising lack of any clear relationship between nationality and personal values, we are left to conclude that the majority of international companies are managing their European markets in a very inefficient manner. One possible explanation is that the national infrastructures create artificially unique markets to such an extent that marketing cannot be standardized. It is certainly evident that national segmentation is not justified in terms of different customer needs!

   The Belgian data confirm this conclusion. It is evident that nationality is a poor segmentation base for the Belgian market; the value differences by spoken language demonstrate the truly divergent nature of the two cultures.
3. *Demographics*. The third interesting result of the analysis concerns the impact of various demographic variables on personal values. Apart from the few relationships one would 'intuitively' expect to find, a substantial trend in relationships was conspicuous by its absence.

   This result is important in that it must question the validity of various demographic variables as both segmentation bases in domestic as well as international markets and predictors of future customer purchase behaviour. Personal values would appear to transcend demographics. The Belgian data are even more emphatic; while sex, life-cycle position and language (culture) show a dramatic effect on personal values, socioeconomic groupings have a negligible effect. Socioeconomic groups are, of course, the standard segmentation bases for almost all media, advertising agencies, market research agencies, etc., who obviously have vested interests in the continuation of the system.
4. *General*. The overriding conclusion to be drawn from the analysis is that a relationship clearly exists between spoken language and personal values. Most importantly, the analysis, by showing that a relationship is present, provides the crucial justification to proceed with the investment required to properly delineate and accurately measure the relationships. Such measurement is essential before companies will consider an appraisal of their current international practice.

PART 3. WHERE NEXT?

THE NEED FOR FURTHER RESEARCH

It is worthwhile beginning this section on the all-important future research by repeating the illustrative diagram originally produced in Part 2. This diagram (Figure 5.4) reminds us of the conceptual flow of influences which has led us to investigate the existence of relationships in Part 2. These established relationships will remain confined to the world of academic theory unless measured in a way which makes them more practical for operating management.

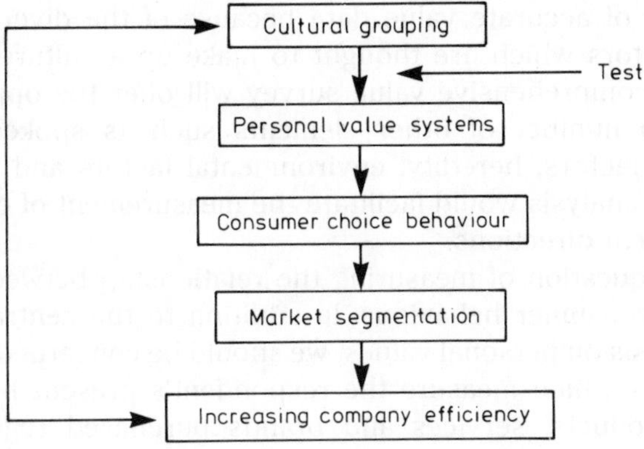

Figure 5.4

It was the declared aim of this research to demonstrate the existence of a relationship between culture and personal values and thus, by definition, an international market segmentation opportunity. This relationship is represented by the first downward arrow in Figure 5.4. Now that the relationship has been exposed, the final stage of this work must be to offer as much guidance as possible to aid in the formulation and implementation of the next level of research projects.

The following sections will deal with the principal elements of the flow diagram represented in Figure 5.4 and concentrate respectively on personal values, market segmentation and improving company efficiency.

PERSONAL VALUE SYSTEMS

We have already made mention of the ideal approach to the

measurement of personal value systems. Our intention here is to consider the problem on a slightly wider scale.

The analysis of personal values is central to the whole concept of cultural segmentation, and properly designed research in this area will achieve a number of objectives. We have already considered the various evidence presented in the literature and concluded that primary research is required at the level of the individual, and that possibly portable computers could be used to present the respondent with a series of 'triads' for pairing to determine both 'terminal' and 'domain-specific' value systems. This approach can be extended as follows.

Cultural groupings are defined as groupings of people with similar value systems. Cultural groupings are notoriously difficult to define in the absence of accurate value data because of the diversity of contributing factors which are thought to make up a culture's 'sense of identity'. A comprehensive value survey will offer the opportunity of overlaying a number of other elements such as spoken language, sociological factors, heredity, environmental factors and technology, etc. Such an analysis would facilitate the measurement of culture from two convergent directions.

Next, the question of measuring the relationship between personal values and consumer behaviour. In addition to the central questionnaire emphasis on personal values, we should be concerned with entering questions which measure the respondent's present behaviour in terms of products, services and brands purchased regularly. This would have the obvious benefit of differentiating between the personal values of purchasers and non-purchasers of any given brand or product/service group.

In addition to simple purchase/non-purchase responses, we will also need to understand more about how values relate to brand choice; key here is the respondent's perception of the product attributes. In more detailed terms, we need to incorporate questions which measure the customer's perception of the different benefits promised by competing brands — these benefits may not be the same benefits that the company considers it is actively communicating! These types of comparative data are best obtained by using the 'open-response' type of question where the respondent is confronted with three brands (triads) normally available in that region and is asked to isolate the 'odd man out', giving reasons for the choice.

Finally, we also need more general information about the respondent's general lifestyle, types of shops preferred, leisure interests, holidays, family background, etc. In this way we can begin to draw up a complete picture of the respondent's preferred way of living. This picture will help clarify and consolidate the hierarchy of values uncovered and also aid with the subsequent marketing plans in approaching the respondent in a more effective manner; we have already seen that the traditional socioeconomic groupings are not efficient descriptors of modern segments. The better overall understanding we can obtain about the salient ways of living, the more accurate the company's marketing and communications can be.

MARKET SEGMENTS

The next step in the ideal analysis must deal with the question of market segmentation. We have already considered the problem of segmentation and what 'rules' must be observed before any grouping can be considered a good market segment. The key to the question of segmentation we have already isolated as the predictability of the future buying behaviour of an identified group, and it is here that the traditional socioeconomic groupings are signally inefficient.

The original research considered the various relationships between personal values and consumer choice behaviour and how these relationships could be measured. The data collection, however, was based upon questionnaire response and related to historical information. Obviously, past behaviour can be a good guide to predicting future behaviour, especially if supported by robust theory. The 'acid test', nevertheless, must be regular testing over time to allow direct measurement of results against a detailed prediction. Thus the company or syndicate of companies undertaking the analysis must wait for one or more periods to elapse before being able to measure accurately the degree of certainty offered by value data.

Such a follow-up test need not be in full value analysis style but can be a simple investigation, ideally of the same respondents, to determine the actual response to a change in marketing of both target value groups and non-target groups. The design of such a test will naturally depend heavily upon the type of activity being measured and the original marketing change initiated.

As far as longer-term changes in personal value systems are concerned, the existing research data available in the area have tended to support the theoretical view that values are durable over time, that they do not change drastically as do attitudes but will evolve slowly as people progress through life and their circumstances gradually change. This stability must, however, be quantified if any precise use is to be made of values in segmentation, especially where the company is active in markets which traditionally enjoy long product life cycles or the gestation period for new products is long. In such cases the company will need to be able to predict both the size and status of different value groups well into the future. Longer-term trends of this type can be measured by a yearly value survey of the type described above. Possibly the RISC group of companies may be able to offer such a commercial analysis in the future.

A second area of concern should also be addressed at this point: the question of national infrastructures. We have already seen that nationality as a factor has a surprisingly inconsistent effect on personal values. Nevertheless, the 'nation' is by far the most popular basis upon which Europe is commonly segmented. We need to understand more about this relationship. Nations tend to produce different infrastructures in terms of political, legal and fiscal systems. Differences in the commercial infrastructure are now slowly being eroded by the growth of the EC and customer mobility and so differences in media, production, transport and distribution systems, etc., although still present are becoming less important. The effect of these structural differences must be measured. This can be best done if integrated into the various analyses.

The importance of the infrastructures can be measured by incorporating the various factors (factors studied will depend upon the commercial considerations of the products or services under analysis) into the value study as external variables and effects can be measured against the value system. It may be that in specific instances some structural factors have an important effect on personal values. On the other hand, it may be that personal values remain unaffected but the company's belief in the existence of structural differences has affected the distribution system and produced a restricted choice for the consumer, who then is unable to purchase completely according to the dictates of the value system.

IMPROVING COMPANY EFFICIENCY

It will be remembered that the improvement of company efficiency in its international operations is the principal long-term objective of this research. Nevertheless, academic research, no matter how profound the arguments or how convincing the data analysis, is no substitute for hard commercial experience in the marketplace.

A lengthy case has been made for the adoption of personal values as a prime determinant of behaviour and value groupings as a good and efficient base for international segmentation. So where should the interested company now turn? The current work on personal values tends either to the highly specific (one product in one market, e.g. Hofstede (1980), Boote (1981), etc.) or to the highly general (RISC).

The results so far achieved in the various studies all support the underlying theory and importance of values in behaviour. Unfortunately, the small number of practical tests conducted means that we do not have enough practical experience in dealing with value data to be able to extrapolate company- or product-specific guidelines from a general value system database, especially on an international basis. We can expect the adoption of value data to grow in the same way as attitude studies grew in popularity, by more and more companies conducting *specific* application studies.

We can expect the next advance in these studies to come from a dominant multiproduct multinational corporation or a syndicate of non-competing companies who can recognize enough potential to justify the considerable investment required by an international study as described here. A company (product-market) specific study will have two crucial advantages over the existing, general, studies which exist in the international field.

First, a specific study will be able to concentrate on those personal values which are especially salient to the consumer choice decision under investigation. Specialization of this type will enable the analysts to concentrate their attention on the important areas of personal values while discarding the peripheral. The value–behaviour relationship is a complicated one and the removal of extraneous (to the company) variables will facilitate understanding at the required depth.

Secondly, a specific study will be properly designed, that is, designed with the specific intention of *applying* the eventual results in a known market.

Only when the concept of international segmentation by personal values has been *implemented* (possibly alongside an unchanged 'control' region) and the results analysed over a number of months or even years will the concept have been truly tested. Only at this point will we be able to say that 'It works for company X'. After company X will come companies A, B, C and D. Slowly the depth of knowledge will increase and we will move towards a more general value system database.

It was stated at the beginning of this section that this work was dedicated to improving company efficiency, but that academic research is no substitute for implementation or 'field-testing' by a company. The role of academic research, however, is clear: it should constantly question accepted wisdom, it should ask 'What if . . .', it should produce practical ideas based on good theory. Most importantly, it should aim to stimulate practising management to the extent that they are anxious to test the theory where it matters — in the marketplace.

If this work achieves this latter objective it will have been successful.

IMPLICATIONS FOR THE WOULD-BE EUROMARKETER

At this point it is probably worthwhile looking at where we have reached as far as the practitioner is concerned. For the international organization pondering either its entry or its ongoing operations in the European market, we should recall the diagram from Part 2 (see Figure 5.5).

So what now? Steps 1 and 2 are (or should be) common practice already and need no further explanation here. Steps 3 and 4 have been the subject of this research and the findings have implications for international marketers.

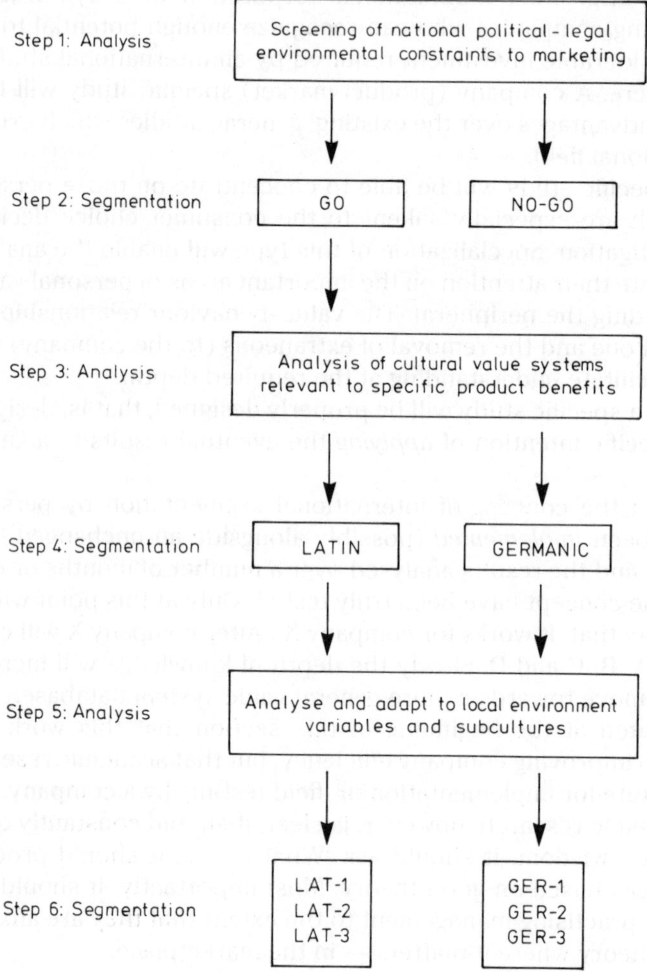

Figure 5.5

Although the benefits which can be expected from cultural segmentation will vary with each company, its level of involvement in international business, etc., the principal benefits to the company can be generalized as being the following:

1. Economies of scale. Fewer segments produce larger numbers and permit advantages of large-scale organization such as product variety, packaging, promotional material, etc.
2. Mobility. Reduction in the number of product platforms allows for benefits of cross-national media and satisfies increasingly mobile populations.
3. Predictable segments. Focuses marketing attention away from artificial (in behavioural terms) groupings of consumers within nations and towards groupings based on similarities of consumer needs and motivations.
4. Centralized planning. More centralized planning control over the marketing mix.
5. Improved control. Since plans are generally only as good as the control procedures installed to monitor their progress, increased controls lead to more effective planning. A much used control device in international marketing is that of intercountry or interunit comparisons. Currently such comparisons are dangerously erroneous, as with the market emphasis on nations there are usually differences in emphasis within the product platforms. This means that comparisons are being based on essentially different products (in terms of the benefits which they are offering). National comparisons of sales penetration, etc. when conducted within a cultural segment where the product benefits are the same will produce a far more powerful tool for controlling plan implementation. Corrective action when needed can be instituted in the knowledge that comparisons have contrasted like with like.

We have seen that there is a strong relationship between personal values and culture (as read by language) and that in most cases the organization could expect a more efficient result from cultural rather than national segmentation of its marketplace. This research, however, aimed to demonstrate that a relationship existed; this it achieved. Now more detailed research is required in order to quantify the nature of the relationship for a given organization or type of product or service offer. Once this additional information has been acquired, the organization will be in a position to segment its market on a 'macro' basis and to position its products or services in the major cultural segments.

Naturally enough, the broader cultural markets will have 'knock-on' effects on how the firm organizes itself on a European basis. A rationalisation of offices and decision-making centres will logically accompany this more simplified view of the European marketplace. The results: greater control, less overlap and duplication of effort and reduced costs.

Step 5 involves the local operating management in the next order or 'micro' segmentation of the products or services to match local needs. All the while keeping intact the overall cultural positioning, local management should make adaptations to the offer which take account of local differences in language, distribution systems, pricing requirements, promotional channels, etc., as is already common practice. The difference at this stage is evident in the degree of freedom given to local (national) operating management. The brief will be for local 'tailoring' to smooth over local market characteristics. The organization will be looking to establish standards within the cultural macro-segment and to keep deviations from this standard to a minimum. In short, the local office will carry out a tactical marketing role, the strategic direction being determined at the Latin or Germanic segment level. Again, clear distinctions of individual roles will contribute significantly to profitability.

WHAT OF THE FUTURE?

The future is more uncertain now (1990) than it has ever been. Already 'Europe of the twelve' contains within its boundaries 30 distinct cultural and subcultural groups as defined by Krejci and Velimsky (1981). The EC is heading full speed towards political union and 'harmonization' with very little understanding of cultural difference and its likely effect on consumption patterns. Industry and commerce are reacting to the unknown in a variety of ways. Some organizations are rushing into 'strategic alliances' with foreign partners, one feels often without a true understanding of what such marriages may bring. Other organizations are sitting on the fence 'biding their time' or 'waiting until the dust settles'.

In the meantime the Eastern bloc has suddenly undergone a popular revolution and now capitalism is expected to produce the standards of living previously just glimpsed on TV. If we are to broaden our definition of Europe to cover the land mass from the Arctic to the Mediterranean and from the Atlantic to the Urals, the problem for the international marketer grows exponentially.

With the decline in central power in the west as well as the east of Europe, how many nations will we have to deal with? Is Czechoslovakia one country or two (Czecho-Slovakia)? How many nations will there eventually be in Yugoslavia?

While all these questions rage, it should at least be clear to all that the premise of Europe as a trading bloc to compete with America and the Pacific Rim lies in the size of its domestic market and the inherent economies of scale. European companies cannot hope to compete on a global scale if the European domestic market continues to fragment.

CONCLUSIONS

This research has shown that broad cultural segmentation offers a robust strategy for European marketing. More research needs to be carried out, but even if we include Eastern Europe we would likely find that, say, five cultural macro-segments are likely to account for up to 90% of the variance in actual consumer demand.

Back in the early eighties when the original research was conducted, a case could be made for changing from national to cultural segmentation. Few practitioners would have been interested then, mostly because everyone was used to dealing with a multinational market. Now, of course, all that has changed. Apart from the Germans, the East has been largely ignored by most West European marketers for the past 40 years. It also looks likely that the European corporations will have to have significant operations in the East as well as the West. We had some problems in dealing with 'Europe of the twelve'; how will we manage 'Europe of the twenty-eight'?

In the nineties the Euromarketer will be forced to move beyond the nation-state as the *de facto* segmentation base; the logistics will be simply impractical. Culture will be the obvious first choice, especially for organizations in the consumer markets. As the first pioneering companies learn how to identify and market to cultural rather than national groups our store of information and understanding of the role of culture and personal value systems will grow to permit others to follow.

We live in changing times. The challenge is to find new solutions for the new problems that now face us. The market is there, and waiting.

REFERENCES

These references form the complete list as appended to the original research document; some have not been mentioned in this, abbreviated, résumé.

Allport, G., Vernan, P., and Lindzay, G. (1960) *Study of Values*. Houghton Mifflin, Boston.

Bales, R., and Couch, H. (1969) The Value Profile: A factor analytic study of value statements. *Sociological Inquiry*, **39**, 00–00.

Becker, B.W. and Connor, P.E. (1981) Personal values of heavy users of mass media. *Journal of Advertising Research*, October, 37–43.

Benedict, Ruth, F. (1934) Anthropology and the abnormal. *Journal of General Psychology*, **10**, 59–80.

Berry, J.W. (1975) An ecological approach to cross-cultural psychology. *Nederlands Tijdschrift voor de Psychologie*, **30**, 51–84.

Boote, A.S. (1981) Market segmentation by personal values and salient product attributes. *Journal of Advertising Research*, February.

Brown, F.E. (1980) *Marketing Research — A Structure for Decision Making*. Addison-Wesley, Reading, Mass.

Buzzell, R.D. (1968) Can you standardize multinational marketing? *Harvard Business Review*, November–December, 102–113.

Calvi, G. (1982) Five years of psychographic research in Italy: Social and political results. *European Research*, July.

Cateora, P. (1983) *International Marketing*. Irwin, Homewood, Illinois.

Council of Europe (1980) *Provisional Report on Minority Languages and Dialects*. Reporter M. Cirici Pellicer, EEC Publications.

Dichter, Ernst (1962) The world customer. *Harvard Business Review*, July–August, 113–22.

EEC (1983) *Yearbook of Regional Statistics*. Office for Official Publications of the European Communities, BP1003, Luxemburg.

Ehrenbeg, A.S.C. (1969) Towards an integrated theory of consumer behaviour. *Journal of the Market Research Society*, **11**(4), 305–337.

Engel, J.F., Kollatt, D.T., and Blackwell, R.D. (1973) *Consumer Behavior*. Holt, Rinehart & Winston, New York.

Euro-Barometer. *Public Opinion in the European Community*. Commission of the European Communities, 1049, Brussels (quarterly).

EVSSG (1980) European Values System Study Group. Background document published by Gallup, London.

Ewell, A.H. Jr (1954) The relationship between the rigidity of moral values and the severity of functional psychological illness: A study with war veterans of one religious group. Doctoral disserations, New York University, Ann Arbor, University Microfilms Inc.

Fishbein, M.A. (ed.) (1967) *Readings in Attitude Theory and Measurement*. Wiley, New York.

Fishbein, M.A., and Ajzen, I. (1975) *Belief, Attitude, Intention and Behavior*. Addison Wesley, Reading, Mass.

Fishman, J.A. (1974) A systemisation of the whorfian hypothesis. In Berry, J.W., and Dasen, P.R. (eds) *Culture and Cognition*. Methuen, London.

Frank, R.E., Massey, W.R., and Wind, Y. (1972) *Market Segmentation*. Prentice Hall, New Jersey.

Gordon, L. (1960) *Survey of Personal Values*. Science Research Associates, supplementary revised material, Chicago.

Graves, C. (1966) Deterioration of work stadards. *Harvard Business Review*, October.

Graves, C. (1970) An open system theory of values. *Journal of Humanistic Psychology*, Fall.

Green, R.E., and Tull, D.S. (1978) *Research for Marketing Decisions.* Prentice Hall, New Jersey.

Guildford, R.R. (1959) *Personality.* McGraw Hill, New York.

Gutman, J. (1982) A means end chain model based on consumer categorization processes. *Journal of Marketing*, Spring.

Hair, Jr., J.F., and Anderson, R.E. (1972) Culture, acculturation and consumer behaviour. American Marketing Association, Combined Proceedings, Spring and Fall Conference.

Haley, R. (1968) Benefit segmentation — a decision oriented research tool. *Journal of Marketing*, **32**, 30–35.

Hall, Edward T. (1976) *Beyond Culture*, Anchor Press/Doubleday, New York.

Hammond, P.B. (1975) *Cultural and Social Anthropology — Introductory Readings in Ethnology.* Collier Macmillan, London.

Hansen, F. (1972) *Consumer Choice Behaviour.* Free Press, New York.

Harding, S. (1979) Towards an empirical evaluation of values — an open-ended approach. Polytechnic of North London.

Harris, P.R., and Moran, R.T. (1979) *Managing Cultural Differences.* Gulf, New York.

Headey, B. (1983) Quality of life studies: Their implications for social and market researchers. *European Research (UK)*, April, 56.

Henry, W.A. (1976) Cultural values do correlate with consumer behaviour. *Journal of Marketing Research*, 121.

Hereberger, R.A. (1972) The impact of concern for ecology factors on consumer attitudes and buying behaviour. *Dissertation Abstracts International*, **32**.

Herskovits, M.J. (1964) *Man and his Work.* Alfred Knopf, New York.

Hoebel, A. (1960) *Man, Culture and Society.* Oxford University Press, New York.

Hofstede, G. (1977) The measurement of human values. European Institute of Advanced Studies in Management, Brussels, Working Paper No. 77–10.

Hofstede, G. (1980) *Culture's Consequences.* Sage, London.

Howard, J.A., and Sheth, J.N. (1967) A theory of buyer behavior. In Mayer, R. (ed.) *Changing Marketing Systems.* American Marketing Association, Conference Proceedings, Winter.

Howard, N. (1981a) How good is value analysis. *Dun's Review*, **117**, March.

Howard, N. (1981b) New ways to view consumers. *Dun's Review*, **118**, August.

Inglehart, R. (1977) *The Silent Revolution.* Princeton University Press, Princeton, NJ.

Institute fur Demoskopie Allensbach (1978) Value research — an evaluation based on the scientific literature.

Jackson, R.G. (1973) A preliminaty bicultural study of value orientations and leisure attitudes. *Journal of Leisure Research*, **5**.

Jaffe, E.D. (1974) *Grouping — A Strategy for International Marketing.* American Management, New York.

Jones, R.A., Sensenig, J., and Ashmore, R. (1978) Systems and values and their multidimensional representations. *Multivariate Behavioural Research*, **13**, 255–270.

Kanter, D.L. (1978) The Europeanization of America: A study in changing values. In *Advances In Consumer Research*, Vol V. Proceedings of the 8th Annual Conference of the Association for Consumer Research, USA.

Kelley, L., and Worthley, R. (1981) The role of culture in comparative management: A cross-cultural perspective. *Academy of Management Journal*, **24**, 164–73.

Kiesler, C.A., and Munson, P.A. (1975) Attitudes and Opinions. *Annual Review of Psychology*, **26.**

Kinder, H., and Hilgemann, W. (1982) *The Penguin Atlas of World History*. Penguin, Harmondsworth.

Kluckhohn, C. (1951a) Values and value orientations in the theory of action: An exploration in definition and classification. In Parsons, T., and Shils, E.A. (eds), *Towards a General Theory of Action*. Harvard University Press, Cambridge, Mass.

Kluckhohn, C. (1951b) The study of culture'. In Lerner, D., and Lasswell, H.D. (eds) *The Policy Sciences*. Stanford University Press, Stanford, CA.

Kluckhohn, F., and Strodtbeck, F. (1961) *Variations in Value Orientations*. Row Paterson, Illinois.

Kotler, P. (1972) *Marketing Management — Analysis, Planning and Control*. Prentice Hall, New Jersey.

Krech, D., Crutchfield, R.S., and Ballachey, E.L. (1962) *Individual in Society*. McGraw-Hill, New York.

Krejci, J., and Velimsky, V. (1981) *Ethnic and Political Nations in Europe*. Croom Helm, London.

Kroeber, A.L., and Kluckhohn, C. (1952) Culture: A critical review of concepts and definitions. *Papers of the Peabody Museum*. Vol. 27, Harvard University Press, Cambridge MA.

Kroeber, A.L., and Parsons, T. (1958) The concepts of culture and of social system. *American Sociological Review*, **23**, October.

Lee, J.A. (1966) Cultural analysis in overseas operations. *Harvard Business Review*, March–April, 106–114.

Levitt, T. (1960) Marketing myopia. *Harvard Business Review*, July–August.

Levitt, T. (1983) The globalisation of markets. *Harvard Business Review*, May–June, 92.

Linton, R. (1973) Culture. In Kassarijian, H.H., and Robertson, T.S. (eds) *Perspectives in Consumer Behaviour*. Scott Foreman, US.

Majaro, S. (1977) Standardisation for international markets. *Marketing (UK)*, May.

Majaro, S. (1982) *International Marketing — A Strategic Approach to World Markets*. Allen & Unwin, London.

Manzler, L., and Miller, S. (1978) An examination of the value attitude structure in the study of donor behaviour. Annual Meeting of American Institute for Decision Sciences, St Louis, November.

McGuire, W.J. (1972) Social Psychology. In Dodwell, P.C. (ed.) *New Horizons in Psychology*.

Mitchell, A. (1983) Consumer value systems. *Across the Board (USA)*, March, 45.

Mitchell, A., and Macnulty, C. (1981) Changing values and lifestyles. *Long Range Planning*, **14**, 37–41.

Morris, C. (1956) *Varieties of Human Values*. University of Chicago Press, Chicago.

Morton-Williams, J. (1972) Questionnaire design. In Worcester, R.M. (ed.) *Consumer Market Research Handbook*. McGraw-Hill, London.

Munson, J.M., and McIntyre, S.H. (1979) Developing practical procedures for the measurement of personal values in cross-cultural marketing. *Journal of Marketing Research*, February.

Murray, I. (1981) Jung at the heart of marketing. *Sunday Observer (UK)*, July.

Oliver, G. (1980) *Marketing Today*. Prentice Hall, London.

Perloe, S.I. (1967) Social responsibility and individualism in college students. Final Report to Office of Education (US) on project S-308, Bureau No. 5-8210.

Piercy, N. (1980) Company internationalisation — active and reactive exporting. *European Journal of Marketing*, March.

Rapaille-Bouee International (1981) Cultural archetype research. Private documents obtained by the author; contact RPI, 19 Rue de Bievre, 75005 Paris, France.

Reich, B., and Adcock, C. (1976) *Values, Attitudes and Behavior Change*. Essential Psychology Series. Methuen, London.

Rettig, S., and Pasmanick, B. (1959) Changing moral values among college students: A factorial study. *American Sociological Review*, **24**.

Reynolds, T.J., and Jolly, J.P. (1980) Measuring personal values: An evaluation of alternative methods. *Journal of Marketing Research*, November.

Reynolds, W.H. (1965) More sense about market segmentation. *Harvard Business Review*, September–October.

Ricks, D.A. (1983) *Big Business Blunders*. Irwin, Illinois.

Ricks, D.A., Arpan, J.S., and Fu, M.Y.C. (1974) *International Business Blunders*. GRID, Columbus, Ohio.

RISC. International Research Institute for Social Change, Frankenstrasse 9, 6002 Lucerne, Switzerland.

Robinson, J.P., and Shaver, P.R. (1973) *Measures of Social Psychological Attitudes*. Institute for Social Research, Michigan.

Rokeach, M. (1968) *Beliefs, Attitudes and Values*. Jossey Bass, San Francisco.

Rokeach, M. (1969) The role of values in public opinion research. *Public Opinion Quarterly*, **132**, 547–559.

Rokeach, M. (1973) *The Nature of Human Values*. Collier Macmillan, London.

Scott, J.E., and Lamont, L.M. (1973) Relating consumer values to consumer behavior: A model and method for investigation. In Green, Thomas V. (ed.), *Increasing Marketing Productivity*. American Marketing Association, Chicago, pp. 283–288.

Scott, W. (1965) *Values and Organisations: A study of Fraternities and Sororities*. Rand McNally, Chicago.

Shorr, J. (1953) The development of a test to measure the intensity of values. *Journal of Educational Psychology*.

Smith, W. (1956) Product differentiation and market segmentation as alternative marketing strategies. *Journal of Marketing*, July.

Sturdivant, F.D. (1973) Sub-culture theory, poverties, minorities and marketing. In Ward, S., and Robertson, T. (eds) *Consumer Behaviour — Theoretical Foundations*. Prentice Hall, New Jersey.

Tertpstra, V. (1978) *The Cultural Environment of International Business*. South Western Publishing Corp, USA.

Terpstra, V. (1983) *International Marketing*. Dryden Press, New York.

Truzzi, M. (1973) The problem of relevance between orientations for cognitive dissonance theory. *Journal for the Theory of Social Behaviour*, **3**.

Vinson, D.E., and Gutman, J. (1978) Personal values and consumer discontent. Annual Meeting of American Institute for Decision Sciences, St Louis, November.

Vinson, D.E., Scott, J.E., and Lamont, L.M. (1977) The role of personal values in marketing and consumer behavior. *Journal of Marketing*, April.

Wadia, M.S. (1967) The concept of culture in the analysis of consumers. In Mayer, R. (ed.) *Changing Marketing Systems*. American Marketing Association, Conference Proceedings, Winter.

Wind, Y. (1967) Cross cultural analysis of consumer behavior. In Mayer, R. (ed.) *Changing Marketing Systems*. American Marketing Association, Conference Proceedings, Winter.

Wind, Y. (1978) Market Segmentation. *Journal of Marketing Research*, August.

Wind, Y., and Douglas, S. (1974) Some issues in international consumer research. *European Journal of Marketing*, Winter.

Williams, R.M. (1951) *American Society — A Sociological Interpretation*. Alfred A. Knopf, New York.

Williams, R.M. (1968) *International Encyclopedia of the Social Sciences*. Sills, E. (ed.). Macmillan, New York.

Withey, S. (1965) The US and the USSR: A report of the public's perspective on United States – Russian relations in late 1961. In Bobrow, D. (ed.) *Components of Defense Policy*. Rand McNally, Chicago.

Yankelovich, D. (1964) New criteria for market segmentation. *Harvard Business Review*, March–April.

Zetterberg, H.L. (1981) Sociological change in Sweden. Paper presented to The Shell Workshop, Midhurst, Kent. Contact: SIFO, Angermanngaten 174, PO Box 131, 16212 Vallingby 1, Sweden.

INDEX

Index compiled by Geoffrey C. Jones